Have you ever experienced, in dreams or fantasies, glimpses of the future? Apparent spiritual messages? Strong hunches which have turned out to be correct?

If so, you are probably one of the ever-increasing number of individuals now standing on the threshold of a vast new world of sensitivity, a world of such sufficiently documented inexplicable phenomena that only the most close-minded would deny its existence.

In this book, today's leading authority in psychic research reveals *how* you can release your own mysterious powers of ESP. By explaining the very nature of extrasensory perception, Harold Sherman illustrates how time, distance, and often death itself can be transcended with full realization of this birth-given potential, this extraordinary means of communication more powerful than the most advanced technical networks, this amazing cosmic consciousness just waiting to be recognized, accepted, and unlocked from the secret recesses of *your* mind. . . .

YOUR MYSTERIOUS POWERS OF ESP

SIGNET Titles of Related Interest

YOUR MYSTERIOUS POWERS OF ESP

The New Medium
of Communication

BY HAROLD SHERMAN

Founder and President of
ESP Research Associates Foundation

A SIGNET BOOK from
NEW AMERICAN LIBRARY
TIMES MIRROR

Library of Congress Catalog Card Number: 69-19631

The author gratefully acknowledges permission to reprint
excerpts from *Croiset, the Clairvoyant* by Jack Harrison
Pollack. Copyrighted 1961, 1965 by Jack Harrison Pollack.
Used by permission of Doubleday & Company, Inc.

This is an authorized reprint of a hardcover edition published
by The World Publishing Company. Published simultaneously
in Canada by Nelson, Foster & Scott Ltd.

THIRD PRINTING

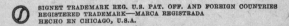

SIGNET TRADEMARK REG. U.S. PAT. OFF. AND FOREIGN COUNTRIES
REGISTERED TRADEMARK—MARCA REGISTRADA
HECHO EN CHICAGO, U.S.A.

SIGNET, SIGNET CLASSICS, SIGNETTE, MENTOR AND PLUME BOOKS
*are published by The New American Library, Inc.,
1301 Avenue of the Americas, New York, New York 10019*

FIRST PRINTING, DECEMBER, 1969

PRINTED IN THE UNITED STATES OF AMERICA

With Love

To MARY and MARCIA,

Who Have Put Up With
This "Oddball" of a Dad
All These Years

CONTENTS

1
Thoughts Through Space

IT'S COMING! It will be here for most people in fifty to a hundred years; for some of us, in far less time than this; for a few of us, *today or tomorrow*. . . . Mind-to-mind communication is just a few experimental steps away. Man's exploration of the inner space of his own mind will soon match his exploration of outer space.

This will come about because man, at last, has a compelling need of these hitherto undeveloped higher powers of the mind, not only to enable him to live in more understanding and harmony with his fellow man but also to prepare him to live peacefully with other intelligent life systems from other planets with whom he will soon, given the most authentic present evidence, be in knowing contact.

An astronaut, for instance, might be bound for Venus shortly, in solitary confinement within a space capsule a hundred million miles from earth. He would be surrounded by a black void, broken only by pinpoints of light from distant stars. Let's say he is suddenly cut off from two-way radio contact. It has usually taken nine minutes for him to transmit a radio message back to earth, and nine minutes to get a reply—eighteen minutes in all. His isolation now seems to be for an eternity, faced as he is with this mechanical failure.

But, instead of surrendering to fear and panic, the astronaut simply switches to mental control. He relaxes. He concentrates. He sends out a strong feeling impulse. He makes almost instant contact with a trained human receiver, standing by on earth, and he maintains mind-to-mind communication while the radio circuits are being re-paired.

Fantastic? Impossible? Not at all.

A Long-Distance Experiment

Sir Hubert Wilkins, the famed Arctic explorer, and I did this very thing, on a regularly scheduled basis, separated by a distance of two to three thousand miles, three nights a week for a period of five and one-half months as long ago as 1937. Two or three thousand miles, a million miles, a hundred million miles—it apparently makes no difference. Telepathic faculties are not limited by time or space.

The complete account of our pioneering experiment in long-distance telepathy (I was in New York while Wilkins was searching for lost Russian fliers in the Arctic) is contained in the book written for Creative Age Press, N.Y., by Wilkins and me in 1942, *Thoughts Through Space*. It was witnessed by competent observers, one of whom was Dr. Gardner Murphy, then head of the Psychology Department of Columbia University (now Director of Research for the Menninger Foundation, Topeka, Kansas), who testified by affidavit:

> When Harold Sherman informed me that he was attempting to get long distance telepathic impressions from Sir Hubert Wilkins in the Arctic, I told him I would be glad to receive and file his daily communications regarding his impressions. He proceeded methodically to record and mail to me the impressions received. The postmarks showed that he was giving me an up-to-date record. I have all these communications in my file with their original postmarked envelopes. I am not able to evaluate the series of impressions as a whole but this statement is to be construed only as testimony that Sherman did send me promptly the dated impressions which he received.

> (*Signed*) GARDNER MURPHY

> Subscribed and sworn to before me
> this 11th day of June, 1938
> NANCY D. BAINES
> (*Notary Public*)

How dependable did this test of possible mind-to-mind communication prove to be? When the experiment was concluded and the hundreds of impressions I had recorded over this period of five and one-half months had been checked against Wilkins' diary and log, as of each specific date, it was found that roughly *seventy percent* of the specific mental images and strong feelings I had received and interpreted in my own words had been precisely *correct*.

Was I surprised? Of course I was—and so was everyone else. When Wilkins had suggested to me that we undertake such an experiment, after learning that I had been privately practicing telepathy with Mrs. Sherman and a few trusted friends for quite some years, I told him I could not guarantee that I would get more than chance results.

"My conscious mind always tries to argue me out of any impressions I seem to receive," I explained. "This is natural because *it* is limited by the five physical senses and it just will not accept thoughts or feelings which come into the field of awareness from the subconscious. I have had to discipline myself to put the conscious mind aside and not let it interfere when I am attempting to receive impressions from the mind of another. This is most difficult to do because the conscious mind instinctively sets up a resistance to anything foreign to its so-called normal operation. However, I am convinced that telepathy can be performed only through developing a technique of at least partially bypassing the conscious mind, since thoughts are transmitted, apparently, from the conscious and subconscious mind of the sender to the subconscious mind of the receiver. The trick is, then, through relaxed concentration, for the receiver to bring these mental images or feelings over into the field of conscious awareness.

"Once these mental images or feelings appear, they must be put in words and written down or spoken before the conscious mind can begin to cast doubt on their authenticity—or the receiver is lost. He will find himself tormented as to whether what has come to him might not be pure imagination or mental or emotional distortions of one kind or another. How can any impressions possibly be correct which have no physical basis for origin? All science is opposed to this. If it is proved to be true, however, present textbooks would have to be torn up and new concepts of the mind established, crediting to it the possession of potential powers unlimited in nature. This is a radical change most scientists are not prepared to accept. On the contrary, they will fight it to the death, since it challenges everything they have been taught about animal man and his way of thinking."

Wilkins, listening with absorbed interest to my comments, then said: "Sherman, all my life I have had premonitions of events, many of which later came to pass. I have long wondered about this. It shouldn't happen, but it did. This has led to my conclusion that the greatest unexplored area yet left to man is the area of his own mind. Perhaps our proposed experiment will not have any significant results, but if you are willing to act as the attempting receiver, I will try to get off by myself, each scheduled night, and relive and review, in my mind's eye, the outstanding experiences I have had that day in our search for the lost Russian fliers—and *will* them to your mind. Put them down in your own words—whatever impressions come to you—and they later can be checked against my diary and log. I doubt that we will be able to reverse the process—with me attempting to receive and you sending—because I will be out of touch with civilization for great stretches of time, except for the radio contacts I hope to have with *The New York Times* shortwave radio station. However, we can pretty well control this sending and receiving arrangement we have agreed upon—Mondays, Tuesdays, and Thursdays, from 11:30 P.M. to midnight, Eastern Standard Time. You sit in your study in your New York apartment, and I will synchronize my time with yours, wherever I may be as I fly north, joining you in mental concentration in these appointed periods."

This is how the pioneering experiment in long-distance telepathy started. That it succeeded beyond any expectations—and has come to be regarded by many today as one of the classics of thought-transference demonstrations—has stirred in me a feeling of profound gratitude for the intestinal fortitude of Sir Hubert Wilkins, who was willing to risk his worldwide reputation as a scientist to undertake what must have seemed to most people an utterly senseless and wholly impossible adventure. Certainly, the personal extrasensory experiences Wilkins had had must have motivated him to propose this far-out telepathic project with me. A scientist who had not been so exposed could hardly be expected to risk the scoffing and criticism of his peers. Already plunged into psychic research, I had nothing to lose. Since most scientists held strong convictions that telepathy was a nonexistent faculty, my failure in the role of the attempted receiver would only serve to confirm their preconceived concept. If I succeeded in scoring consistently above chance, scientists would most likely still refuse to accept the results as evidence of extrasensory perception, and could be expected to imply that there had to be some physical explanation—I must somehow have been able, coincidentally, to have "leaped at conclusions," or else I had engaged in some form of deception or collusion.

These were the hazards as to possible public and scientific reaction that Sir Hubert Wilkins assumed when he suggested to me that we engage in this highly problematical experiment.

That this test in long-distance telepathy, which began on October 25, 1937, and continued almost half a year, ending March 24, 1938, had an amazing outcome could not have been predicted by either Sir Hubert or me. We followed through on our assignments as sender and receiver, under varying conditions of physical, mental, and emotional pressure often difficult to surmount. For my part, I ended up with stomach ulcers brought about by the unexpected strain, as I continued recording impressions, week after week, not knowing for long stretches of time what percentage, if any, of them might be "on target." Once it had been discovered that I seemed to be scoring consistently above chance and that these tests might produce some significant scientific results, the pressures on me mounted. I could not control a growing feeling of responsibility, as well as human feelings of apprehension, for Wilkins' safety, since I had on several occasions received precognitive flashes of plane accidents, which later occurred.

During all these nerve-trying months, I had remained stationed, at the appointed times, in the study of my New York City apartment, while Wilkins, with his crew, flew over great wastes of the Arctic in search of the lost Russian fliers. They had been headed by Sigismund Levanevsky and his companions, who had sought to make a nonstop flight from Moscow, in a multimotored plane, to Fairbanks, Alaska. Something had gone wrong with their plane some four hundred miles this side of the North Pole; the radio had gone out of commission, and they had either crashed or made a forced landing.

The last radio message received from Levanevsky, sent partly in code, had read:

MOTOR ON RIGHT SIDE GIVING TROUBLE . . . WE ARE FLYING AGAINST A HUNDRED-KILOMETER-AN-HOUR WIND VELOCITY . . . AND HAVE LOST ALTITUDE FROM 6,000 METERS TO 4,300 METERS . . . WE ARE GOING TO LAND IN . . .

The rest of the message was lost in a jumble of sound. This was on August 12, 1937. On August 13 the Soviet Embassy in Washington, in a public statement, expressed great concern for the safety of the crew. It was thought that a forced landing may have been made between the North Pole and Alaska. Shortly after this announcement, the Soviet government contacted Sir Hubert Wilkins and requested that he prepare a search expedition as promptly as possible, to fly north in search of the Soviet airmen, in the hope that they still might be alive and awaiting rescue.

Their approximate position could not be established. Moscow had reported that Siberian radio stations had heard indistinct signals, from an irregularly working radio station, considered likely to be from Levanevsky's airplane. This led to the speculation that the plane had made a forced landing between the 82nd and 83rd parallels, some four hundred and fifty miles from the North Pole on the American side.

Within thirty-nine hours after Wilkins had begun preparations, with authority from Moscow, he had taken off in a Consolidated Flying Boat lent by Richard Archbold, a member of the Explorers Club. This was eight days after the Soviet plane had gone down.

With Air-Commodore Herbert Hollick-Kenyon of Toronto and Alderman Al Cheeseman of Port Arthur serving as pilots, and Wilkins acting as navigator, a distance of ten thousand miles was flown over the Arctic Ocean in the next ten days—more than the equivalent of four transarctic flights—but no trace was found of Levanevsky. The search was continued for thirty days, with a total of more than thirty thousand miles. Of the thirty nights, twenty-three of them were spent either flying or sleeping aboard the flying boat, with only seven nights ashore. Some of the flights were of long duration, the longest being almost three thousand miles over the Arctic Ocean, zigzagging back and forth over the area in which Levanevsky was supposed to be. Still no trace of the missing men was found.

The season for using flying boats in the Arctic came to a close when the temperature lowered to the point at which a skin of ice formed over the surface of the lakes and rivers being used for landings.

Forced to return to lower latitudes, Wilkins was requested by the Soviet government not to abandon search, but to continue the flights throughout the winter. This would require equipment other than that which had been used throughout the period from August to mid-September, and Wilkins immediately began to look for another machine. This he located almost at once—the *Good Will* airplane, which Richard Merrill had flown from the United States across the Atlantic to Liverpool and back, during the activities in connection with the coronation of King George VI and Queen Elizabeth. It was a Lockheed 10E airplane equipped with extra tanks to give it a range of nearly four thousand miles. It had all available instrument aids to blind flying, and Wilkins had the latest in radio apparatus installed.

The original search with the Consolidated Flying Boat had been carried out in a period of almost continuous daylight; but the search to be carried on throughout the winter would have to depend on moonlight, the light of the stars and the Aurora Borealis (Northern Lights) as aids to visibility. This complicated the difficulties of navigation. To be effective, each of the flights would have to be a distance of more than fifteen hundred miles. If Wilkins and his crew were to cover all the area allotted to them, they would have to make some flights of more than three thousand miles. Winter flying was obviously much more hazardous. In summertime one could get some indication of one's position by taking sextant observations of the sun. In winter, having to work in a restricted cockpit behind frosted windows, with the temperature ranging to 60 degrees below zero and with only the moon or stars to observe as astronomical points of reference, Wilkins had his work cut out for him.

About four months had now passed since Levanevsky had set out on his flight. Many people had given him up as lost. Many thought the proposal to seek the missing fliers by moonlight was fantastic, and they classed Wilkins and his veteran Arctic fliers, who proposed to carry out the search under these conditions, as romantic optimists who believed in miracles. They pointed out the extraordinary danger involved, and believed it would be impossible to see anything on the ground from an airplane flying high above the Arctic in the depth of winter.

However, the vast and almost totally snow-covered area would act as a vivid reflector for the moonbeams, and the relatively clear polar air permits more light from the heavenly bodies to reach the Arctic surface than would be the case in the neighborhood of smoke-hazed cities in low latitudes.

In Wilkins' opinion, the time since Levanevsky had last

been heard from was comparatively short. There was no real reason to believe that if he and his crew had landed safely, they would not be still alive. It was known that Levanevsky and his companions had set out with full rations for a period of eight weeks. These might be stretched to last twelve weeks; supplemented by food obtained by hunting seals, the rations might have lasted for a considerably longer period.

This was the dramatic setting that served as a backdrop for the Wilkins-Sherman long-distance telepathic experiences. Had the world known in advance of the attempt Wilkins and I were to make to transmit and receive thoughts, I am certain that the famed Arctic explorer would have been branded as "completely off his rocker." His moonlight attempt to find the lost Russian fliers was considered fantastic enough. All that would have been needed to discredit Sir Hubert entirely would have been the news that he was devoting serious time and thought toward an experiment in extrasensory perception.

Several years later, in 1942, Dr. J. B. Rhine of Duke University, pioneer investigator in psychic phenomena, was to publish his first much-discussed book, *New Frontiers of the Mind* (World Publishing Company, Cleveland), and the Zenith Radio Corporation had produced a thought-provoking radio program on telepathy, publicizing Rhine's famous ESP cards. Thousands of men and women were trying out their own extrasensory powers through the use of these cards, attempting to send and receive mental impressions of the five card symbols—a square, a circle, a star, a cross, and a wavy line. The possible existence of telepathy as an actual fact was being debated, but scientists at large were skeptical and scoffing. Dr. Rhine, who had brought psychic phenomena out of the wilderness of the ismic and the often fraudulently practiced occult and had given it the name of extrasensory perception, could present laboratory evidence of tests which he claimed proved telepathy, clairvoyance, and other psychic manifestations beyond a doubt.

Into this arena of highly controversial investigation Wilkins and I were about to tread.

Prior to Wilkins' second departure, in late October—while his rescue plane and crew were being assembled—he took me to *The New York Times* shortwave radio station and introduced me to the chief operator, Reginald Iversen. We explained to Iversen the telepathic test we had planned, and he listened to us in open-mouthed astonishment.

"You have to be kidding!" he said, and laughed outright.

"No," Wilkins assured him, "we're quite serious. Inasmuch as I hope to keep in regular touch with the *Times* by shortwave radio, in filing news reports, it occurred to Sherman and me that I could inform you each week of some of the outstanding experiences I have tried to transmit to Sherman, and since Sherman will already have recorded his impressions on these then past dates, a check can determine the number of 'hits' he may have made."

Iversen looked his utter incredulity. "Okay!" he said. "I'll cooperate. But I think this is the zaniest experiment I ever heard of!"

Providentially for me—from the standpoint of skeptical scientists who would have seized on any possible physical contact I might have had to explain away any possibility of genuine telepathy—the weather conspired, throughout the next five and one-half months, to prevent Wilkins from maintaining dependable contact with Iversen through shortwave radio. This plan of checking the accuracy of whatever impressions I might receive was therefore almost immediately out of the question.

At the conclusion of our experiment, Iversen then testified by affidavit as follows:

This is to certify that I, Reginald Iversen, radio operator for *The New York Times,* was in contact with Harold Sherman off and on during the period of his telepathic tests with Sir Hubert Wilkins. It had been thought that some of Sherman's impressions could be checked by shortwave radio with Wilkins and thus expedite the report on the tests, but magnetic and sunspot conditions were so bad during this entire time that I was unable to communicate with Sir Hubert Wilkins except on a comparatively few occasions.

One Monday evening, February 21, 1938, my wife and I visited Harold Sherman in his home and were present in his study at 380 Riverside Drive, New York City, when he was receiving impressions from Sir Hubert Wilkins. At that time Mr. Sherman recorded the impression that Sir Hubert Wilkins was trying to get some messages through to me by shortwave radio. I was dubious that this was so, because Wilkins knew that the next two days, Tuesday and Wednesday, were my regular days off duty at the *Times,* and he rarely tried to contact me when he was certain that I was not on the job. But I learned the following morning that these messages had been received the night before by our night operator at the *Times,* who had tried to reach me by phone, and that the messages contained additional information which Harold Sherman had also telepathically received in my presence.

At no time during this period of six months did Harold Sherman ever seek such information as I might have known concerning Sir Hubert Wilkins and his activities in the far north. In fact, despite my skepticism, as it turned out, Sherman actually had a more accurate telepathic knowledge of what was happening to Wilkins in his search for the lost Russian fliers than I was able to gain in my ineffective attempts to keep in touch by shortwave radio.

(*Signed*) REGINALD IVERSEN

Sworn to before me this
9th day of June, 1938
(*Signature of Notary
on original affidavit*)

In addition to this testimony, Iversen prepared a chronological report of *The New York Times* shortwave radio communication with Sir Hubert Wilkins as further substantiation that I had no way of securing reliable or continuous information from this source. His report was as follows:

Due to the emergency conditions prevailing, Sir Hubert Wilkins left on his second search flight for the lost Russian fliers with much of his equipment having to be arranged for and shipped to Canada after him. It was one of my duties to assist him in lining up this equipment, acting upon instructions from Wilkins.

Because of unprecedentedly bad communication conditions extending over the entire Northern Hemisphere— brought about by magnetic and sunspot disturbances—our intended schedule of shortwave with Wilkins was almost completely disrupted.

There were long periods of time when contact with Wilkins at Aklavik or Point Barrow was made, but no traffic could be handled. On many occasions the signals did not come through at the appointed times, and when they did, they were so weak that we could pick up no messages. But the dates when we did make successful contact with Wilkins, and received press dispatches from him, were as follows:

December 2, 1937	January 27, 1938
January 11, 1938	February 3, 1938
January 24, 1938	February 17, 1938

March 2, 1938   March 10, 1938
March 4, 1938   March 11, 1938
March 7, 1938   March 14, 1938
March 15, 1938

The balance of the dates on our log from October 25, 1937, to March 18, 1938, when Wilkins' radio station at Aklavik was dismantled, show ineffective attempts to contact Wilkins, with signals too weak for communication, or signals "unheard" or "unreadable," or contact made for testing and little or no "traffic" handled.

It should be borne in mind, however, that the news contained in these press dispatches had, in most instances, happened some days before, and Harold Sherman, recording his telepathic impressions three nights a week, had already noted whatever he had been able, telepathically, to pick up concerning these events, the copies of his impressions having previously been mailed and in the hands of Dr. Gardner Murphy of Columbia University and Samuel Emery of the City Club of New York.

Even so, I never notified Mr. Sherman on these few occasions, or at any other time, when communication of any sort took place. Mr. Sherman's first knowledge of my having received a press dispatch came when he saw it published in *The New York Times*.

(Signed) REGINALD IVERSEN
Chief Operator, New York Times radio station,
June 12, 1938

At this point I feel that the reader might be interested in the actual recording of impressions received by me on the night to which Reginald Iversen has referred in his affidavit, when he and his wife and Mrs. Sherman seated themselves in my study to witness my attempted reception of Wilkins' thoughts. These are taken from the book *Thoughts Through Space* * and tell their own documented story:

Test 53
February 21, 1938   11:30–12:00 P.M.

Tonight, we had Mr. and Mrs. Reginald Iversen as guests for dinner. Iversen, a *New York Times* radio operator, who has been frankly skeptical throughout these months, expressed great interest in many of the impressions, asking me: "Well, how in the world did you get an impression like that?"

It was Iversen's comment that many of the impressions

---

* Master Publications, 1957, New York City.

were so personal and also so accurate that he didn't see how anyone could now deny that something unusual was happening. . . .

An exact transcription of impressions received tonight is as follows. I will be interested to learn whether the presence of the Iversens and Mrs. Sherman in the study with me has in any way inhibited my "sensitivity." I seemed to feel Wilkins' thought strongly.

SHERMAN	WILKINS
Installing of engine has been completed and testing of it carried on today. Very difficult job—feel that weather delayed your work one day . . .	Cold south wind made for delay.
Someone of crew seems to have hurt left leg during work on plane—someone else has skinned hand or finger. . . .	Dyne had hands spotted with frost "burns," which blister, or else the skin is pulled right off when the hand is pulled away after being frozen to any metal.
See great clouds of smoke or vapor about plane and hear uneven coughs of motors. . . .	With a wood stove going inside the "tent" over the motor, there are always clouds of steam and smoke on cold days.
Use made of part of damaged engine—see someone tinkering with it—removing some parts. . . .	Some parts of old engine fitted to the new.
You have some wine with several friends who welcome you back to Aklavik. . . .	They have had some liquor that I brought with me. I didn't have any.
Your cold which you mentioned in your letter to me, has given you a little trouble —in your head and throat. . . .	Cold really bad.
You brought back to Aklavik several boxes of cigars, cartons of cigarettes. . . .	One box of one hundred cigars for Wilson.
Seems as though Dyne wanted you to bring him something special, or some member of crew requested you get some	Kenyon wanted receiver radio.

SHERMAN	WILKINS
article—can't make out what it was. . . .	
Someone has had toothache—sore condition mouth. . . .	I had tooth filled evening before I left Edmonton. Was still tender and jumped each time I trod heavily.
Think you would like to get some word through to Iversen if you could reach him before Thursday—wonder if this thought in your mind tonight as you think of me? . . .	Sent word to Iversen.

In my report, mailed to Wilkins about above "coincidences," I ventured a deduction, as follows, which Wilkins later commented upon—his comment placed in parallel column:

SHERMAN	WILKINS
My repeated reception at different sittings concerning the radio equipment Kenyon wanted seems to indicate the ability of a sensitive mind to follow a trend of thought in the mind of the "conscious" or "unconscious" sender, as it pertains to one subject. Apparently this "radio" business for Kenyon had been one of the details Wilkins had been following through on and thus often in his mind.	Correct. Gave this intense thought. Kenyon wanted me to bring it in as expedition equipment, and so avoid "duty"—but I finally decided not to do this.

Confirmation Through Iversen of Impressions Received Night of February 21, 1938

On the night of February 22, the evening following the Iversens' presence in my home, they attended a lecture with us, given by Dr. A. E. Strath-Gordon at Steinway Hall. I was shown, at that time, several radio dispatches received by the relief operator at *The New York Times* shortwave radio station from Wilkins, the night of February 21, confirming impressions which had come to me in the "sitting" that the Iversens witnessed that same night.

Iversen said he had not learned until that morning (February 22) that these radio dispatches had reached the

Times, and that he had made a special trip in to the office to pick them up. Iversen expressed amazement that I had recorded: "Think you [Wilkins] would like to get some word through to Iversen if you could reach him before Thursday—wonder if this thought in your mind tonight as you think of me?"

Iversen further stated that he could not recall Wilkins having put through a message to him during his "off-time days at the radio station" in all the months he had been north. This was the reason he had expressed doubt the night before, when I had finished my "sitting" and read this impression to him. He had expressed even greater doubt when I had read to him this impression: "Installing of engine has been completed and testing of it carried on today. Very difficult job—feel that weather delayed your work one day. . . ."

Iversen had gone on to say that the mounting of a new engine was a difficult job and that he thought it would take Wilkins considerably longer to complete it. Here is a copy of the radio message which had even then been received at the *Times* for Iversen from Wilkins:

Feb. 21, 1938

ENGINE ON PLANE MOUNTED WON'T BE READY TILL THURS-
DAY . . . QTC 1

LOP

I read to Iversen some past impressions, now confirmed by Wilkins, and also read some of later impressions received, which Wilkins had not yet seen. One of these impressions had come through on the night of February 14 and was as follows: "You in communication Aklavik today. Kenyon seems to want more supplies or parts of equipment. . . . You have to delegate New York, through Iversen, to secure some pieces equipment and rush through in relation to repair job on plane's motor—also in connection radio. . . ."

Again, on night of February 17, I recorded: "Radio attempt tonight which seems to have been more successful —report on operations Aklavik—need for several more pieces mechanical equipment. . . ."

Iversen confirmed that "contact" was made the night of February 17, the most successful communication since Wilkins went north, despite magnetic predictions to the contrary. The night of February 21, when Iversen was present at the "sitting," I once more "tuned in" on Wilkins, having done something about the request of one of the men for mechanical equipment: "Seems as though Dyne wanted you to bring him something special, or some member of crew requested you get some article—can't make out what it was. . . ."

This persistent thought, coming to me through three "sittings," hooking up first with Kenyon, in a very definite manner, the night of February 14, was substantiated by a radio message for Iversen the night of February 21, received by the relief operator while Iversen was present in my study:

IVN:
UNLESS YOU ALREADY ORDERED HOLD EVERYTHING REF: KENYON'S RECEIVER HE WILL PROBABLY NOT GET UNTIL AFTER RETURN.

WILKINS
10:10 P

Iversen, when showing me these messages, said that Wilkins had ordered him, about the time I had picked up the first impressions regarding Kenyon, to secure radio receiver for Kenyon. He had been working on this since.

The reader will have observed the specific nature of the impressions received; these continued from the first to the last of the five-and-one-half-month period of our experiments.

Samuel Emery, a resident member of the City Club of New York, was enlisted by Sir Hubert and myself as an additional witness to these experiments. He had expressed great interest, but also doubt that this experiment would prove anything but a waste of time and effort. His testimony follows:

This is to certify that I, Samuel Emery, resident of the City Club of New York, 55 West 44th Street, New York City, being a friend of both Sir Hubert Wilkins and Harold Sherman, was asked by them to be a lay witness of their telepathic experiments and that I received from Harold Sherman complete typewritten copies of his impressions the day following their reception. I was able subsequently to check them, as confirmation was eventually received from Sir Hubert Wilkins, and I can testify to the honesty and sincerity of Harold Sherman, the receiver, who could not possibly have access to the intimate knowledge of Sir Hubert's many personal and expedition activities in the Far North except through the agency of extrasensory perception.

(Signed) SAMUEL EMERY
May 9, 1938

I herewith attest to the genuineness of
Mr. Samuel Emery's signature.
JOHN J. CASSIDY
Chief Clerk, City Club of N.Y.

Henry S. W. Hardwicke, M.D., was research officer for the Society for Psychical Research of New York and a friend of mine. I had often attended the meetings of this society and had addressed its members. When these tele-pathic experiments were about to get under way, I con-fided this fact to Dr. Hardwicke, who expressed immense interest. He said he would like to follow these tests closely, and I granted permission, on his promise not to mention them to anyone until they had been completed and an op-portunity had been afforded to analyze and evaluate the recorded impressions and their percentage of accuracy. It was possible, I emphasized, that the results would disclose nothing beyond chance.

Here is Dr. Hardwicke's notarized testimony.

This is to certify that I, Dr. Henry S. W. Hardwicke, have been in weekly contact with Harold Sherman throughout the period of the telepathic tests he conducted with Sir Hubert Wilkins; that I have known of many of Mr. Sherman's recorded impressions shortly after they were received by him and weeks before Sir Hubert Wil-kins could be reached for the purpose of determining and verifying the experiences he had undergone as described by Sherman on those dates.

There is no question of the authenticity of these tele-pathic phenomena. The distance alone, between sender and receiver, of over two thousand miles—and the fact that most of Mr. Sherman's impressions pertained to Wil-kins' activities on the very day of their reception—should answer any reasonable skepticism, it being perfectly ob-vious that it would be humanly impossible for any person to accurately record the experiences of another, at such a distance with the time element as closely synchronized, and accomplish such a feat, consistently, week in and week out for a period of six months, without the exercise of a telepathic faculty.

(*Signed*) HENRY S. W. HARDWICKE, M.D.

Dr. A. E. Strath-Gordon, who served as chief of staff of brain surgery for the British government during World War I and who was a member of the First Triangulation Survey Committee to enter and study the Great Pyramid of Egypt, became acquainted with me shortly after he took up residence in the United States. He was a member of the British Society for Psychical Research, an authority on metaphysics, and a man whose confidence I could also enjoy during the period of these telepathic tests.

Dr. Strath-Gordon, as the tests progressed, asked if I thought it would be disturbing to my concentration if he sat in the study with me and witnessed my recording of impressions at first hand. I told Dr. Strath-Gordon that there was no way I could answer this question unless we tried it out. I knew that if I could not keep from being self-conscious while I was being watched, it might well inhibit my reception of thought impressions from the mind of Wilkins.

The first night that the Strath-Gordons sat in my study, with Mrs. Sherman, as witnesses to my recordings, was February 17, 1938. Their presence did not seem to make me self-conscious, and impressions appeared to come through in normal fashion. They were later shown to have their usual percentage of accuracy.

The second time that the Strath-Gordons witnessed me undertaking "thought reception" proved to be the last of the series, on March 24, 1938. Since it concluded what has now come to be regarded as a "historic adventure in the realm of the mind," it seems fitting that you should see an exact transcription of the impressions that came through:

SHERMAN	WILKINS
Feeling just as strong that you have left Aklavik some days ago—first to Edmonton, where skis changed to wheels —then—yes, I feel you are now in Winnipeg—Fort Garry Hotel—I now know the name of this hotel—believe you stopped at MacDonald in Edmonton, name of hotel I also since have come to know. . . .	Stopped at Fort Garry on night of 24. Left there on 25. Correct.
I hear you making address in Edmonton—seems that you are thanking different countries for cooperation which made search flights possible— Canada, United States of America, and Soviet Russia.	Correct. Spoke of value of our activities in relation to international friendship and cooperation.
I seem to see mental picture of Russian fliers walking toward shore across ice. Did you say in your talk you consider it possible they still could be	Yes.

SHERMAN	WILKINS
alive, and making way across drifting ice floes toward land? Drift would be tremendous by this time. Feel this is speculation in your mind—though strong probability Russian fliers have perished. . . .	Correct.
Think these comments made at luncheon club at Edmonton, and repeated in address at Winnipeg.	Correct. We arrived at Winnipeg just in time to attend a luncheon at the Aviation Section of Department of Commerce. They did not know we were coming until we actually arrived at airport, where luncheon was to be held. Ten minutes after landing, I was giving a talk.
The nerve tension which I have had to combat for past month or so is almost completely gone, and I seem to see these mental pictures clearly, as though obstruction removed. "Feeling" contact with your own consciousness seems different, clearer nature—will be interested to discover if this is actually true. . . .	Correct. Mental strain of not being able to fly more often was over.
I see welcoming committee at landing field, Winnipeg, to greet you—feel Kenyon at controls, flight from Aklavik to Edmonton—also enroute to Winnipeg. . . .	Correct.
See Cheeseman and Dyne, I believe, seated at soda counter, tanking up on ice-cream sodas. . . .	Not while the Scotch lasted.

Herewith is Dr. Strath-Gordon's testimony:

This is to certify that I, Dr. A. E. Strath-Gordon, have had occasion to check Harold Sherman's recorded impressions during the six months' telepathic experiments conducted with Sir Hubert Wilkins in the Far North.

On two different nights, that of February 17, 1938, and March 24, 1938, I sat in Mr. Sherman's darkened study at 380 Riverside Drive, New York City, and witnessed his actual recording of impressions as he received them from Sir Hubert Wilkins.

Mr. Sherman wrote rapidly and filled a number of pages of his notebook. My presence in the room did not seem to inhibit his ability to place himself in a receptive mental state, because most of his telepathic impressions recorded on these two nights were subsequently proven to be what I would term "photographically" correct.

In my many years of study and research all over the world, in the field of mental and psychic phenomena, I have never observed such continued clarity and exactness of telepathic vision as that demonstrated by Harold Sherman. To witness his receiving and recording thoughts or thought forms is to give one the feeling that Mr. Sherman is taking what amounts to dictation from some invisible intelligence.

The test conditions under which these Wilkins-Sherman telepathic experiments were conducted were ideal. Sir Hubert Wilkins was, for the greater part of his six months' expedition in the Far North, beyond the regular reach of air mail and shortwave radio.

Thus, any possible day-to-day channel of communication, other than that of extrasensory perception, was automatically ruled out.

(*Signed*) A. E. STRATH-GORDON

On this day appeared before me, Henry Borger, Notary Public in and for the Borough of Allendale, County of Bergen in the State of New Jersey, the deponent, A. E. Strath-Gordon, who states that the above, to the best of his knowledge and belief, is true and correct. Subscribed and sworn to on this fourteenth day of June, 1938.

The intervals between the times I recorded impressions regarding Wilkins and those when I learned what might be happening to him and his search expedition varied from weeks to months. He was often beyond the reach of air mail for long periods, but I kept on regular schedule, feeling increasing strain and wonder as to what percentage of my impressions and feelings might be right or wrong. This as much as anything brought on the stomach ulcers from which I eventually suffered.

The lost Russian fliers were never found, and during the course of these experiments I regretfully expressed this conviction. They had perhaps broken through the ice and gone down without trace.

Current Research into ESP

As I review these most exacting, mentally and physically grueling, intensely exciting, and highly emotional test months—and study and evaluate once more the evidence, so well documented—I can now more plainly see how these pioneering telepathic experiences were pointing years ahead to a time when man would have to look within his own mind for answers he can no longer find in the world about him.

Current Manifestations
of Extrasensory Perception

Understandably, skeptical scientists studying the Wilkins-Sherman telepathic experiments have remarked that they took place more than thirty years ago, and it is most difficult to judge them in the light of today's technical knowledge. The question most often asked is: "Can Sherman still demonstrate these powers that were apparently evidenced in his mind-to-mind communication with Sir Hubert Wilkins?"

For this reason I feel it will be helpful to report on two current case histories, wherein I was able to receive accurate, fairly detailed impressions of what had happened to two missing planes, one in the state of Washington, and the other in Arkansas. In each case, quite a period of time elapsed before the planes were found and the correctness of my impressions was established.

The Missing Plane in Washington

On Sunday, May 16, 1965, at 1:05 P.M. Sidney Gerber of Seattle, the pilot of a single-engine Cessna, a four-passenger float plane, radioed the airport at the town of Wenatchee, Washington, for weather conditions in the Cascade Mountains and the Seattle area. He was told that adverse weather, in the form of high winds and snow, prevailed in the mountains and passes. He reported his position as being over Lake Wenatchee. Two friends were in the plane with him, Wing Luke and Kay Ladue. This was the last radio report heard from them.

On Wednesday night, May 26, 1965, I received a long-distance phone call from my niece Jennifer and her husband, Don Winter, close friends of Sid Gerber, who told me of the missing plane and the fruitless search thus far, and asked me if any immediate feelings came to me concerning them.

I said at once that I sensed that Gerber's plane had been forced off course, to the right, in a storm; that it had crashed; and that I felt all occupants were dead. The Winters stated that they had hoped Gerber had been able to set down safely in some inaccessible spot and that he and his two passengers might still be alive, awaiting rescue. I could give them no such assurance.

They asked me then: if they sent me some article of Gerber's, did I think I could get more detailed impressions? I said it was possible, but I couldn't promise anything. I then explained that I was shortly to depart by car for Denver and the West Coast on a lecture tour, and that this was not a good time to concentrate on such matters, but that I would do the best I could.

They sent me a yellow slip of paper containing Gerber's handwriting, which had been addressed to "Jennie." I sat from 9:30 to 10:15 A.M., Saturday, May 29, in our house in Mountain View, Arkansas, holding this piece of paper in my hand and directing my mind to make contact with the conditions that existed at the time of the Gerber flight.

Within a few minutes a flood of mental images and feelings poured in on me, and I recorded them in the following words:

About forty miles beyond Lake Wenatchee, the full force of the storm hits Gerber. I feel as though I am in the plane and being buffeted. It is carried to a higher altitude in an updraft, barreling off to the right, keeping a halfway forward motion against the force of the wind hitting the left side of the plane.

I feel we are being carried off course, and the pilot is trying desperately to get out of this weather, which has been steadily worsening. The velocity of the wind, with snow and hail now pelting the plane, makes it almost impossible to control it.

Sid hopes to get above the storm, since it is dangerous to go down through it for an emergency landing . . . but the storm ceiling is too high. I know nothing about the geography of the country, but sense its ruggedness and wildness. There are heavily timbered areas and mountain crags below, deep canyons, small lakes of different sizes and streams, but few of them permit a safe approach for a landing, especially in foul weather.

Sid decides he must get down at all costs, since he cannot get out of the weather—nor can he turn back. The force of the wind makes the plane almost unmanageable, and I hear creaks and straining sounds and wonder if the plane is icing up. It begins to lose altitude—and the engine reacts to the hard going.

Sid and his companions now recognize the desperateness of their plight and brace themselves for a possible rough landing. It seems that Sid has an area in mind—a body of water he hopes to reach—one he has landed on before . . . but he has lost visibility and his sense of direction. He realizes that he cannot call for aid—nothing can be done for him; whatever can be done, *he* must do. . . .

The plane is being carried far right from his intended course, and Sid has great trouble keeping it on an even keel. He is now losing altitude fast—hoping he can get a ground view—to level off for a crash landing.

The plane narrowly skims a crag and treetops, shoots across a canyon . . . and runs into an updraft, a swirling one from a deep ravine. It is blown like a kite . . . and hits into trees and a mountainside . . . about a quarter of a mile above what seems to be a river and a small waterfall.

I feel Sid was killed outright . . . and as the plane cracks up . . . the other two may have been thrown clear, badly injured. They are still in a bad storm area, and if the other two did temporarily survive, I feel it was not for long. I do not get a "live" feeling as I put my mind on the three. I am sorry to have to report, for whatever these impressions may be worth, that I do not sense survival.

You may be able to figure their approximate position —forty miles beyond, and to the right of, Lake Wenatchee, when I tell you that I feel they were down within ten to fifteen minutes after their last radio communication.

If the wind velocity at their altitude was around one hundred miles an hour, someone who is technically qualified, figuring the forward speed the plane could make under these conditions and the amount of drift under wind pressure in this time span, might almost pinpoint the area where the crash occurred.

I feel, some weeks later—under ideal weather conditions —a pilot flying over the area may sight some spots of color from plane fragments, and perhaps a forestry parachutist might be dropped, or a helicopter make it down to within a quarter or half a mile of them. . . .

After mailing these original impressions to Jennifer and Don Winter, who lived on Mercer Island, Washington, I was busily engaged in lecture work, and it was not until June 15, 1965, when I was at the Garden Court Apartments in Hollywood, California, that I was able to give intensive thought to the Gerber case again.

The Winters had then sent me a shoe that had been worn by Gerber, one of a pair he had passed on to Don, and asked me if I could get any further impressions, since no trace of the plane had yet been found.

I sat from 8 to 8:30 P.M. on June 15 and recorded the following impressions:

Gerber a powerful man—fearless—sure of himself—almost reckless at times. . . .

Same sensation . . . plane in storm . . . veering off to right . . . Gerber fighting to keep on course . . . gives up and has only one thought—to get down out of weather. He tries for a water area and a water landing. But I still feel he does not make it. . . .

He is blown into the side of a mountain . . . trees . . . and I get sliding sensation, as though fragments of plane drop into ravine. Difficult to detect from air . . . if I am right . . . about a quarter to half a mile from stream or lake—old logging road . . . or camper's road . . . to left of area where plane crashed. . . .

Could be wrong, but still seem to be spots of snow nearby . . . strips of white. . . .

A cabin or two, a mile or more ahead of place where plane down. No one seems to be there at present—wild—main highway possibly ten miles . . . and to right of location. . . .

Looking down from the air, I seem to see land sloping to the left from higher elevation on the right, where plane crashed. . . .

I never get direction—north, south, east, or west—and never consult map or want to know layout of country, so mind will not invent or activate imagination. . . .

Sorry, this is first time mind has been free to attempt further impressions—have been enormously busy with lecture work. . . .

The fact that the shoe has been worn by Don Winter as well as Sid Gerber makes it difficult. Is it Don who hurt his leg some time ago? Has he or Gerber been skiing? I see some overland tramping—and outdoor action. . . .

This is all that comes to me at present.

In mailing these added impressions to the Winters, which amounted to a reiteration of my first feelings, I made these comments:

In many cases, when sudden death occurs, we are now getting evidence that, for a time, those involved in a sudden death experience often do not realize they have been divested of their physical bodies. They find themselves in a higher vibrating body form, as seemingly substantial as the physical. It is possible that their entities are still remaining in the vicinity of the crash scene—concerned over their plight—and hopefully awaiting rescue, fixated in that "time bracket." Eventually they will adjust to the "change" or will be met by other discarnate entities interested in them —and released from their temporarily "frozen state."

Every thought and feeling that emanates from the mind of any human creature, in my opinion, still exists in vibratory form—for want of any other words to describe the phenomenon—and can be sensed under certain conditions. Those who have gone on are much more difficult to contact, because they exist in a different "wave band," or dimension, so to speak, and few humans have developed the sensitivity to establish verifiable communication.

On October 7, 1968, Jennifer and Don phoned to tell me that the Gerber plane had been found on October 3, approximately *forty miles from Lake Wenatchee*, and that "my description of what had happened was amazingly accurate throughout."

Jennifer said that she was dispatching newspaper accounts of the finding and that Don was preparing a detailed report, with marked maps, showing point after point covered in my recorded impressions, as they tallied with what was now known of the plane's crash and what had apparently led up to this tragic happening.

News stories pretty well confirm the impressions:

Gerber, apparently thinking that the weather along his intended course, despite the report of snow showers to the west and southwest, was not too bad, did not land at Lake Wenatchee.

But to the south, at Stampede Pass, the visibility was down to half a mile, with snow showers and winds gusting to 36 miles an hour. The temperature was 29 degrees.

Across the mountains, at Boeing Field, a line of cumulonimbus clouds was moving northeasterly, pushed by winds up to 55 miles an hour.

Thick clouds formed a ceiling to obscure the tops of all mountain peaks. . . .

By now, the weather throughout the mountains had deteriorated. Icing conditions prevailed at relatively low altitudes, and clouds shrank the distances the fliers could see.

The pilot, perhaps disoriented, at some point in the flight turned into a canyon with a wide entrance; it was possibly the only avenue open to him. But it was a dead-end canyon.

The plane, now flying almost south at about 4,200 feet, clipped off the tops of some trees in level flight and slammed into the rock face of 5,800-foot Merchant Peak, six miles east of Index. . . .

—*Seattle Times*
October 13, 1968

Establishment of the downed aircraft's identity ended one of the most intensive and baffling searches in state aviation history. . . .

A Seattle helicopter pilot, Robert E. Nokes, sighted the wreckage Thursday afternoon on a sheer cliff on the north-east face of Merchant Peak at about the 4,000-foot level. Nokes, 3248 45th Ave., S.W., was on a geological survey of the area.

Nokes reported his sighting to the Aeronautics Commission Friday afternoon. He and Pretti flew to the crash site in a rented helicopter; Pretti said the state-owned copter was inadequate for the high-altitude mission.

Pretti said Nokes let him out at the 4,500-foot level of Merchant Peak, about 500 feet above the wreckage. . . .

Pretti said: "Terrain in the area is extremely steep, approximately 75 to 90 degrees, and movement was difficult and dangerous. I waited until Nokes flew in Bill Hamilton, the commission's operations officer. Then we descended to the wreckage together, using a rope to insure our own safety.

"The aircraft was totally destroyed. It was resting in a log jam on a rocky ledge, actually in a waterfall, at the headwaters of Trout Creek.

"Close inspection revealed the aircraft engine had been broken into several pieces, and the cylinders were scattered in the general area. Other pieces, including a wing tip and part of an elevator, were found about 200 feet from the major portion of the wreckage. The propeller, a door and other fragments of the plane were located down waterfall."

Nokes and Pretti described the accident as one of the unsurvivable type.

"They were evidently sucked up the canyon and struck the cliff full force," Nokes said. "No one could have survived the impact."

Pretti explained that if anyone did survive the initial impact, it would have been nearly impossible to successfully descend the mountain to seek help.

"It would have been extremely difficult for search airplanes to sight the wreckage," Pretti said. "It would have been almost equally impossible to distinguish the white aircraft from patches of snow, falling water, and foliage and other natural cover."

Human bones were found scattered near the wreckage, and evidence that the bodies had probably been eaten by bear or cougar, which abound in the area. . . .

—*Seattle Post-Intelligencer*
October 6, 1968

Of course it is gratifying to me when my recorded impressions in cases like this are subsequently proved to have been what many term "amazingly accurate."

I only regret that it has not been possible for searchers to locate the planes, in the areas my impressions have indicated, before the expenditure of such a vast amount of time and effort and money.

As a sensitive, I cannot guarantee that a plane will be where I feel it has crashed, but since such wide areas are always searched by those who have little or no idea where the plane may be down, it might be helpful to explore first the vicinity my impressions have earmarked.

The Missing Plane in Arkansas

On the morning of October 13, 1967, Marvin Melton, a prominent farmer and businessman, took off from his home airport at Jonesboro, Arkansas, for an intended two-and-one-half-hour flight to Dallas, Texas. He checked the weather in Texas as he reached the Little Rock area. There were two cloud layers at the time, one about 2,500 feet up and another starting again about 4,000 feet. A frontal system was advancing across the state, and wind from the northwest was at about twenty miles an hour. Since the weather report for the area toward Texarkana and Dallas was good, he apparently decided to go on through—but all trace of Melton and his plane vanished from that point on.

I knew nothing about this because I was out of the country, visiting Japan and the Philippines, when the tragedy occurred. Arriving back in Little Rock on October 16, I went direct to the offices of the ESP Research Associates Foundation, 1750 Tower Building, to report the results of my trip to Executive Director Al Pollard.

During the course of our discussion about psychic surgery, Mr. Pollard suddenly said to me, "Harold, you knew Marvin Melton, didn't you?"

"I only met him once," I replied. "Heard him speak. But I was deeply impressed and, of course, I know of his great humanitarian work on behalf of the have-not countries, in agriculture. Why?"

"He disappeared on a plane flight from his home in Jonesboro, en route to Dallas, last week," said Al. "And no trace of him has been found. Do you suppose you could get any impression of what happened?"

I had a shock reaction to the news. Melton at one time had been a candidate for governor, one of Arkansas's most beloved and distinguished men; no one, I think, could come within his influence without having a warm personal feeling for him.

An instant impression hit me, and I heard myself saying, almost at once: "Melton is down one hundred and seventy-three miles from his takeoff point at Jonesboro. Please give me a piece of paper. I am seeing a scene in my mind's eye of the area where he crashed. I'd like to draw it."

Frieda Helmich, Mr. Pollard's secretary, handed me a notepad.

"He ran into bad weather," I continued. "It closed in around him. When he saw he couldn't get through it, he tried to get down. He was briefly in sight of what he thought might be a landing area—some flat land beyond two mountains—lying like the blades of a jackknife. The mountain nearest him sloped to the left; the mountain just beyond, with a ravine between, sloped to the right and was higher." Here I drew a sketch picturing the terrain as I mentally saw it. "The feeling I am getting is that Melton missed the first sloping mountainside, but either plowed into the other or sheared off trees and slid into water just beyond. Pieces or fragments of the plane are not easily discernible. I doubt if he will be found for a while."

Al looked at the drawing. "That's interesting," he said. "There's a big search on. I think I'll phone the Civil Air Patrol and tell them about your impressions. No one seems to know where he may be, and they're covering a wide area."

For some weeks nearly one hundred aircraft, including Army helicopters and giant Air Force C-130's, combed south and southwest Arkansas, looking for the wreckage. The Air Force finally pulled out of the search, but the Arkansas Civil Air Patrol decided to carry on an "indefinite" hunt for the plane.

In April, 1968, the Mountain View Chamber of Commerce, of which I am a member, held a community-betterment program, attended by state leaders, one of whom was Eddie Holland, a pilot and administrative aide to Governor Winthrop Rockefeller. I sat next to him at the banquet table, and Mr. Holland, when we were introduced, said he had heard about me and my work in ESP. The conversation veered to Marvin Melton, and when asked if I had had any feelings about him, I repeated the impressions I had given to Al Pollard some months before. Then I drew the same sketch of the crash scene on a napkin and gave it to him.

I particularly stressed my persistent feeling that the plane was down approximately one hundred and seventy-three miles from its takeoff point at Jonesboro and that this was the region where I thought a concentrated search should be made. Mr. Holland said that he would communicate this information to the proper authorities and would let me know if anything came of it.

A few days later, on April 18, I received a letter from the office of Lieutenant Governor Maurice Britt, written by Eddie Holland, in which he reported:

I met with Colonel Bob James, head of the Arkansas Civil Air Patrol, today and briefed him on our conversation at the banquet in Mountain View the other night.

You will be interested to know that after pinpointing the map, from the information you gave me, Colonel James stated that more than fifty calls had been received in this general area from people who had seen or heard a low-flying airplane on the day Marvin Melton was lost.

Colonel James has not given up the search and will have CAP planes over the area this weekend. Their primary mission on the flights now will be to try to locate the two hills and flat land that you described to me. After these have been located from the air, ground crews will then search the area. I am hoping they will find something this weekend. I'll keep you informed of anything Colonel James has to report.

Despite this "lead," no trace was found until some months later, on Wednesday, July 17, when members of a timber-spotting team, working for the U.S. Forestry Service, came on the remains of Marvin Melton and the plane, which had burned beyond recognition on the side of a mountain, about four hundred feet from the top.

I had not received an impression of the plane's burning, but all other impressions were determined to have been correct.

Colonel James and Lieutenant Colonel Joel Wall of Hot Springs, director of emergency services for the Arkansas

Civil Air Patrol, visited the crash scene. Wall said the wreckage was not totally visible from the air. He said he flew over the area, and "I could see a little glint by knowing where to look." He said he could understand how easy it was to miss it during the widespread search for the plane after Melton was reported missing. This search was the largest and longest in the state's history.

A letter confirming the accuracy of my impressions was written to me by Eddie Holland on November 8, 1968, with apologies for having taken so long in making ac-knowledgment, due to his involvement in the political campaign from midsummer on. His letter read as follows:

I have talked with Colonel Bob James, head of the Arkansas Civil Air Patrol, and Mr. Hancock of the local FAA office. From these conversations, I would like to give you the following information concerning Marvin Melton and the facts pieced together after his crash and death.

Both of these gentlemen were on the crash scene after Marvin was found by the Forestry workers. Colonel James knew of your impressions prior to the finding of the plane, and I asked him if the area where the crash occurred could, perhaps, compare to the sketch you drew of your impressions. Colonel James stated that it definitely could, with the exception of the aircraft going into water. However, when Colonel James was describing the location on the map for me, he told me to look south of Mount Ida where the river crossed the highway three times, and just west of the last crossing was the valley where Marvin evidently was flying to stay under the overcast. At this point, he apparently crossed over a hill, as you show in your sketch, and suddenly came upon a hill higher, where he clipped a wing and crashed.

The location of the crash marked on my map from the description given me by Colonel James was approximately 175 nautical miles from Jonesboro. Your impression of 173 miles from point of departure to crash is very close.

I hope this information can be of help to you in your studies and research on ESP.

Recently some friends interested in making possible more advanced research in the realms of the mind, the emotions, and extrasensory perception have helped me establish the ESP Research Associates Foundation. I receive thousands of letters from men and women of all ages, relating unusual ESP experiences that they have had, many expressing an eagerness to learn more and to develop their own powers so that they can depend on them for guidance and protection in their everyday lives.

What I have been able to accomplish and demonstrate, thus far, through years of study and experimentation, is nothing compared to what will, one day, be achieved by many. My experience has convinced me that we all possess extrasensory powers that are awaiting activation and development. This book is designed to extract the lifetime lessons I have learned, from my own immensely varied experiences and observations, and to pass them on to the reader for whatever value they may have.

A new world of the mind is opening and unfolding. It is leading to new forms of creativity, new forms of healing, new forms of enlightenment, new forms of awareness. I invite you now to participate with me and explore these new powers of the mind.

2

Evidence for ESP

HAVE YOU, like many people, been reluctant to tell anyone, even your family and closest friends, about unusual impressions, in the form of dreams or fantasies, glimpses of the future, apparent spiritual messages, strong hunches, or other types of extrasensory phenomena you may have been experiencing—for fear they would subject you to ridicule or conclude that you were becoming mentally and emotionally unstable? Have you possibly been somewhat frightened or in awe of these often unsought manifestations? Have you wondered, if you are religiously inclined, whether or not these happenings might be the works of the devil? Perhaps you haven't taken time to consider psychic impressions, but a large number of people have.

My mail, numbering several hundred letters a month, contains sufficient undeniable evidence of mystifying and inexplicable phenomena to convince all but the most closed-minded that something beyond the reach of the five physical senses is definitely happening. A new world of sensitivity is knocking at the door of man's conscious awareness, waiting to be recognized, accepted, and developed.

This chapter deals with a number of typical case histories from the many on file with the ESP Research Associates Foundation. You will observe the wide variety of these extrasensory experiences, which are constantly occurring in the lives of different people of all ages, classes, races, religions, and degrees of intelligence. No doubt you can add some experiences of your own, or of friends or relatives, in substantiation.

ESP is no respecter of persons. These extrasensory faculties exist potentially or in partially developed form in everyone. Very few, thus far, have learned to control and operate these higher powers of mind at will. Most of the verified incidents have been spontaneous in nature and seldom can be reproduced under laboratory conditions. It is largely for this reason that most scientists still tend to dismiss or discredit any claims or reports of ESP phenomena, regardless of what otherwise would be accepted as irrefutable evidence. It should be obvious that a scientist who has never experienced any psychic sensitivity of his own must depend on a study of those who have demonstrated extrasensory abilities in order to arrive at any significant evaluation or conclusion.

It is my contention, however, that these higher powers of mind do not lend themselves naturally to the scientific control methods considered empirical by researchers in other and allied fields. New approaches and procedures must be created to enable us to achieve the breakthroughs in knowledge we are seeking with respect to the challenging mysteries of our minds.

The sheer weight of the numerical evidence in support of ESP, as illustrated by these case-history samples, which can be multiplied by the thousands, should give all honest skeptics pause for thought. The usual attempt to dismiss such cases by attributing them to an overexercised imagination, self-delusion, hallucination, mental or emotional imbalance, fraudulent practices, or mere coincidence will not hold up as you, yourself, may be the first to concede upon examination of the following reports.

The real names and addresses of the people concerned are on file, but because most of them have requested anonymity for personal or business reasons, this information is withheld. Wherever and whenever possible, except for little deletions of extraneous material, I am presenting these case histories in the actual words of those who have reported them so that you will have the feeling and the color of their own personalities and comments.

ESP in One Woman's Life

One of my earliest memories was one day when I was playing in the yard alone. (I was always happier playing alone.) I suddenly knew that my older brother, Fuller, and his wife were coming to our house that day.

Filled with delight, I rushed into the house and announced this fact to my mother. She looked at me sternly and said, "How do you know? Who told you?" "Nobody told me, I just know," I replied.

Mother was kneading light bread. She rubbed the dough from her hands, strode threateningly to me, grabbed my shoulders, and shook me so hard I was dizzy, demanding repeatedly, "Who told you?" Then: "Answer me or I will half kill you!" she said.

Frightened and crying, I answered, "I guess God told me. No one else was there." For this, I got a whipping and a warning to "Tell no more lies like that"; then she sent me to sit in a corner until suppertime.

As any member of the family came in the house that day, Mother asked them if they had heard from Fuller, and each said no, they had not. Mother told them how I had "lied" to her and why I was being punished.

Late that afternoon Fuller and his wife drove in.

Mother at once asked if they had sent any word that they were coming. (They lived twenty miles away.) They said no, they had not. Mother came grimly into the house and forbade me to go out and greet them.

This was always Mother's attitude toward the gift that I, even as a little child, subtly recognized and held most dear, although I dared not cultivate it. However, I knew ahead of time many things that were going to happen, but said nothing about them.

When I was about eight years old, we went out into the pasture to pick blackberries. We were dressed for the occasion, and each given a large and a small bucket to pick and carry in. The berries were large and plentiful, but I, being smaller, could not reach in the briers like the others could, so decided to go to another patch, alone, so I could pick my share.

My chosen patch was some distance from where the others were working, and the berries were thick and easy to reach. When all the outside berries were picked, I started to push my way into the thicket where the berries were plentiful.

I had taken but one step in, when a voice said, "Don't go in there, Dessie!" I stepped back and looked around to see who had spoken, but no one was near. I did not want to be ridiculed for being afraid, nor of failing to pick my share of the berries. I could reach no more from outside, so I decided to go in after them. I pushed back some briers and stepped in a little; then a voice spoke sharply, saying, "Don't go in there, Dessie! There is a rattlesnake there, and it will bite you!" This time I knew I should obey. I ran back to where the others were working and told my brothers to "Come quick with the hoe. There is a big rattlesnake there, and it has fourteen rattles!"

That did it! That "fourteen" rattles fixed me, but good. Mother scornfully said, "Fourteen rattles, indeed! I suppose you picked it up and counted them." Then, turning to my brothers, she said, "Go on with your picking, boys. It's just another one of her lies."

My father said, "No. We're going over there and find out."

Father and two brothers, each carrying a hoe, went to my patch. I tagged along, not knowing whether to cry or run for the house. Father asked me where I had seen the snake. I pointed to where I had started into the thicket, but said nothing.

They chopped their way in a few feet, then commenced striking furiously, and soon dragged the dead rattlesnake out.

It had fourteen rattles.

My father sent me to Iowa to help my married sister, who was expecting her third baby. I liked Iowa, and since I was not needed to help with the work at home, I decided to stay in Iowa and go to school there.

I went to live with a kindly lady, to help her with her housework, and I had been there about two years and was very happy. One night I awakened from a sound sleep, fully conscious that I was urgently needed at home; also that my youngest brother, Jim, was calling me.

Giving no thought to the time of night, I quickly dressed and packed my things, and was ready to leave, when the nice lady tapped gently on my door. She had heard me stirring around and had come to see if I were sick. I explained that I had to go home, for my brother had called me.

"That can't be," she protested. "There has been no one here. You just had a bad dream. Try to calm yourself, and go back to bed. It is only a little after midnight, and you have school tomorrow."

I protested, determined to go. She firmly pointed out that there had been no message, that it could only be a bad dream. Besides, we did not know when I could get a train for home. If I would stay until morning, she would take me to the train if I insisted, but she thought I should wire home first. I consented to wait, but knew I should go.

While we were at breakfast that morning, a telegram was delivered for me, saying that Jim had been seriously hurt by a horse rearing and falling backwards on him, at eleven-thirty last night.

I think I should add that Jim and I had practiced what we called "mind reading at a distance," secretly, of course, from when I was a small child until I had left home. We could "send a mental message and receive a mental answer" from different parts of the farm, and when one of us was away from home. We thought we were "pretty good at it."

Before I had left for Iowa, we had agreed to let the other know if anything ever happened when we had need for each other.

Jim passed on from this injury.

I married a pharmacist, who owned and ran a drugstore in Pittsburg, Kansas. At that time Pittsburg was largely a coal-mining town, and a very rough element of people lived there, as well as many fine and prosperous people.

Many houses in the better parts of town were built by coal companies for their resident officials. They were always built just alike, and in rows. We moved temporarily into the second house of a string of five when the house we lived in was sold.

It was a winter night, and at eight o'clock my husband had not yet come home for dinner. He was frequently late, and I kept his meals warm and ready to serve, but had to watch that they did not dry out. Tonight the meal was waiting, and I started into the kitchen to check on things.

When I reached the door between the dining room and kitchen (the door was wide open), I was stopped short by my chest crashing against a bar across the door. The force of the contact threw me back a foot or so.

Stunned, I tried to figure what had stopped me, for the doorway was clear. I recalled that I was actually afraid, even though I tried to tell myself that I was not, and decided that fear alone had stopped me.

I started through the door again, more slowly, and again my chest struck a bar that stopped me.

I looked down and saw an opalescent bar, about the size of a broom stick, clear across the door!

While pondering this, my telephone rang, loud and persistently. I felt an urge to answer it. When I did so, a voice said, "Dessie, this is your next-door neighbor. I want you to stay right there and talk to me. Listen carefully, but don't move away from the phone, and I'll tell you why. Your house, you know, is built just like mine, and your phone in the same place as mine. Stay there and you will be safe. I've already called your husband, and he's on the way home with the police.

"Now, don't be afraid, but there is a man outside your kitchen with a gun, and he will shoot you if you go in there. Stay where you are. He can't see you there. Oh, thank God, they are here! Stand still till they come in!"

She hung up the phone, and I froze to the spot.

That was before cars were numerous, and I heard the running horses and rattling cab come to a clattering stop, then voices and running feet around the house. Presently my husband unlocked the front door and rushed in, two policemen with him. After making sure I was all right, they explained that the man who lived in the second house from ours was drunk and wanted to kill his wife.

He thought he was at his house!

I did not tell my husband about the bar across the door, for his attitude about such things was very much like my mother's had been.

After I lost my husband, his twin brother, who was in the drugstore with him, a bookkeeper, but not a pharmacist, beat me out of everything and left me penniless. I had to go to work to support my two little sons. After two years, my health broke down, and doctors ordered complete rest for a year.

Having only a small amount of money saved, I had to hunt a cheap place to live. Through newspaper ads I located a twenty-acre place in southern Missouri, with a good orchard, fair land, and a small house. The place rented for twelve dollars per month. I went there, rented the land out on shares, then decided to raise chickens to boost the finances a little. I bought two used brooders, heated by kerosene lamps, and a used incubator, 250-egg capacity. I bought eggs and set it. Almost every egg hatched a healthy chick.

My brooders were placed on the back porch, which had been enclosed with wide, rough, green boards that had shrunk, leaving big cracks between them through which the wind blew freely when strong.

A blustery March storm blew in one evening, when my chicks were about a month old, and I covered the brooders on the windy side with sacks and fixed a shield for the lamps. I felt sure everything would be all right, so I went to bed early and to a sound sleep.

I was wakened during the night by someone shaking my shoulder and telling me to get up. I lit the lamp and looked around. Both boys were asleep, and no one was near. Being weak and tired, I decided I must have dreamed it, so I lay down again and slept.

Again I was awakened, this time by a hand on each shoulder, shaking me vigorously, and a voice saying, "Dessie, wake up! Your chickens are going to burn up! Get out there, quick!"

I had left the light burning but could see no one. I was, however, wide awake now. I wakened the oldest boy; we lit the lantern and went to the back porch.

The wind had changed. The sacks were smoking, ready

to burst into flame. I saved the chickens, but I should like to know who woke me.

—Mrs. D. L.
Long Beach, California

A good question, indeed. Who wakened Mrs. D. L.? Whose voice spoke to her? What intelligence or force materialized a hand (or what she felt to be a hand) and shook her shoulders vigorously? On the occasion that she was prevented from entering her kitchen by what she describes as an "opalescent bar"—how was this formed, and by whom, and of what energy was it composed?

An Actress Is Saved

These types of ESP experiences are by no means rare, but not too many people have the temerity to report them. Miss C. S., a well-known actress, swore me to secrecy before she related a happening similar to the "bar" episode just recounted.

"I was on Broadway in a play," she said. "On my way to the theater, about to cross Fifth Avenue, the lights changed, and I stepped off the curb. I had taken no more than two steps when an invisible arm struck me with forceful impact across the abdomen, encircled my waist, and actually lifted me back onto the sidewalk. As it did so, a car swung sharply around the corner and narrowly missed striking me down. It seemingly came from nowhere, and I certainly would have been directly in its path, had it not been for this unaccountable force that rescued me. If you mention my name, I'll deny it, because I just can't afford to be called 'kooky.' "

There are countless case histories of men and women who have had impressions of the recent death of loved ones or friends, or premonitions that death was going to occur. These experiences have occurred in the form of dreams, or fantasies while awake, or what many call hunches, unmistakable yet unexplainable feelings.

Here are a few:

A Black, Foreboding Feeling

In 1949 I had gone to work one morning as usual, when suddenly I began to have a black feeling. This was the only way I could describe it to the girls with whom I worked. They only laughed at me and said it was the meanness coming out of me. But at our afternoon coffee break, I told a close friend, who is still living and can verify this fact, that I ought to go home. She wanted to know why; but all I could say was, "I don't know why—I just feel strongly I ought to go." But I fought the feeling off and went back to work. I had not any more than sat down when the office girl came in and said I was wanted on the telephone: My husband had dropped dead in a grocery store.

—Mrs. I. P.
Cardin, Oklahoma

A Warning of Approaching Death

My mother had been dead for about twelve years. I lost her back in my home town of Utica, New York, and had not been thinking of her.

At this time, I dreamed mother was with me, and, without saying anything, she put her arms around me and, with tears in her eyes, was comforting me. I said to her, "Mother, why are you sad for me? I am very happy. I have a wonderful husband and a good and very beautiful ten-year-old daughter."

She just held me closer and looked sad. At that time, our daughter did not even have a cold. But three days after, we lost our darling with encephalitis, sleeping sickness, from an insect bite.

—Mrs. A. R.
San Diego, California

A Daughter and
Mother Foresaw Fatal Accident

On Wednesday, September 13, 1961, I had a dream in which I saw my mother lying on her side on the street in a pool of blood. I woke up immediately in a cold sweat. I called her the next day and told her of my dream. Then I called on her the following Sunday and woke her up from a nap. I apologized for doing it, but she said, "Oh I'm so glad you did. I had a terrible dream. I dreamed I was killed!"

She went on to tell me about the big truck that hit their car. She mentioned her coat and said, "If anything happens to me, I'd like my brother's wife to have it, and I'd like you to have my fur stole."

I pooh-poohed her remarks. When we left that day, I kissed her cheek and said, "I'll be seeing you." She said, "Yes, if I'm still here."

We waved good-bye from the car. That night I had another dream. I seemed to be with friends and relatives at a party. Different people were passing trays of food and drink. As they came to me they would say, "Have you met Mr. Barron?" This was repeated over and over: "Have you met Mr. Barron?" Also, someone gave me a number, like a license number, which I couldn't recall.

The next morning, as I was getting ready to go out, a neighborhood dog howled and groaned. It bothered me so, I froze on the spot. I couldn't explain why.

Outside I met a mere church acquaintance. As she chatted with me, all pleasant-like, I wanted to burst out crying. Tears came over my eyes. I left her quickly, as I was sure she would think me odd. I couldn't understand my own miserable feelings.

I did later, though, because it was about that time that my father hit a huge trailer truck in Lynn, Massachusetts. My mother was thrown out and was found lying on her right side in a pool of blood, just as I had dreamed. She died three hours afterward of severe head injuries. My father was uninjured—but the Mr. Barron of my second dream was the driver of the trailer!

—MRS. G. M.
Danvers, Massachusetts

A Presentiment About a Father

It was in the year 1945. At that time I was living on the French Riviera (Cannes) with my husband and child. My family was on the Atlantic coast (near Bordeaux). After being released from a German prison, my father had been in very poor health, but his condition was improving steadily that summer. On this particular October day I was on the beach with my daughter; I felt wonderful, and the weather was glorious. Around noon I very suddenly became frighteningly oppressed and depressed; I left the beach and started crying as soon as I got home, and was unable to stop, although my husband was bringing a guest for lunch. I could only apologize and went on crying until four o'clock, when I received a wire that my father had died during his sleep somewhere between twelve and one o'clock. I must make it clear that I did not have any premonition, nor did I think of my father, but I have never felt that way before or since this incident, and the awful feeling is impossible to describe. I was my father's favorite child.

—MRS. M. M.
Chicago, Illinois

A Son's Vision
of His Deceased Mother

My most outstanding ESP experience was on February 19, 1919, when I was in billets east of Mons, Belgium, after the end of World War I. It was evening, and about a dozen of us were lying on our bunks, waiting to roll in, but all carrying on small talk. All at once a white curtain started to appear at the right side of my bunk. It crackled like a series of electric sparks. It appeared to be about three inches thick and extended from the floor to the ceiling, and it progressed down the side of the bunk, across the bottom, and up the left side. I followed its progress till it had reached the wall behind me. Then, turning my eyes, I saw my mother sitting there.

She greeted me, wanted to know how I was getting on, and we carried on a most pleasant conversation, until one of the boys kicked me on the sole of my boot. My mother and the curtain disappeared at once.

"What's the matter with you?" he said. "You have been talking and jabbering a long time."

I replied, "I guess I've been asleep." He said, "Asleep, nothing! You have had your eyes wide open and appeared to be talking with someone, but nobody was in front of you."

I do not recall what I replied to him, but I remember feeling queer and disturbed. When I got back home three months later, in May, 1919, my sisters told me that my mother had died on that same date, February 19. They said they had sent me a cablegram, which I never received. When I told them my story, they gave me a blank look, then exchanged glances with each other without saying a word. But I could tell by their reaction, they were thinking to themselves: "Too bad, it's a shame—his mind has been affected."

—MR. H. P. L.
Morgan Hill, California

It will be noted that most of these impressions of death, preceding, at the time of, or following the demise, have been related to loved ones—a mother, father, or daughter. This would indicate that the close emotional affinity existing between relatives has made them more sensitively aware of happenings connected with each other.

You have observed how deeply moved the percipients of these impressions have been. Whether or not they could specifically determine the motivation behind their shock or grief, they had to give way to feelings that seized them, and they remained disturbed until they knew the cause or until their impressions were verified. It was only then that relief came. There is a conviction related to a genuine extrasensory feeling totally different from one's imagination or fears or wishful thinking. People just "know" without knowing *how* they know. Once these impressions hit them, they can seldom be talked out of them. They may be ridiculed, but they will often insist in acting on them. Once they have done this, and an event they have sensed has come to pass, friends and loved ones still may not accept what has happened as evidence of ESP.

How would you explain this case? It was sent to me by Mrs. M. C. K. of Elba, New York:

A Dream
About a Neighbor's Daughter

A few years ago, my sister dreamed about her neighbor's daughter. It was a horrible dream. My sister saw (while asleep and dreaming) the girl being attacked and raped in front of a local supermarket, which she called by name. She knew what the attacker was wearing in detail. She awoke afterward, feeling rather guilty and wondering whether or not she was the victim of a dirty mind.

Later the next day, her neighbor came to her house, crying. My sister already knew why the tears flowed. The incident that had been dreamed actually happened at the same time my sister was dreaming about it.

The attacker was caught. The clothing he wore was exactly as my sister dreamed it had been!

Cases like this indicate that many experiences may be automatically broadcast in the form of mental images into what I call the "mental ether," and can be picked up when sensitive-minded men and women, either asleep or awake, happen to "tune in on the same wavelength." There is as yet no adequate scientific explanation as to what energy is involved in the transmission or reception, except that we know that the degree of intensity of the feeling involved plays a vital part.

She "Knew" What Had
Happened to Her Soldier Husband

The year was 1940. I met and married a fine student who was attending the University of Alabama. My husband's home was in Delaware. He had been commissioned a second lieutenant in ROTC. He went into the military for one year, the year President Roosevelt called on them to serve. Unfortunately, Pearl Harbor kept everyone in, including my husband. He left one month after Pearl Harbor for the South Pacific, to a lonely island by the name of Bora Bora. I worked in a war plant in Baltimore.

One night I was awakened from a deep sleep. I sat up in bed and saw my husband plainly, as if he had been beside the bed. He was bending over and holding his leg. He said, "Oh, God! My leg!" Naturally, I did not hear his words. They came to me very plain in my mind. I did not sleep any more that night. I was restless and told the girls with whom I shared an apartment about my terrible feelings that something was wrong with my husband's leg.

When a bunch of his letters arrived about a month later, sure enough, one letter told exactly about a piece of steel going into his leg. He walked on crutches for three months.

—Mrs. F. A. J.
Hollywood, New Mexico

A Dream
of an Accident to a Sister

I dreamed of my sister in Mexico. I saw her, in her bedroom, crying desperately and waving her arms, while uttering unintelligible words of distress. After this kind of demonstration, she would return to her bed, but only to rise again and repeat her same distressful performance. This happened three or four times before my dream faded, but I awakened in the morning with a profound feeling of foreboding and uneasiness.

I lost no time in writing my sister, not speaking in detail of my dream but urging her to answer me immediately and let me know if all was going well with her. Her letter was quick to arrive. In it she described a painful accident she had experienced in the kitchen the week before, when a pan of hot grease overturned as she was lifting it from the stove and scalded her arms. She was now quite comfortable, she explained, and the burn was healing normally, but she had been in considerable agony for several days and was unable to sleep. The date of this unhappy occurrence coincided exactly with that of my dream.

—MRS. E. F. P.
Wilmington, California

When Mrs. E. F. P. wrote me of this experience, I was reminded of an impression I had received years ago while living in New York City. I was dozing on a Sunday afternoon in our apartment when I suddenly had a vision of my father-in-law, Bryant G. Bain, then visiting a brother in California. I "saw" him with blood streaming down his face from an injury to his forehead. It seemed to have some connection with a car. I reflected a moment and felt he had not been seriously hurt, however painful the experience might have been.

I immediately told Martha, my wife, about my impression. She sat down at once and wrote her father, describing my feeling and asking if there was any truth to it. He replied that, allowing for the difference in time between New York and California, *as* I had "seen" the vision in my mind's eye, he had been up on a ladder trying to help his brother install the coil springs that operate the overhead garage doors. One of the springs broke loose and struck him a glancing blow on the forehead, cutting a gash which required six stitches. In falling, he landed on his brother, who had been holding the ladder, knocking the brother unconscious.

I had not "seen" this part of the accident, only that which related to my father-in-law. Somehow, in my relaxed and receptive state, the emotionally charged happening had been instantly transmitted to my mind.

You can imagine the emotional intensity involved in the next tragic case, evidently one of many of this type:

A Good-Bye from
a Twin Brother

The afternoon of this happening, I lay down for a nap and fell into a groggy, deep sleep. I saw my twin brother standing in front of the couch, looking down at me in a most sad and depressed way. He said, "I'm leaving now." Then he seemed to wait for me to say something. When I didn't, he again said, only more loudly, "I'm leaving now, and I'm not coming back!"

I believe I said impatiently to him, "I know it!" (My brother, then separated from his wife, had talked about going to another state to look for a job.) I thought this was what he was talking about and felt only relief that Mother wouldn't be worrying so much about him if he did go away. By this time, I was desperately trying to wake up. (I didn't know if I was dreaming or if this was truly happening.) In all of these experiences, from the first one when I was a child, I felt that these occurrences were real, but it was as though my mind was awake but that my body was weighted down to the point that I couldn't make it move. My brother still stood, staring at me with that sad, defeated look, and I heard him say once more, "I'm really leaving now."

He then turned and stepped right through the front door.

I finally managed to roll off the couch and promptly regained control of my body upon hitting the floor. I remember strongly feeling that I should call him by telephone, and this thought persisted for approximately a half-hour, and then suddenly it vanished.

That evening my aunt called and said my brother was gone. I replied, "Yes, I know he has" (still thinking he had gone to look for a job in another state). After several attempts to break the news to me gently, she finally had to tell me he was dead—and I learned then, that at the time I thought I saw him, he had committed suicide.
—Mrs. P. J.
Des Moines, Iowa

The fact that so many of these case histories have been reported by women does not mean, necessarily, that they receive more impressions than men. Psychologically they seem more willing to recount such experiences and to depend more on their intuitive faculties. Then, too, they may have more time, or are more disposed to take the time, to recount their "psychic adventures" and to seek an explanation for them. They are, I'm convinced, temperamentally less afraid of ridicule.

But here is an experience, related by a man, which rivals, on a miniature scale, a Biblical story.

A Premonition of a Flood

My home is situated on the beach right in the middle of a development of thirty homes. We are only three feet away from mean-tide level, and when we bought the house we had no idea there were any dangers. Eighteen years ago, I owned a small ten-foot boat.

On the evening of November 24, 1950, I got the compulsive urge to move the boat off the beach itself, drag it up, and tie it to the porch of my house. As I did so, I remarked to my amazed daughter, Pamela, "I'm tying this boat here, as we are going to need it before morning."

For some reason I said these exact words. It was beautiful weather that evening, and the reports all said "fair and mild" for the following day.

At six A.M., before dawn, something woke me up quickly. I knew something was wrong! Upon looking out the window, I saw that we were surrounded by the ocean. Through the early light, I saw homes floating across the meadows and over the nearby state highway. I woke up my wife and daughter and got them into the boat and up the street to higher ground.

Whatever made me tie that little boat to the porch? The spirit of *Noah?*

—Mr. R. W.
Laurance Harbor, New Jersey

An Advance Warning of a Crash

At seven A.M. one day, in a moment of anxiety out of nowhere, I warned my husband not to go to work. We argued on this, and my husband said I was crazy. Finally he left, and I shouted after him, "There's going to be an accident . . . and I see an awful fire!"

Later that day I myself could no longer remain at work and returned home to find my husband there ahead of me. This is what he told me: he was behind a great big oil truck, it skidded, and he almost crashed into it, but for some strange reason he pulled to the side of the road. As he did, another car hit my husband's car, and there was a forty-two-car crackup, one hitting the other, on the road. Up in front, the big truck had turned over, the driver having lost control. There was a big fire, and oil was spilled all over the road—and if my husband had not stopped when he did, he and other cars would have been right in the middle of it. As it was, no one was hurt, and all the cars, except the big oil truck, suffered only slight damages.

—Mrs. J. C.
Fall River, Massachusetts

A Vision of a
Deceased Mother and a Newborn Baby

My most dramatic experience with ESP was in July of 1944. We had just welcomed the arrival of our second son fourteen hours before. On that Sunday, July 9, about seven P.M., while my first son and husband were visiting me in my hospital room, I "saw" my mother (who had departed this life, July 19, 1942) go toward the nursery of the hospital, and a few minutes later she went back the other way, carrying our new son in her arms. A cold, almost icy chill had gone through my frame at about the time she would have been taking him from his crib.

I told my husband the baby was gone, before the nurse called him to the doctor's office, where they meant to plan a strategy of how to tell me. My husband informed them that I knew he was gone. Of course, there was a "logical" explanation, but I never told anyone except my husband what I had seen. I had always adored my mother. She was very talented and lovable, but even with this apparent assurance that the baby was now in her care, there was fear, for a few days, that I would follow my newborn son in death.

—Mrs. M. H. D.
Lindsay, California

A Warning That Arrived Too Late

My favorite sister and I were very close, and on many occasions I had phoned her when I felt something was wrong, and my feelings had always proved to be true. I was on the other side of the continent, and when this feeling of great apprehension for her safety came to me, I was having small problems of my own and did not phone her.

I had received a letter from her about a week to ten days before, and from the time I took the letter from the mailbox, I felt an inner chill that continued up to the time that the tragic event took place. There was nothing in her letter—just the usual chatter about her children and other family matters.

While answering her letter, I felt as if I were writing to someone who was not there. Of course I did not tell her that. I asked her how she was, and cautioned her to be careful. The letter arrived the day of the happening, and I learned later that she did not have time to read it and had set it aside to read when the children were quiet and in bed. My nephew was sick that night, which was another reason why she could not get to the letter.

That day and night, the feelings persisted in me that something dreadful was going to happen to my sister. I felt sick and helpless to do anything about whatever it was. I tried to go for a walk and shake it off. My disturbed feelings grew worse and worse. There was a time difference of three hours. Then the feelings gradually faded, and toward four A.M. I finally slept. I actually had not slept much from the time I had received her last letter.

This time, as I slept, I dreamed of being in a dark place, and there was only a small light. I saw a long, dark object pointed toward me. Then there was a large flash of light, followed by a terrible burning feeling in my abdomen. I awoke around five A.M. to hear someone banging on my door. I answered, and as the boy handed me a telegram, he said, "Someone has been shot."

I opened the telegram, and it contained the information that my sister had been shot at about the same time the icy chill had left me.

Now, this is what had happened. My sister was murdered by a young demented boy of seventeen. She was tricked out of her house at night, asked to hold a flashlight under the hood of the boy's car (the small light I had seen in the dream), so the boy could see to fix it. He made an excuse that he needed a wrench, and as my sister held the flashlight for him, he reached into the back of the car and got a rifle and shot her. (This was when I saw the big flash of light and felt the pain in the abdomen.)

As you remember, I told you my sister had a ten-year-old child who did not feel well and could not sleep that night, and she and the child were the only ones awake at that hour. The child witnessed the shooting of his mother through the living-room window.

The seventeen-year-old boy who shot her was a neighbor's child, said not to be "quite right." He had no friends and from the time he was seven years of age had been welcomed in the house—and was treated as one of her own children.

Somehow, when I got her letter that day, I must have picked up impressions of this boy's demented intentions, and as they grew stronger, I felt more and more concerned about my sister—but I just couldn't get the "whole picture" of what was getting ready to happen, and, for the first time, didn't phone her, as I usually did, when I felt disturbed about her. I will always regret this.

—MRS. V. D.
Toronto, Ontario

The Mystery of
the Watch That Stopped

My husband died of cancer on Saturday, May 1, 1954. Although he knew he would not recover, we never spoke of his dying. However, I know that he absolutely believed that death was final, the end of all. He did not believe in any sort of hereafter or have any thought that any part of a person lives on. We made no plans to "communicate"; we didn't either of us ever even mention it, because neither of us believed it possible.

I had not noted the exact time of his death. When I received his watch from the undertaker, it was still running on Sunday, May 2, but it stopped at 3:55 P.M. on the next day. Later, when I got the death certificate, this was the exact time of death. I thought it only an odd coincidence.

It was not until Sunday, May 1, 1960, that *my* watch stopped at 3:55 P.M. I couldn't believe it. I had had a strong feeling of his presence all that day, more than at any time since his death. I had married again and was trying to rebuild my life, so this was rather a shock to me.

On Saturday, May 2, 1963, it happened again, the same feeling all day, and the watch stopped at 3:55 P.M. But this time I was not aware of it until about ten or fifteen minutes after the watch stopped.

On Saturday, April 30, 1966, I had that "closeness" feeling again all day. This time I was alone (other people had been with me before), and I watched my watch reach the 3:55 time—and stop! I could not believe it a coincidence any longer, nor do I believe I have the power to do this myself, because I willed it to happen. Some force beyond me did it—and, actually, I would rather prefer it not to happen. How would you explain it? All this bothers me more than it should.

—Mrs. N. M.
Chico, California

I always try to answer these letters as carefully as I can, in terms of my discoveries in the area of ESP. In some instances, my responses will be given in this book.

Studies have been made in parapsychological laboratories of what is termed psychokinesis defined as "the alleged power of controlling the behavior of physical objects by the direct influence upon them of emotional states, strong desire, or extrasensory factors." In this particular case, could it have been the "spirit" influence of her "dead" husband, trying to impress his wife not only of his presence but also of his survival? Or could she herself, once having accepted the suggestion, have exerted an energy which stopped her watch? This is not likely, since the time her husband's watch stopped on the first occasion, 3:55 P.M., had no significance to her until she learned it was the time of his death. Also, in succeeding years, when her watch stopped at the same time, she was not always giving conscious attention to it. This is one of the many mind mysteries that science has still not been able to explain or to solve.

A Prediction of a Rock Slide

Mr. R. H. E. of Harrisville, New York, wrote me that he had put his ESP "gift" to good use during his war service in the South Pacific.

"Of course," he stated, "everyone in the outfit put me down as a nut, but whenever something came up that threatened our well-being, then they called on me to pull some of my mental tricks out of the bag.

"I had been a construction carpenter most all my life," he continued, "and here again, I found many fine uses for this 'gift' in my every working day."

About that, he told me this story:

One time on a heavy construction job, I told a general foreman that at two o'clock in the afternoon, on a certain day, there would be a cave-in of rocks near an underground concrete pour. The foreman just smiled and walked away. But just before the "appointed time," I told the men about what was to happen, so they started to follow me out of the hole. The last man up the ladder was caught by the legs in the rock slide. The fellow was not badly hurt, but, here again, everyone gave me a funny look, and next day I was looking for a job.

I have been told since by a friend, who was also "sensitive," to keep these things to myself, as he had experienced the same trouble. You may think I am giving you some kind of a line, but I swear that everything I have reported is true.

I believe this man, as I accept the authenticity of every case I am presenting herein. Years of research and a study of thousands of cases, as well as personal experiments and experiences in various phases of extrasensory perception, have enabled me, I'm sure, to distinguish the imaginary, the self-deluded, and the hallucinatory from the genuine phenomena. Few people are going to put forth the time and effort to give long, detailed reports of psychic adventures unless they actually did occur. Where possible, I have gotten documentation. In a number of cases, due to the understandable lack of records for these emotional experiences, this has not been possible, but the genuine quality of these cases should, I think, in most instances speak for itself.

Consider now this remarkable case which has the ring of truth in every word. It was written to me by a retired registered nurse, whose initials are N. J. M., now living in Hilo, Hawaii.

A Case History Involving a Nun

In 1929, I was a student nurse at St. Vincent's Infirmary, 2000 High Street, Little Rock, Arkansas. I was also a recent Catholic convert but knew very little about how prayers were answered.

There was an old nun whom I loved very dearly, and I know she loved me too. She was from Ireland, and her only living relative, a brother, still lived in that country.

One morning she received a cablegram telling her that her brother was dying, that he had suffered a heart attack and the doctor had given him two more hours to live.

Sister was just crushed—there is no other word for it—and so was I. But I asked her permission to go to the chapel and pray.

While I was in the chapel I "saw" her brother sitting in a platform rocker with white marble wheels (small), eating from a brown crockery bowl, something that looked like cream of wheat. I "saw" a handmade afghan of unusual design across his lap. I "saw" Irish lace panel curtains at the window. I "saw" the design in the rug—all these things I can still see thirty-eight years later.

I returned to my floor, told Sister her brother was not dead, that he was sitting up eating. I even drew the design of the chair, afghan, and rug and described her brother in detail. She was furious with me, said I was sacrilegious! I was heartbroken and bewildered. I was only seventeen years old, and I thought that was the way prayers were answered.

A few days later, Sister got a letter from her brother's wife, stating that he had "snapped out" of his heart attack within an hour after she had sent the death message, and had insisted that she help him to his chair and wheel him to the window to watch for the mailman. She helped him up, put the afghan across his lap, and gave him a bowl of "gruel," and that's where I saw him!

I've had many such visions since then, and only this summer I was able to save a two-year-old child's life because I had "seen" the accident three weeks before it happened, and so was able to act in time when I saw it happening for real.

These feelings always leave me feeling weak and exhausted, with a splitting headache, and I might add that they frighten me no end. I can't keep them from coming. I certainly don't invite them, can't understand, don't want them, and I never mention them to anyone, not even my own husband. What I'd like to know is this—does everyone have them and, like myself, keep it a secret for fear of ridicule—or do I really have something? . . .

I think that Mrs. N. J. M. does have something, something quite priceless, and she is trying to the best of her ability, however much this power disturbs her, to use it for service to others. This was how it was meant to be, and how it will ultimately be used by humankind, when man is sufficiently developed mentally as well as spiritually.

Do Animals
and Birds Possess ESP?

This question was asked me by Mrs. H. B. D. of Rochester, New York, who may have answered her own query with this touching little story about Paderewski, the famous Polish pianist.

I have read of animals that seemed to have foreknowledge relating to someone they loved. I am wondering if any experimentation has been done with thought transmission from animal to human and vice versa. J. Allen Boone (now deceased, a dear friend of mine), author of *Kinship with All Life* [Harper, New York, 1954], tells of such communication with the wonderful movie dog Strongheart.

Someone told me that when Paderewski was on one of his concert tours in this country, he heard his parrot, in England, calling to him for help. Next morning he received word that the parrot had been shut between door and screen by mistake the night before and had died of the cold.

Can you tell me if anyone has had an identifiable message from an animal that has died? Some horses and dogs and dolphins and cats, I understand, have seemed to sense, at times, what their masters have said to them or have reacted to thoughts in their minds.

Terhune* used to tell about his dogs walking around the spot where one of his dogs had always lain, outside his door, after the dog's death, as if he were still there.

Mrs. H. B. D. has raised some profound points that I hope will be answered, in part at least, in later chapters of this book. There is so much we do not know as yet about what takes place in the consciousness of all forms of life.

A Deceased Grandfather Reappeared

This is the report of Mrs. L. W. of Chula Vista, California, of an experience she had when she was a girl of thirteen, in late August of 1938, which she will never forget.

My maternal grandfather had been very ill, and in the last weeks of August he went into a coma. (He had cerebral thrombosis.) During the five months he had been ill, he seemed to worry about me all the time. At Grandfather's request, he had been kept at home rather than at the hospital, with nurses around the clock. Anytime my mother was present he always wanted her to go to her own home and "take care of Babe." ("Babe" is my family nickname.)

My grandfather and I had always been very close, and there was a deep and abiding love for one another. I am also the "baby" of the family, so it is perhaps understandable that he was worried about me and how I was taking his illness.

On the afternoon of his death, I suddenly had a feeling that he was gone, and proceeded to dress and prepare to catch a bus to my grandparents' home. As I was leaving the house, the phone rang and I answered it. It was my sister calling to inform me that Grandfather had died. I told her I already knew and was on my way to catch the bus.

When I arrived, I walked into Grandfather's room and looked at him. A feeling of peace invaded my being, and I knew that all was well now. He had no more pain.

Two days later I went to the funeral home to see Grandfather. My grandfather had the most beautiful

---

* Albert Payson Terhune, the well-known author who wrote so extensively about his collies.

hands, and he had always been very careful of them. During his illness, his nails had grown very long. I asked Mr. Preston to please cut them and take the rough off Grandfather's face, as I knew Grandfather would have been very displeased about this.

The evening of my visit to Grandfather, we had what is called a Santana here in Southern California. It is a very strong wind, and the sand even comes through the windowsills and cracks under doors.

At this time, I had a dog called Lady. She was half shepherd and half collie. She was strictly my dog. When I went out to play, Lady had to be brought into the house, as she would bite anyone who chased me or anything of this sort. She was a wonderful watchdog and always preferred to sleep outside on the front porch. No one could come into the yard without Lady alerting us by barking.

That particular night, she howled like a banshee. I "saw" Grandfather walk across our lawn, through the walls of the house, and come to stand in my bedroom doorway. I felt no fear. Just warmth and love. He simply said, "Babe, be a good girl." Lady quit barking, and Grandfather went away. Then he came again, and the same statement was repeated.

After this second visit, my mother brought Lady into my room, and she crawled under my bed. Then Grandfather came for a third time. Lady whimpered and fussed. At this time, I told Grandfather that I would call Mother so he could talk to her too. He said that she could not see or hear him and that he would have to leave now. He did. Lady was quiet the rest of the night. Oh, there was a phosphorescent substance that completely encircled Grandfather each time I saw him.

At thirteen, a person may be highly imaginative but would hardly conjure up an experience like that. The dog, too, was sensitively aware of something taking place or of a presence. There have been countless similar cases testifying to after-death appearances.

The After-Death Return of a Dog

Last December I had to have my dog put to sleep. We had Jack for sixteen years. He was an English shepherd and had been given to us when a puppy. He adopted the oldest boy, and remained faithfully his until John left for the Air Force, June, 1961. Jack then adopted me. He slept by my side of the bed and kept a vigil out by the driveway when I left home. He was a very dignified and intelligent dog. He had a weak heart, but this was controlled by medicine. He finally got arthritis in his front shoulder. I had him doctored, but the condition gradually got worse. I knew that I had to have him put to sleep, because I could not stand to see him suffer. I had it done on a Saturday morning in December.

The following Monday, at 3:30 A.M., I heard Jack snuffling at the bed and could feel him nudging me the way he did when he wanted me to wake up. I opened my eyes and saw him standing by my bed, wagging his tail and looking at me. It took all my willpower not to reach out and touch him. I was afraid that if I did, he would disappear. I don't know how long I lay there looking into his eyes. He was so joyous to see me. Then he was gone.

—Mrs. M. F.
Redding, California

Several years ago my wife, Martha, and I had two beautiful black-and-white cats, of undetermined breed, whom we dearly loved: Whitey, a male, and Spot, a female. Whitey was a manly little animal, quick in his defense of Spot, and would fight other stray cats and any other threatening wildlife to the death. We have our home in the Ozark hills, surrounded by thickly wooded areas, almost junglelike. One day Whitey went off into the night and never came back. We feel that some hunters, looking for something to shoot, practiced their marksmanship on him.

Of course, Whitey was missed by us, as well as by Spot. She would sit out back and watch and watch for him to return. At night the two cats had had the habit of sitting side by side on an ottoman in front of my reclining chair. Often Whitey, especially, had rubbed against Martha's and my legs as we were seated in the living room, reading or listening to music.

One evening shortly after Whitey's disappearance, Martha and I unmistakably felt something brush against our feet and legs. Martha noticed it first and looked down, expecting to see Whitey, but there was nothing there. My reaction, a few moments later, was the same. Spot, at that moment, was perched on the ottoman, quietly looking at us. We exchanged comments about this phenomenon and wondered if this might have been Whitey's way of letting us know he was "still around." Since this time, there have been at least half a dozen other occasions when the experience has been repeated.

I report this in support of like experiences that have been recounted, such as the one just related by Mrs. M. F.

Who are we to say that ours is the only form of life that may have survival value?

A Dying Brother
Sees Something Beyond

This last summer I lost a brother with cancer. He had an unusual passing. The doctors had said he would go into a coma, but he was conscious to the last breath and kept saying, "This is all so wonderful!" We felt he must be seeing something. It makes a person want to break through all these barriers.

—MRS. R. B. E.
Wichita, Kansas

A Visit and a Message After Death

On June 1, 1967, at 10:30 P.M., my intended second husband died. His death was unexpected, but he realized he was dying, and I was with him to the end.

I went to bed about 4:30 A.M. June 2, after having gone with my son to his home. I had been asleep about one-half hour when I heard my beloved calling me. I woke up, and my departed Joe said, "Jane—Janie, I have not gone yet. I have come to say good-bye. I must leave soon."

In a circle of light, I saw my beloved, and he was growing smaller and smaller, until the light disappeared. I was not dreaming. I was wide awake and heard and saw my departed Joe. I have dreamed of him twice since his death. We had strong telepathy between us.

—MRS. J. C.
Pennsville, New Jersey

It is significant to observe that in a great number of these cases wherein people who were loved apparently return for a final message, they all indicate that they "must leave" and that they are "going somewhere." They do not usually express regret at their going; this departure from people they love seems to have been accepted, and they are apparently aware that they will meet again sometime, somewhere.

Needed Help from the Other Side

On occasion it would appear that loved ones return to convey information in moments of great need and, in reaching the mind of the percipient (in this case, the daughter), create formerly familiar sounds, sights, and actions in order to establish identity.

As an only child who lost my mother when I was five, and living alone with my father in backwoods country, I grew up very close to Dad. One of my childhood memories is Dad's nightly prayers, which always ended, "God have mercy on Mary's soul." (Mary was my mother's name.) Dad remarried when I was eleven, and home was never home for me afterward.

Thirty-six years later, as Dad was dying, I had a fleeting picture of Mother, with her hand outstretched to him. Very lonely, with Dad gone, I had received an odd impression, as if a voice said, "Don't wish me back; I'm happy with your mother."

Shortly after Dad's death, I was handed a will, but my stepmother's niece turned up with a later will just about the reverse of the one I had. Litigation followed. As my dad could neither read nor write, both wills were signed with crosses, and my lawyer said it was practically impossible to identify crosses.

The later will was probated, but because of my rights through my mother, certain settlements were still necessary. My lawyer urged me to sign; I held off. Finally I was given only so many days to sign or move out of the house I was in. My husband was ill, I had two infants less than two years old, living on unemployment insurance, and no bank account.

Days ticked off. I had to give an answer the next day. It was nighttime. After tucking the babies in their crib, I lay down to await my husband's return from a nearby neighbor's.

Suddenly I heard horses drive into the yard. Thinking it was my husband, I sat up. The door opened and in walked Dad! He went to the stove to warm his hands, as was his habit, and sat in his usual chair. Then, looking intently at me, he said, "You sign nothing. I never made that will of theirs."

A step on the veranda signaled the entry of my husband. Dad faded slowly from sight, and I was called back by my husband's remark, "What's wrong? You seem to be far away."

I told him what had occurred, and he told me to follow the advice. The next day, my lawyer practically branded me as crazy to try to fight the matter. I felt that if I told him why I was so positive the second will made was a fake, he would be sure I was crazy, so I said nothing as to why I was so sure.

Within a few days a technicality turned up, holding matters as they were, and gradually one thing led to another, and the second will was disqualified completely and the first will took its place. As years went by, it turned out, without a doubt, that the second will was a fake.

Imagination, perhaps—or what?

—MRS. M. L.
Farrellton, Quebec

Mrs. M. L. has raised a good question. If we accept the visitation of her father's spirit, she must have slipped into the "next dimension," or certainly a higher state of consciousness. The door apparently opened; it actually did not. Her own husband observed, when he came in, that she seemed to be "far away." Unquestionably her mind had gained access to knowledge beyond her normal awareness that gave her the conviction to take a stand and impressed her husband sufficiently to cause him to support her. Whether or not we accept the "spirit-communication" premise, we are confronted with a baffling, evidential mystery.

His Dead Stepfather Waited for Him

My stepfather, who had been a Chicago ward boss and legislator, died of poisoned alcohol during Prohibition. He had been a TB patient and had removed himself from home when discharged in order not to endanger my health. I saw him shortly before his death.

A week or so after this event, I returned home one evening to a house and room he had never visited, stripped for bed, turned out the light, and discovered him waiting for me.

He told me he had been afraid he would have to leave if I didn't get there in time. At the end of his and my conversation, he said, "I'll have to go now, and I won't be back. But I'll see you again someday."

I awoke in the morning with the bed covers and my pajamas sweat-soaked, and with the feeling that we had conversed all night about things I cannot recall, but that I was rested and completely at ease.

One comment did remain with me, in conjunction with his remark: "Tell the Swede not to worry; it's all right." "Swede" was his nickname for my mother. Years later I recited this to her. She thought back and said that several nights, at the time of her husband's death, she had been awakened by a hand nudging her, and turned on the light and found no one there. She then told me what she had never revealed to anyone before. My stepfather had told her that he would not share her with anyone else, and that when he died, he would take her along.

I spent that night with Mother and her then husband, and awoke in the morning with the uncanny feeling that there had been a tremendous stir about me during the night. I wondered what must have been going on. I was later informed that the room in which I had slept had been the bedroom of a couple whose arguments had ended one night by the husband locking the bedroom door, then killing his wife and butchering her into strips and sections.

—Mr. K. H.
Marin City, California

The before-death "intent" of individuals apparently survives, together with the desire to carry it out on the so-called "physical plane" if at all possible. It appears necessary, however, to function through mortals, loved ones or others, with whom an emotional attachment has previously been formed, and with whom recognizable contact can hopefully be made.

An Out-of-Body Visit to a Mother

A doctor from Clarkston, Michigan, after reading my book *How to Make ESP Work for You* (DeVorss, Los Angeles, 1964), was intrigued enough by my description of the technique used by some sensitives to leave their physical bodies that he decided to try it. He thought, "How convenient it would be to be able to put my physical body to bed and asleep, and then travel instantly in astral form, spending my free evenings entertaining myself with visits to distant cities." He reported:

My first successful experience was brought to my attention by an alarming letter from my mother who lives in Iowa. She wrote that, on a certain Sunday afternoon, she awakened from a nap to find me standing in the bedroom. "I" apparently was talking to her, but she was so startled that she didn't grasp what I was saying. I immediately wrote her, requesting more details, and she replied as follows:

"I was asleep and I thought I heard you calling. I awoke and you were standing there in the room. You had a look of intense urgency on your face, and you were talking to me in great earnestness. I was frightened that this must mean something terrible had happened to you. I called for Dad, who was in the next room, but you disappeared then. You were wearing a dark, plain sport coat and a pair of slacks of contrasting color, with some design in it. Your hair was disheveled, and your skin seemed darker than usual."

At that time, I was asleep in my home in Pontiac. I had been up all that night before, working in the local hospital. I had finally arrived home about 10:30 A.M., thoroughly exhausted. As is my custom, I picked up a book to read for a few minutes to "unwind" before going to sleep. It happened to be your book, *How to Make ESP Work for You,* and I opened it to the chapter on out-of-the-body experiences. I thought I would just lie there and imagine myself visiting home. Then I apparently went to sleep.

After I received the first letter from Mother, I dimly remembered having a "dream" in which I returned home as I used to do when coming home from college in the fifties. I walked to the back door, which is always unlocked, right into the bedroom, where I found my mother napping. She awoke with a start, seeming to leap a foot off the bed. I started to express some sort of greeting, when I thought to myself how inconsiderate this was of me to so startle her, and turned about and walked out.

The description of the clothes fit the type of clothes I was wearing earlier that day, although at that exact time I was actually in pajamas. My skin was darker than usual since I had just returned from a California vacation.

This experience caused me to do some more experimenting. Several nights later, before dropping off to sleep, I imagined myself visiting a close friend, an architect, via "astral projection." Nothing apparently happened after about ten days of such trying, so I decided to forget it.

Then, a few days ago, this friend told me he awakened at 4:45 A.M. to find a dim shape of a man, having my appearance, standing at the foot of his bed. As it was dark, he could not see my face distinctly, but he said it definitely resembled me. He described this form as holding an object in his outstretched hand as if to give it to him. He was quite sure he was wide awake and not dreaming.

In checking back, at the time this "visitation" occurred, I had just gone to bed to catch a brief nap at the hospital. I was very tired and very relaxed. To my knowledge, I did not consciously try to project myself to his home at that moment, but the conditions must have been right, and my mind seemingly acted on a delayed suggestion from one of the previous times of concentration when I did try to reach my friend. Anyway, it is all very mysterious and quite exciting.

Out-of-Body Travel During Illness

There are many accounts from men and women who have experienced leaving their physical bodies while under the influence of an anesthetic or during a serious illness, almost as though a higher force within them starts to take over and prepares them for a possible departure into another state of being. The attempts of skeptics to ascribe all these adventures to hallucination or dreams or imagination, even though we must accept the testimony of the individual, on occasion without external proof, just will not suffice. The evidence is too overwhelming.

Here is a case, recounted by Mr. H. D. E. of Evansville, Indiana:

> The year 1938 was the year of my ulcer episode. I was apparently bleeding to death internally, and left the body quite comfortably and gladly. Looking back from the window and seeing my body lying on the bed, I reflected that leaving it was a most happy experience. Then I recalled that I had two small sons (twins aged nine) who needed a father, so I decided to get back into the body on the bed. Soon, the ambulance arrived and took me to the hospital, where I remained a month.

I myself had a similar experience when given an overdose of chloroform at a time, in 1920, when I had a gangrenous toe lanced. This experience is described in detail in *How to Make ESP Work for You.* I apparently saw my brother, Edward, who had been "dead" six years, waiting for me and ready to take me somewhere. Then, as I thought of my parents in Traverse City, Michigan, I suddenly left Detroit and found myself visiting them. They were unaware of my presence, even though I tried to attract their attention. I reached out to touch them, and my hand went right through them. This is characteristic of all reports of so-called "astral travel."

Further Evidence of "Soul" Flight

From reading the account of my own out-of-the-body experience, Miss Z. V. of Denver, Colorado, wrote that she had been reminded of a pamphlet that described a similar adventure, which her mother had acquired when Miss Z. V. was a child in Russia.

We were fascinated by it. I recall the details vividly after all these years. The pamphlet told of a young man who had been an avowed atheist until he became very ill, I believe, with pneumonia. Suddenly he found himself in the middle of the room and saw the doctors working over something in the corner—it was his body!

He tried to speak to them and touch them but could not attract their attention, and his hand went through them [as mine had done when attempting to contact my parents].

At first he was indignant that the doctors did not pay attention to his real self; then he became frightened. His old nurse, who lived with him, knelt down and began to pray. As he was watching her, two angels appeared, took him into their arms, carried him through the walls, and began to fly upward. A swarm of evil spirits clamored for his soul but could not take him away from the angels. They kept speeding upward, until they reached a realm of dazzling light. He tried to shield his eyes from it with his hand, but the light went through it.

The angels finally stopped, and he heard a voice: "Not ready!" and they began to descend. How he did not want to return to earth! After a time, difficult to determine, he experienced suffocation and the feeling of entering a dark, narrow prison. He was back in his body, and they were preparing it for burial! His signs of returning life and consciousness just barely saved him.

From that moment on, the account in the pamphlet went on to say, this young man became a believer and a lover of God. This story made a great impression on me, and I never forget it. I am sure, if all of us could experience astral projection, we would not be afraid of death or fear the unknown. Perhaps our dreams that we are easily and quickly floating through space are often more than dreams. Who knows?

The references made in this account to "angels" who were in attendance upon this young man's "spirit" when he left the body are often a part of these out-of-body reports. This gives them a certain religious overtone, but it is commonly held that some intelligences may be present when the possible death of the physical body is involved. Whether "angels" is the right word for them is a matter of conjecture at this point. Much remains to be known about what takes place in the realm beyond this life. We will have more to say about this in later chapters.

I hope that the reader is ready to agree, after a perusal of these varied cases of psychical phenomena, that the subject is worthy of serious and comprehensive research and examination. It has been a most difficult task to choose these extrasensory experiences from the vast number on file, and the temptation has been to include more and more, because of their enormous interest and significance. You, the reader, don't of course have access to these files, but I have felt a responsibility to give you, insofar as possible, a comprehensive sampling of what they contain.

My gratitude to those who have come forward to tell their stories, in spite of the skepticism and disbelief of friends and relatives, and the fear of ridicule, is unbounded. It has long been my contention that the greatest laboratory for the discovery of the meaning, purpose, function of extrasensory perception has to exist in the field of human experience—in the lives of men and women and children through whom these psychic adventures come. Most of these people have been subjected to these manifestations, often spontaneously, when they were unsought, and occurred under stressful conditions. Their contribution to demonstrable knowledge of these higher powers of the mind *has* to be significant—and a study of their case histories as well as of those individuals who can and have demonstrated extraordinary sensitivity will lead openminded scientists and researchers of the future to great breakthroughs in mind expansion. It should help, too, in determining just who and what man is, and the part he really has been designed to play in the infinite scheme of creation.

3

The Universal
Language of Feeling:
Some Major Breakthroughs

WHAT WOULD YOUR reaction be if it could be substantially demonstrated to you that a sensitively developed person can "tune in," on occasion, with your thoughts and feelings—can describe these experiences so accurately in words as to be apparently reading from a literal record of them? However skeptical you may be, we now have increasing evidence that such an amazing recording system does actually exist. For want of adequate definitive words, this phenomenon must be termed as a vibratory form of thought transference.

For a human sensitive to be able, further, to see the past, present, and future as though they exist all at the same time, and to relate past, present, and future happenings to one another in an unbroken series of mental impressions, is a phenomenon that most scientists are not yet ready to accept. But there are highly developed men and women today who have demonstrated and are demonstrating these abilities.

Gerard Croiset

There is Gerard Croiset, the Dutch sensitive, for example, whose mental feats have been reported by Jack Harrison Pollack in his book *Croiset, the Clairvoyant* (Doubleday & Company, New York, 1964; and Bantam Books). Pollack says of Croiset and his ESP powers: "He sees things not visible to the normal human eye or mind. His images aren't confined to the limits of coventional time and space. He not only describes events occurring in the present, hundreds of miles away, unseen by anyone else, but constantly dips into the past and future as if into an endless sea. The past, present and future, according to Croiset, are difficult for him to separate."

Croiset, whose developed telepathic, clairvoyant, and precognitive gifts have been studied in Holland by his mentor, Professor W. H. C. Tenhaeff, director of the Parapsychology Institute of Utrecht, has solved many criminal cases in various parts of the world, such as robbery, rape, and murder. He has located hundreds of missing children as well as adults, living and dead; has helped people find documents, artifacts, and hidden treasures. In addition, he has also unraveled, through his exercise of extrasensory perception, numerous other mysterious happenings and problems which have baffled police, parents, and all concerned.

Croiset often performs what is called psychometry, as reported by Pollack, using a photograph, ring, glove, letter, brick, piece of clothing, bone, or stone as an inductor. He can repeatedly "know" a person he has never met by simply holding something belonging to him. This implies, of course, that these objects are impregnated vibrationally, in some way, with the thoughts and feelings of the person with whom they have been associated; Croiset and other similarly endowed sensitives can sense past experiences as well as the character and nature of the individual from contact with these articles.

But to a sensitive of Croiset's amazing capability, it is not necessary to touch or have access to an object. Some of his most accurate and, at the same time, most unbelievable extrasensory performances have been demonstrated over the long-distance telephone. Says Pollack, "Over the phone, he doesn't 'fish' for information. Instead, he prefers to let his sensitivity guide him toward relevant facts. Actually he asks as few questions as possible. He prefers telephone consultations because they eliminate extraneous influences and reduce confusing or overlapping impressions. He helps many individuals over the phone or in person, but tape-records only cases that he considers important."

Peter Hurkos

Another sensitive who possesses powers similar to those of Croiset, and who has gained a worldwide reputation, is Peter Hurkos. He, coincidentally enough, also came from a Dutch town, Dordrecht, a few miles from The Hague, capital of the Netherlands. When thirty-two years of age, he fell from a scaffolding and was in a coma for three days. After he recovered consciousness, Hurkos discovered that he could shake hands with, or make contact with some object belonging to, a person he had never seen before, and that vivid mental images would then flash through his mind, having to do with experiences this individual had undergone.

An injury to the brain had apparently activated certain sensitized areas which other sensitives have been able to stimulate through methods of concentration. In any event, Hurkos soon came to the attention of the police in different European countries and was also helpful in solving, through his telepathic, clairvoyant, and precognitive powers, many perplexing cases of robbery, rape, and murder. Brought over to the United States, he was able to demonstrate his extrasensory faculties under test conditions.

In his book, *Psychic,* Hurkos attempts to explain the nature of what he calls his "gift." He says:

> When I shake hands with a stranger, I know all about him; his character, his private life, even the house in which he lives. For, in simply touching his hand, I receive a series of images like those thrown on a screen by a motion picture projector. They are often unrelated images, one picture flashing to another quite different from the one before, but I see them. After a single handshake, I know as much about the man as an old friend would know—often much more. . . .
>
> I have never claimed more than eighty-seven and one-half percent accuracy in my readings, the percentage established by scientists after performing thousands of tests with me. With that small margin of error, however, I can tell what has happened to people I meet, or to people at a distance, what is happening, and what will happen to them in the future. . . .
>
> No one knows how this is done. We are sure, however, that emanations from a person or an object do exist, just

as heat waves, radio waves and electric impulses exist. . . .

Every man has the power of ESP within himself, but he must learn to use it. . . .*

I am in agreement with the reports on the unusual psychic abilities of these two men and their statements pertaining to extrasensory powers, because I, in a lifetime of experimentation and research, have been able, on occasion, to demonstrate these same faculties. Their existence indicates that there are higher energies and forces functioning through your mind and body of which you as yet have little conscious awareness or knowledge, and that, since everything is recorded with the degree of intensity that it has been experienced, you may be carrying in your consciousness *all* that has happened to you up to the present moment.

Let me present a few documented case histories of my own in support of this, and then point out to you what I consider the significance of these facts as applied to yourself.

I am quoting below from an affidavit contained in my personal files, which reads as follows:

Impressions Relating to the Murder of L. Jane Braden,† a Seventeen-year-old Babysitter Who Was a Murder Victim in the Early Hours of December 28, 1965, in Wyoming

At about 9:30 A.M. Friday, January 7, 1965, I, Burleigh K. Allen, a special investigator from Billings, Montana, who was retained to conduct titled investigation, telephonically contacted Mr. Harold Sherman . . . who, at that time, was located at the Lafayette Hotel in Little Rock, Arkansas.

I advised Mr. Sherman that a young woman, age seventeen, a baby-sitter, had been stabbed and her body found in the North Platte River near ——, Wyoming, and

---

* From *Psychic: The Story of Peter Hurkos,* copyright © 1961, by Pieter van der Hurk and V. John Burggraf, reprinted by permission of the publishers, The Bobbs-Merrill Company, Inc.

† Fictitious name.

asked for his impressions and cooperation in developing facts concerning this case.

With only the above information, and without the victim's name, Mr. Sherman advised that the person who had committed this crime was a young, tall, blond individual with sallow complexion and high cheekbones. He was described as inwardly psychotic, highly nervous, and with a tendency to twitch his eyes. This man enjoys pornographic literature and may be addicted to dope or liquor. This individual drove a dirty secondhand car of light color with a dented or damaged left-front fender. It was further stated that he lived in a small house of about five rooms which had some type of dug-out cellar underneath. It was possible some item connected with the crime could be hidden under this house or buried nearby.

He has committed at least two previous assaults; and, if not apprehended, would repeat this type of offense. The subject was believed to still be in the area. The weapon the subject used was a knife of the switchblade type. The crime, according to Mr. Sherman, occurred between one and two A.M. He visualized the subject removing the victim from the back of the car, carrying her body some distance, and dropping it from a high point. He said that subject then cleaned up and went home. Mr. Sherman visualized further that the figure "5" is a factor in this case, and also that the letter "L" is a very prominent letter in the case.

With the above observations and impressions, I will now set out the facts of instant case as known at this time, but not entirely known at the time of my conversation with Mr. Sherman.

The man who was arrested, Robert Samuel Evarts,* is age twenty, height six feet, three inches, weight one hundred and eighty pounds, light brown hair, sallow complexion, slightly noticeable high cheekbones, and one who has been believed inwardly psychotic for some years. He is a very highly nervous person; and, when arrested, was attacked with stomach-cramp convulsions, which wore off only after his admissions of this murder and two prior assaults on local young women in the past four months. He ordinarily wore glasses, but when he takes them off, which he does quite often, his eyes have a tendency to twitch and blink.

At the time of the crime, he was driving a dirty secondhand 1958 Ford, white over light blue, with a dented left-front fender and damage to the right side of the car. It has been ascertained that the damage to the left-front fender occurred less than thirty minutes before the death of the victim. When the information relative to the car

* Fictitious name.

was given to me, I told Mr. Sherman that the right side of the car was damaged, not knowing of the damage to the left side.

At no time was Mr. Sherman advised of the weapon used, but it has been ascertained that a long, narrow fruit knife was used, and in many ways resembles a switch-blade type.

It has also been ascertained that the crime was committed between 12:45 and 1:45 A.M., December 28, 1965. Subject admitted stabbing the girl twice in the chest with this long knife, picking up her body, and carrying it approximately fifty feet, where he placed her on the floorboards of the rear seat and drove onto a bridge, dragged the body from the rear of the car, carried it to the edge of the bridge, and dropped the body about fifteen feet into the North Platte River. He said he threw the knife along the highway as he returned to the city at that time.

No connection has been found in this case to the figure "5" as a factor, but it is pointed out that the letter "L" is very prominent. This is the initial of the first name of the murder victim, and the names of the two prior victims were Linda and Linda Lee.

As previously stated, he admitted to two prior assaults, and it is believed that he attempted entry into a home the night before his arrest but became frightened when the young girl came to the front door with a butcher knife in her hand.

At the time I talked with Mr. Sherman, I was not acquainted with the type of home in which the subject lived. I can now state that it is a small five-room house which has no basement but which has a cellar underneath part of the house, which can be entered only through an outside door.

The only information furnished by Mr. Sherman that I have had difficulty reconciling is that of the direction and distance which he described. Since they play no part in particular, these impressions and facts are not being set out in this paper.

(*Signed*) BURLEIGH K. ALLEN
Special Crime Investigator
Billings, Montana

Like Croiset and like Hurkos, as I fixed my mind on the case, given only a simple statement of the crime by a man I hadn't known existed until I received his telephone call, I was able to tune in on the existing vibratory records. As I did so, I almost instantly seemed to "take on" the conditions and the feelings and actions concerning this murder. I felt, in my own body, as the killer felt; I felt the stabs in the body of the murder victim; I saw mental pictures of the actions of the killer as he picked up the body, carried it to the car, and drove to the bridge, where I saw him "drop the body from a high point."

It was almost as though my body and mind were serving as instrumentation for a "playback" of all that had happened. I could sense that this killer had attacked two women prior to this attack; I could feel his sensuous desires building up again as he prepared to make an assault on still another young girl. As I talked to Mr. Allen on the phone, without a word of coaching from him, I put these thoughts and feelings into words, just as I was getting them. He made a tape recording of my comments.

While I could not distinguish the names, I saw the letter "L" flash across the screen of my mind and felt it had specific significance. I have had to discipline myself to speak out or to record impressions as quickly as the mental images and feelings come into consciousness; otherwise my conscious mind will try to argue me out of them, tell me they couldn't possibly be true.

With reference to the dirty secondhand car with the dent in the left-front fender, I saw it momentarily in my mind's eye, as clearly as you can remember the appearance of your own car. I was not getting the impression from Mr. Allen's mind, because he was not aware of this damage until later. In fact, he thought I had made a mistake and had picked up the impression of the damage to the right side, wrongly identifying it.

There is always a percentage of error in this pioneering type of extrasensory work, as both Croiset and Hurkos have remarked—but seventy to eighty percent of detailed accuracy achieved, in most cases, by each of us should indicate that these higher powers of mind not only exist but also can be developed and used for practical purposes.

A Lost Boy

Here is a case of a different sort. Note that previously there has been a high degree of emotional intensity involved in these experiences; again, the deeper the feeling, the more intense the projection of thought.

This affidavit concerns a lost little boy:

121 West Grand
Hot Springs, Arkansas
February 17, 1966

DIVING ASSOCIATES

Underwater Salvage and
Inspection—Year-
Around Service.

Mr. Harold Sherman,
ESP Research
Associates Foundation,
1750 Tower Building,
Little Rock, Arkansas

Dear Mr. Sherman:

As you will recall, I telephoned you last Tuesday, February 15, and requested your help in locating a three-year-old boy who had been missing from his home on Lake Hamilton late Monday afternoon.

I reported to you that bloodhounds had been used in searching for the child in the woods and that divers were also searching in the lake for the body.

You advised that you did not feel that the child was lost in the woods but that he had been drowned and his body would be found in the water at a location which you described as follows:

Two hundred feet to the right from the spot where the child was last seen, there is an obstruction; from this point a tree-surrounded path leads to a steep bank; twenty to thirty feet from the steep bank and in water about twenty feet in depth is the location of the child's body.

I would like to advise that the child's body was found Tuesday afternoon in the exact location which you described to me as noted above.

Thanking you for your cooperation with regard to this tragic matter, we remain,

Yours truly,

DIVING ASSOCIATES
(*Signed*) CARL E. BROOKS
LOUIS BRODRICK
Divers

When this phone call was received early that Tuesday

morning, I instantly instructed my mind to determine for me what had happened to this young boy. Almost at once I seemed to be mentally canvassing the wooded area and received the positive impression that the child had not been lost in the woods, as many had surmised.

My attention became fixed on the boy, and I felt myself to be in the yard where he had been playing. I moved with him to the right, as I reported over the phone to Mr. Brooks, and "saw" the boy, in my mind's eye, encounter a low obstruction (which proved to have been a fence surrounding the property). He had reached this fence after traversing a tree-lined path, and somehow managed to clamber over it. I suddenly felt as though I were the little boy, as he continued on to the edge of a steep bank and toppled from it, into the water. I felt myself cry out and my mouth fill with water. I struggled briefly as water closed over my head and I felt my body being carried out away from shore, perhaps some twenty to thirty feet, where I sank slowly to the bottom of the lake. It was here that my mind disengaged itself from attachment to the boy's body, and I left it, as I mentally saw it huddled on the bottom in some twenty feet of water.

It is clearly evident that my mind was not in attunement with the mind of the boy who had drowned. This had been an act of clairvoyance—an extrasensory perception of something that had happened at a distance far beyond the reach of the five physical senses. Again I must voice my conviction that this entire drowning episode, together with the feelings the boy experienced at the time, had been somewhere recorded—and that I, through a method of inner concentration learned through years of experimentation, had managed to pick it up.

One more example should suffice to substantiate the existence of these higher powers of mind, and perhaps the fact that nothing that has ever happened to you, or can happen, is ever lost.

You are today the end result of the effect that all your past experiences have had upon you, physically, mentally, emotionally, and spiritually. There is no stopping the recording. It is continuing as you read these lines. Every page you turn, every move you make, every thought you think is being photographed, is being registered, I feel sure. Much of the recording will be weak or faint because very little feeling is associated with what you may be doing; but let something vital happen which arouses you emotionally or calls for intense thought, and the grooves in your life's record will run deep. This is the reason that a sensitive can get accurate impressions of tragic experiences more easily than of ordinary events.

A Sister Who Disappeared

Here is a letter recently received from Ralph E. Glasgow, 216 W. Baltimore Street, Jackson, Tennessee, which bears this out:

Dear Mr. Sherman:

You will recall that I wrote you about the disappearance of my sister, Mrs. Ida G. Meals. She left her home September 18, 1966.

You wrote me back that she left in a highly confused state of mind. Also that you could not contact her mind. You also stated that her body would be found in a rough, wooded place, near a stream or river, about seventeen miles from her home.

I wish to tell you how highly accurate you were.

Her body was found September 26 at 3:30 P.M. by two men who were bird hunting. Her body was just 99 feet from Highway 20, going northwest. Although close to a prominent highway, the body was behind a bush and lay near some large trees. Now it was only about 10 feet from the bank of a large drainage ditch. This ditch is as large as some small rivers. Also it was only 10.7 miles from the city limits of Jackson but was 17 miles from her home. You asked me to let you know when the body was found.

(*Signed*) RALPH E. GLASGOW

Mr. Glasgow went on in this letter, as a postscript, to comment: "The autopsy left much to be desired and did not pinpoint the actual cause of death. We would like for you to determine for us the cause of death. If you can take the time to give this matter sincere concern, it would be one more real testimony for the power of ESP. You were so highly accurate on the other, if you could come up with the cause of death, then it would be one to relate in a book if you wish. Please let us hear from you soon. Help us find the actual cause of death, as this is still a major mystery with us."

It is difficult for men and women, confronted with tragedies or pressing personal problems, to realize that I am barraged at all times with many letters and long-distance telephone calls from various parts of this country and the world, making similar requests of me. Utilizing these higher powers of the mind in this way is not a parlor game. I have often had stomach upsets and solar-plexus reactions from having taken on the vibratory conditions relating to a savage and revolting crime, and reliving and experiencing these sensations in my own mind and body; or, in the case of this woman, sensing her confused state of mentality at the time she left home and trying to follow her movements mentally.

As Mr. Glasgow reported, I wrote to him that "I could not contact her mind." She was dead at the time, and there is a difference in *feeling*, difficult to describe, when a person is no longer in this life. But even when a person has passed on, nature continues its recording of everything that is happening. A clairvoyantly endowed sensitive can, therefore, often "get" conditions and events related to an individual after the individual himself is out of the picture. As Hurkos has stated: "No one knows (or can explain) how this is done," except that there must be some emanations or vibrations that translate themselves into images and feelings in the mind of the receiver, and then can be interpreted in words.

Since I had been so accurate in my impressions of what had happened to his sister, Mrs. Ida Meals, Mr. Glasgow was equally confident that I could, by calling upon such extrasensory powers as I possessed, determine the cause of her death. This assumption does not necessarily follow.

I did put my mind on the case once more, and the feeling that came to me was that Mrs. Meals, having wandered away from home in a confused state of mind, suddenly recovered her senses after dark. I saw her, in my mind's eye, panicked and bewildered, rushing from the woods, running out into the highway and trying to flag down a motorist. Still somewhat dazed, but now wanting to have help, she ran into the path of a car, was struck down, and killed. The motorist, in a state of shock, finding that the woman was dead, and noting that no one had seen the accident, picked up her body, carried it off the road, and hid it behind the bushes.

This is the scene that crossed the screen of my mind, and there is probably no way of discovering, at this late date, whether or not any part or all of these impressions are correct. I cannot guarantee that they are, and I always am tormented by my conscious mind, which tries to tell me that there is no foundation in fact for the things I see mentally.

Every genuine sensitive stresses the point that you cannot *force* yourself to get impressions. If you do, you activate your imagination and cause it to embroider or build upon any true impressions that may be coming through and thus distort them. Since it has become rather widely known that I have been successful in locating missing planes and missing persons and in helping to solve murder and other mysteries, the pressures on me have been growing.

I have finally had to refuse most requests for aid, as I could be devoting full time to this work alone, and I never charge for such services as I can perform. To be placed under any feeling of obligation, or to be asked to prove that it can be done, to satisfy their skepticism, or for "show," repulses me. I have too deep a respect for this higher power to permit it to be abused or misused in any way.

Can you now begin to accept the probability that there are vast areas of your mind of which you have been only vaguely, if at all, aware? When the ancient wise men suggested that thoughts were things, they were not giving expression to an empty phrase. Thoughts are a form of creative energy with *feeling* behind them. Whatever you desire or fear, once *imaged* in mind, seeks to objectify or materialize itself in your outer life.

Everything comes from the *invisible* into the *visible*. Its launching pad is the mind. The more intense the feeling behind the image, the more apt it is to reproduce itself in some future moment of time.

4
Behind the
Mystery of Your
Individual Existence

THERE ARE FOUR basic questions that have obsessed the human race—young and old—from the advent of life on earth, and there was never a time in any history of which we have record when these questions were being raised with more persistency and urgency. They are:

"Where did I come from?"

"Who am I?"

"Why am I here?"

"Where am I going?"

No one, including the wisest men of all ages, has been able to come up with conclusive answers to any of these four fundamental, challenging questions. This failure of man to find satisfactory answers in his quest for an understanding of himself, his relationship to his fellow creatures, and to the world about him, is responsible to a great degree for his basic inner feeling of insecurity.

You, in keeping with every other form of life, have come on the earth as the result of a creative sex act. On arrival, you found, as you developed self-conscious awareness, that this ball of earth, with all the ingredients necessary to your existence here, was waiting to receive you. The earth, like yourself, as judged by our limited five physical senses, came originally from the invisible into the visible.

All the elements composing it, everything on it and in it, first emerged from a gaseous state. It was once without form, and void. Yet, billions of years ago, some intelligence beyond comprehension designedly gathered these gaseous clouds traveling through space, whirled them into a gigantic vortex, crystallized and solidified these gases

83

into the spinning, speeding globe on which you have now appeared, in this fleeting moment of time, in the company of some billions of your fellow creatures.

The number of potential identities that might have originated throughout all time, but for premature deaths due to abortions, accidents, illnesses, and wars is unthinkable. And we must now accept the probability that there are countless trillions of other inhabited planets throughout this limitless universe, many perhaps supporting intelligent beings evolved beyond our capacity to grasp.

What does this mean as applied to you? It means that you are an infinitesimal but still important part of the vast scheme of creation. Perhaps your parents did not consciously plan your conception. You may have been wanted or unwanted. You could have been conceived out of wedlock. The principle of creation is completely impervious to manmade laws. But all creation is sacred and must be attributed to some power; many call it "divine."

Whether or not you know who your actual parents were, you owe your life and your existence, I believe, to the Father of us all. As human creatures, in keeping with the entire animal world, we have been given the creative capacity to reproduce our kind. We cannot create life, we can only provide the physical instruments through which life manifests. This is wonderful enough, but we are surrounded by a host of untold and continuing miracles as well as mysteries.

Perhaps greatest of all is the mystery of who you are—your own identity. Your name is obviously not the "real you," because you can change your name completely and not change your awareness of self. An inner voice keeps on saying to you, "I am I." You are the exclusive possessor of this "I am I" consciousness. Male or female, you are never anyone else but yourself. Your physical body, your mind, and your personality belong uniquely to you. No other man or woman, in all recorded time, has ever looked exactly like you, acted exactly like you, thought exactly like you, or felt exactly like you.

The creator of this universe is not producing any duplicates. When you disappear from this earthly scene, no one will ever appear again specifically resembling you.

But if it were possible for your consciousness of "who you are" to be transferred magically to my mind, and my consciousness of "who I am" to be transferred to your mind at the same time, we both might make the discovery that what says "I am I" to you is saying "I am I" to me with the similar feeling of awareness behind it.

This might have nothing to do with our differences in sex and the facts that we would also differ, quite naturally, in appearance, temperament, environmental influences, educational backgrounds, training, and the emotional reactions to various life experiences we have each had. The feeling in consciousness could be one and the same.

It has long been my conviction that an omnipresent part of the universal creative force, to which we owe our very life and being, including the remarkable sensitized physical instrument through which we are manifesting, exists within our subconscious. We *have* to be a part of what has created us. This is inescapable. Consider then the probability that the reason we each share the same, although individualized, feeling of identity is because God, the one great intelligence, is eternally existent as the "I am I" awareness in the consciousness of all living creatures, in all worlds, including man.

Each form of life could possess its own kind of sense of identity, too, limited by its stage of evolutionary development. This could apply to the ant, the bird, the fish, the dolphin, and the elephant, ad infinitum.

Your identity came into being from the moment of your conception, through an act of sexual intercourse performed by your father and mother. But it is possible that you have always existed, if only as an idea in the mind of the great creator, and that this is the time and place in the scheme of creation for your appearance as a self-conscious entity.

Think of it. You have existed from that split second of conception on. And the intelligence within you, possessing the blueprint or design of your body form, took immediate command, issuing creative orders that caused this single united cell to begin dividing and subdividing into millions and billions and trillions of new cells, each one of these cells coming into life, knowing the exact and specific part it was to play in forming the various organs and structure of your physical instrument.

There is no apparent difference in these cells, yet each is performing its separate and distinct function. Each joins with countless others to help form your lungs, heart, stomach, head, hands, legs, feet, hair, skin, and bones—every smallest part of you—and to accomplish this miraculous construction job inside the body of your mother, without you or your mother being consciously aware of the process.

Where did I come from?

This is as much of an answer as can be given. Sexual creativity at its highest and finest—unperverted by man.

Why am I here?

It is apparently to give you the opportunity to develop greater qualities of character and ability, through the way in which you mentally, emotionally, and physically react to the various experiences that life is bringing to you.

In preparation for what?

Quite possibly, in preparation for where you are going.

Where am I going?

There is increasing evidence, in my opinion, that you will survive physical death, and since you have attained a self-conscious awareness of your identity through your birth on this earth, and actually are a part of this stupendous creative force in process of continuous unfolding, it is my conviction that you will go on to higher realms of existence, as real to you there as this planetary experience now is. When death occurs, you will step out of your physical body as one vacates a house no longer usable, and you will, according to the evidence I have, find yourself in a higher-vibrating body form, just as substantial and just as suited to the environment of the next dimension of *being* as your present body is suited to earth life.

Sex will exist there, as it exists here. It undoubtedly will take different forms of expression, but creativity has to be everywhere present. Isn't it reasonable to presume that, if you survive death, the same creative power that has provided your earth body will have prepared increasingly sensitized vehicles for your "I am I" identity to occupy as you progress from one plane of existence and developing experience to another? Science has proved that energy is deathless. Then why should not intelligence, once identified with energy, continue to manifest through whatever form energy takes? Obviously, you can carry over into the next dimension only what you have developed here—and this should cause each one of us more than passing concern.

The purpose of these comments is to suggest the kinship with all life that is apparently the design of creation—life brought into being, in every instance, by a procreative sexual act. Various species, on up to the human, occupy myriad different body forms, but they have each and all emanated from the same unfathomable creative power that we so inadequately call "God."

We are separated from direct communication with the other forms of life, which we consider beneath us, because ants and birds and fish and dolphins and elephants, for example, speak a wordless language we cannot understand. It is difficult enough to communicate with our own fellow human creatures because of language barriers and prejudicial differences in ideologies, customs, traditions, and beliefs, as well as different skin colors and degrees of intelligence.

When it comes to plant life, we are dealing with still another form of intelligence with which we have not learned to communicate. There is no record of any trees or flowers or vegetables having spoken to man, except as they have appealed to one or more of his five physical senses.

But experiments have been conducted on a feeling level, wherein feelings of love, hate, or indifference have been projected toward flowers or vegetables and the effects on them noted. Scientists report that there is evidence of a response to a loving attitude: flowers or vegetables, so treated, have shown greater growth and vitality, as though influenced by thought vibrations. Hate, the opposite of love, has apparently produced the opposite effect: flowers or vegetables show a retardation of growth and vitality. Indifference produces a like result, even though the same physical care is given to these flowers and vegetables, insofar as watering and cultivation are concerned.

It is well to remember that feeling preceded language. Everything that lives feels. The impact of feeling is everywhere discernible. You are reacting to every feeling you have, and so is every form of life, animal or plant.

On the human level, with man's more highly developed brain structure and capacity, feelings are naturally more sensitized. One day man may well be able to tune in on the feeling levels of other forms of life and then put in words what each is experiencing. Now all he can do is observe and deduce. He cannot as yet attune himself to the type of consciousness that exists in an ant, a rose, or a monkey—although he is getting closer through exercise of new electromagnetic and electrochemical processes.

Exciting proof that feeling is the dominant force in all life is contained in recent experiments with the sensory awareness of babies, the discovery that their minds from birth are ready and capable of registering and absorbing much more knowledge than was thought possible a few short years ago. It is a fact, for example, that even a day-old baby can distinguish between a variety of sounds and smells and, through repetition, become quickly conditioned to them. We know now that babies two to four years of age can be taught algebra and how to spell difficult words. This had led some advanced educators to the conclusion that a formal program of education for all children should be started at three to four instead of six to seven. The child who is given challenges and things to see and do and taste and touch and smell in infancy can adjust himself to the world around and within him much more quickly and effectively. When a baby is left to stare at blank walls and a white, monotonous environment around him and is given no objects, outside of a bottle, a rattle, and a teething ring to use or observe, for months on end—it is small wonder that he has developed little interest or awareness in what is going on around him, or any incentive to do things.

The babies of the future, exposed to these new methods of education, will possess at ten years the knowledge and abilities that other comparable young people may not have acquired now at twenty. This is how far advanced we may soon be in stimulating the minds of the very young.

Pleasurable and unpleasurable feelings are registered in consciousness, and a baby responds to or reacts against them when they are repeated. Many tendencies and patterns are thus developed before the child has learned to talk.

Extrasensory perception is essentially feeling—feeling that goes beyond the five physical senses, and beyond language, feeling that is behind every thought or desire a person has ever had or can have. Feeling, then, *has* to be the universal language, the means through which you comunicate with all life within and around you.

Through feeling, as you develop greater and greater sensitivity, you can expect to solve for yourself more and more of the mystery of where you came from . . . why you are here . . . where you are going . . . and the relationship you bear to the presence of God within you.

5

The Sensitized
Instrument of
Your Mind

I SEE the functions of the mind as taking place on seven levels. There are: conscious level, subconscious body-control level, memory level, creative-power level, restorative-health level, intuitive level, and cosmic-consciousness level. (I have described this in greater detail in my book *How to Make ESP Work for You.*) These levels are all actually interrelated and work together in the mind of the so-called normal individual, with the smooth and unfailing precision of a finely made watch assembly.

But the moment you let some life experience disturb you, this highly sensitized mechanism of the mind becomes affected, upsetting its delicate balance. There then occurs an immediate reflexive reaction in the nervous system, and unless you can adjust your mind to the situation, tensions develop throughout your body, and the organs that your mind controls lose, to a degree, their rhythmic coordination. You might get an attack of indigestion, a heart palpitation, a shortness of breath, a tight feeling in your head and solar plexus, or other signs of mental and emotional distress, with physical repercussions.

To picture for you quickly and graphically the part that each level of the mind plays in consciousness, I urge you to visualize your real self always at the center of your being—or consciousness—encircled by the seven different levels, beginning with the outermost, or conscious, level.

Your identity, your awareness of "I am I," is housed, for the duration of your life on this earth, in the highly intricate but beautifully functioning instrumentation of your physical body. The network of interconnecting nerves, muscles, glands, and arteries and blood vessels extending throughout your various organs is constantly supplying one or more of your five physical senses with experiential stimuli, which are carried to your brain—the tremendous receiving center—and you, as the governing entity, are endlessly deciding what to do about them.

This means that both physically and mentally you are a highly sensitized, multisensory organism and that all stimuli registered through your five physical senses are converted instantly into mental images and feelings in consciousness. This is much like the functioning of a television broadcasting station, which transmits images and sounds, of scenes and people, in the form of electrical impulses; these do not become pictures and sounds again until they are so translated by contact with the converting mechanism of a TV receiving set.

Wonderful enough, but it is important to realize that all that TV transmission and reception can do is photograph a scene or a person and record the associated sounds, conveying them to a distant point. The television instrumentation has no awareness that it has performed this operation, nor can it interpret what it has transmitted or received.

The human mind, however, not only possesses the power of transmission and reception, but it has the built-in sensory apparatus and intelligence to know what it is doing, to be aware of what is going on, and to interpret and give meaning to the flow of images and feelings that are incessantly taking place from one consciousness to another. Of course, you can be consciously aware of only those stimuli that are most strongly transmitted by the emotional intensity of the sender. Countless stimuli are so faint by comparison that they cannot command conscious attention, and are recorded on the subconscious level only.

Nevertheless, it now seems evident, whether science has yet been able to produce laboratory proof or not, that everything that has happened or is happening, has been or is being continuously and automatically recorded, without discrimination, so exactly that not even the wink of an eye is missed. The recording, I am convinced, is taking place not only in the mind of each individual but also in a dimension to which I have given the name "mental ether." The incomprehensibly vast number of mental images and feelings, existent in vibratory form, are apparently kept alive in the electromagnetic field. They are a part of the great subconscious sea of consciousness to which all minds appear to be linked.

I believe it will ultimately be discovered that man's evolution is somehow associated with this boundless storehouse of knowledge of the ages, on which creative intelligence builds in bringing forth new forms of life. Man, often without realizing it, taps this source of total-knowledge, time and again, in conceiving what he feels to be new ideas and inventions.

Your real self, through the medium of your conscious mind, depends on the testimony of what you see, hear, taste, touch, and smell for its contact with, and concept of, the outer world in which you live. What your senses tell you about this world, you generally accept as reality.

It is only in comparatively recent years, however, with the advent of advanced telescopes and microscopes, X rays, and varied forms of highly sensitized instrumentation, that we have come to realize how woefully limited our physical sensory range is—and how vast a universe of reality exists within and without us, of which we have not the slightest conscious awareness. Even so, your creator has equipped you with almost unlimited potential mental power that few are yet aware exists and that, in time, can enable those who learn how to develop these higher faculties to sense planes of being beyond description today.

Dangerous Shortcuts to Mind Expansion

Men and women tend to follow the path of least resistance. Instead of making a sustained conscious effort for self-development to activate the higher powers of the mind, they are seeking mind expansion and greater sensual pleasures by the shortcut methods of hypnotic, electrical, and chemical devices.

Along this devious, uncharted road are many detours, pitfalls, and hazards, laying a person open, without guidance and protection, to collisions with unknown forces, usually destructive in nature, which can prove shattering to the personality as well as the nervous system.

It is often mentally and emotionally unstable people who venture into these areas, because they have had fragmentary experiences with hallucinations, fantasies, distorted visions, and dreams that have aroused curiosity and caused them to believe that if these illusory sensations could be explored, perhaps more could be learned about the mystery of life, including the mystery of their own selves. Young people, new to the field of sensation, willing to try anything once—and more often than that if they discover that there are thrills and kicks in it—are more prone to these mental and emotional adventures that give promise of greater sexual at-one-ness as well as spiritual illumination.

Unhappily, what has resulted thus far has been, in the main, more confusion, bewilderment, demoralization, frustration, fears, insecurity, and despair of finding the ultimate reality or any dependable reality at all.

These are, of course, the staunch supporters of the intelligent use of drugs under proper guidance as a means of releasing one's hidden potentials and liberating the "sleeping genius" within. Opposed are those who just as strongly declare that these methods for expanding one's consciousness and inducing greater creativity are extremely dangerous and self-defeating.

Vast research must still be undertaken before anything reliable is known about the right control factors for those who wish to be "sent" by LSD and other psychedelic drugs. Doctors and scientists are now warning that only individuals with recognized maturity and stability should be exposed, that otherwise mental and emotional disaster may result.

Science is now experimenting with the effect of electromagnetic fields and their influence on human beings. Miniature transistorized devices can be placed in animal and human bodies, bringing about emotional and muscular reaction by remote control or radio waves. Posthypnotic suggestion can be triggered as desired by radio transmission, once the individual is conditioned to receive and react to certain signals. Men and women, under electronic influence, can have their memory of whatever they have done, or are impulsed to do, dissolved. *The New York Times* recently carried a startling front-page story, quoting Dr. David K. Krech, professor of psychology at the University of California, as saying that: "Mind control is coming!" *

The implications of this announcement are more horrific in my estimation than the constant overhanging threat of the damage that can be done to human life through atomic warfare. A completely controlled human creature,

---

* See Dr. David Perlman, "The Search for the Memory Molecule," *The New York Times* (Magazine Section), July 7, 1968, p. 8.

unable to think or feel or act for himself, might better be dead.

Man, through excessive use of barbiturates—the wide variety of pain-killing and sleep-producing medicines—is drugging his own mind and senses. Millions throughout the world are today unwittingly moving more and more into acceptance of control by drugs, breaking down their ordinary subconscious resistance to every form of mind-influencing forces, mechanical, hypnotic, and otherwise.

Nature originally designed that you were to rule your body by your intelligence, that you were to be the sole operator, through your mind, of your sensitized physical instrument. But how would you like to be "turned on and off" by push button—made to feel amorous or not amorous by remote control—no longer able to determine whether your feelings are real or synthetic? How would you like to have someone else either running or using your body—telling your organs when and when not to function, whether to have sex or not have sex, whether to eat or not eat?

The fact that your feelings can be played upon by outside minds and electronic, chemical, and hypnotic influences is evidence that your body can become essentially an instrument that responds automatically to whatever controls are imposed on it. There is contained in this the implication that your soul, or identity—the intelligence that gives you the awareness of "I and I"—exists basically apart from the body that it inhabits, and is simply using the body through which to manifest in this plane of life. If this is true, and there are increasing evidences that it is true, then man's whole concept of his relationship to this physical world and to the universe is in for a fundamental change.

The world of the senses is not a world to be played with by neurotically inclined young or older people seeking to gain a deeper understanding of themselves and to relate more intimately, if not sensually, to others, as well as to the universe about them. You cannot drug or hypnotize yourself into spiritual development or greater awareness. If this were possible, the entire human race should be compelled to take whatever dosages or treatments are necessary to relieve the massive tensions and hatreds, resentments, suspicions, sexual disturbances, and like destructive emotions that are running rampant through the consciousness of mankind today. Each human creature is, however, a universe unto himself. What goes on in his mind and body is strictly individual and must be coped with, essentially, by the self of that individual.

The shock reaction many men and women are suffering today (especially idealistic youth) is not so much from resort to aphrodisiacs as it is due to disillusionment at the discovery of the sham, hypocrisy, and dishonesty that exist in governments and institutions, in religions, and in many business, social, and personal areas wherein these men and women had formerly placed their faith and confidence.

"There must be truth somewhere," many have said to me. "I've decided I'm going to try in every way I can to find it."

Unfortunately, tragically, mind-expanding drugs are not the answer. You do not have to lose your mind to find it. You have to lose, instead, your fear of facing your real self, of facing your past feelings of guilt and shameful conduct; your fear of assuming responsibility for your own thoughts and desires and acts; your fear of adjustment to others, of your own sex drives, of your feelings of inferiority and inadequacy; your fear of death, and the loss of your identity.

These fears are very real, and they have largely grown out of your wrong emotional reactions to past experiences. These fears can be mastered without drugs, and when they are mastered, even in part, you will begin to get flashes of illumination, glimpses of something higher within; a preview of what is to come as you gain greater and greater mental and emotional control so that you can reach the higher dimensions in your mind and find the God of your own concept—a satisfying, exhilarating, ecstatic attunement with the cosmic consciousness you have been seeking.

The Science of
Mind-to-Mind Communication

Few scientific investigators or researchers who have seriously studied the abundant evidence testifying to the existence of extrasensory faculties any longer doubt the ability of the mind, under certain conditions, to transmit and receive thought impressions beyond the reach of the five physical senses. They are still mystified and baffled, however, by the fact that this communication is not limited by time or space.

This fact suggests the functioning of a different form of energy from any of which we yet have physical evidence: its transmission apparently is not diminished by distance or time. Either that is true, or there is something faulty in our commonly accepted concept of what constitute the properties of time and space.

Could it be possible—in the larger and utterly profound sense—that everything in the universe is actually coexistent? If so, when we have developed the proper human instrumentation, could we not, then, be instantly aware of anything we might desire to know, as parts of the omnipresent?

One can program the mind, for example, to ask for answers on the intuitive and cosmic-consciousness levels —set the dial, so to speak, by deep concentration, and wait, in the supreme faith that mental images and feelings will be received from the source containing the desired information. Once received, all we would have to do would be to decode the knowledge if some of it appeared to be too symbolic or obtuse for ready understanding and use on our level of awareness.

The Einsteins of the world did not come by their great scientific, mathematical, or inventive knowledge by physical research, deductive reasoning, and conscious calculation alone. As they applied their minds persistently to the problems confronting them, unexpected but welcome breakthroughs into a higher dimension of understanding and comprehension took place. They "knew," without knowing how they knew, what had formerly been unknowable.

Some ordinarily existing mental barrier had yielded, a flash of illumination had broken through into the awareness of the cosmic-consciousness level: a greater intelligence than man had reached down, as man had reached up, and extended a helping hand. Without this, call it "divine" assistance if you will, either in the form of a vivid dream, a vision, or a sudden sportlike jump in the evolution of an idea, a hitherto unsolvable problem would not have been cracked.

Countless scientists will testify to the miracle of creativity—a communication far beyond so-called normal awareness or intelligence. Acknowledging this, why will many of these scientists still stubbornly refuse to accept the existence of extrasensory perception? They are working constantly in the presence of mental phenomena that are serving them intuitively and creatively at all times, without their seeming to recognize or to so credit them.

As these scientists or other seekers of knowledge assemble data and feed them into the instrumentation of their minds, this creative-power level takes the results of their education and research on up to the intuitive level, enlisting the aid of man's extrasensory faculties, and if this is not high enough to produce the answers needed, the full power inherent in the human mind is commandeered, and the entity lifted to the cosmic-consciousness level, wherein man's mind can be illumined with cognition beyond his own individual capacity to perceive. Such transcendental experiences as are above suggested are a comparative rarity today, but, as man overcomes his egoistic tendency to attribute all advancement in knowledge and science to himself alone, he will be able to make a selfless attunement, more and more, to these higher levels of consciousness, and realize in consequence greater enlightenment not only for himself but also for others.

Of course, what has been suggested here is for the future, even though such illumination has been experienced and recorded enough times throughout history, and in this present day, for us to know that it is by no means fantasy. It does lie within the realm of the attainable.

Most of us are challenged by the more mundane manifestations of extrasensory perception, and these are difficult enough for us to understand, let alone accept.

Here are a few examples:

A Characteristic Sample of Unexplainable Phenomena

Mrs. B. S. of Torrance, California, who has furnished me with a wide variety of ESP experiences, all well witnessed and giving evidence of an unusual degree of sensitivity, reported this case concerning a day in her life.

> My husband had left [the house?] several minutes before, to go to the store, and I supposed that he had already left [our property].
> After a while, our little girl went out to play. Now, our living room is so arranged that when anyone is seated toward the back of the room, it is impossible to see the driveway. Moreover, we have always had heavy draperies across the front window.

I was sitting in a chair in the back of the room, talking to my son, then about thirteen years old, when suddenly I "saw" a clear image of the little girl standing behind our station wagon, and my husband about to remove his foot from the brake.

The vision was so compelling, and I was so certain that it was accurate, I leaped out of the chair and ran out the front door. There my husband sat, in the car with the motor running, about to back out of the driveway.

I screamed to him to wait, and sure enough, when I got to a point where I could see behind the car (she was too small to be seen through the windows), there she stood!

My husband was pale and visibly shaken, but he had only one question: "How did you know?" My son repeated the question when he came to see what had sent me out of the house in such terror.

That is a type of case that has been repeated, in one way or another, countless times. The archives of all psychic-research laboratories and foundations are filled with them.

Mrs. B. S. added a significant comment to her report:

All the instances I have related to you (and there have been many more, less important or certain) seem to bear out your contention, Mr. Sherman, that "anxiety or feeling plays a large part in causing psychic phenomena." I now recognize a genuine experience because of this one I have reported, when the feeling of certainty was so overwhelming as to leave a strong conviction of what was actually happening.

Mrs. B. S. has recognized what I have long pointed out, that there is a distinctly different *feeling* in consciousness which you can learn to distinguish from your imagination, wishful thinking, fears, or anxieties, when a genuine ESP impression comes.

It requires a little experience, on a trial-and-error basis, as well as practice, before you can learn to sense and act on a "real hunch" or "intuitive flash," as Mrs. B. S. did, without hesitation. Had she permitted her conscious mind to question or try to argue her out of the mental warning flashed into her mind so forcefully and vividly, her little girl would have been run over. It is better, when you are developing these higher powers, to act quietly on those that you feel to be genuine, rather than wait to see if they are proved out by some happening—and perhaps live to regret your failure to respond.

Mrs. B. S. made a final statement, relative to her ESP adventures, which should prove helpful to anyone trying out ESP initially: "I find that these things happen only when I am not thinking about such things at all. They come in times of great need."

She is right. Don't make the mistake of trying to get an impression of everything that is happening around you. The mind is extremely suggestible, and you can so activate your imagination that you will confuse yourself with manufactured mental images of things that are seldom associated with reality, and could give you many wrong steers.

Accept, if you will, on faith, the evidence that these higher powers of mind *do* exist, and that they can work for you, giving you guidance and protection in times of need. Then go about your business, without giving any conscious thought to ESP; if you're in a relaxed state, impressions may get through to you when the occasion warrants. Often you will feel impelled to go somewhere or do something for which you have no conscious explanation at the time, only to discover later that your higher self had a reason for causing you to take such action, for your own good.

The case of Mrs. B. S. is worthy of further analysis. She was not employing telepathy, because neither her husband nor little daughter was aware of the existing danger. It was not, then, a matter of "reading" one or both of their minds. Yet some intelligence conveyed to her consciousness a mental image that enabled her to "see" her little girl behind the car, and her husband about to run over her. We are justified in asking the same question that her husband and son asked: "How did you know?"

From a study of numerous cases, I have concluded that there is what might be termed an electromagnetic affinity established on subconscious levels, especially between a mother and her children, or between any two persons who have a deep feeling for each other. This emotional line of communication exists continuously, unless broken off by a change in attitude or feeling; often, when one or the other is distressed, in trouble or danger, the other instantly knows it or senses that something is wrong and is prompted to do something about it—unless his conscious mind talks him out of the extrasensory impression.

The reason that the experience of Mrs. B. S. is so provocative is that she saw, in her mind's eye, a clear image of the little girl standing behind the station wagon and her husband about to remove his foot from the brake. It is important to observe that neither the little girl nor the husband was aroused emotionally—each was unconscious of any danger—so it was not a feeling from either of them which generated the power behind the image, as ordinarily appears to contribute to the transmission of thought.

It must, then, have been the "feeling" that existed subconsciously between mother and daughter, as before suggested, an awareness in the mind of Mrs. B. S. that her two loved ones were facing, unknowingly, a dangerous situation, that excited her to action. The intensification of feeling was on *her* part, not theirs—and so pronounced that she reacted at once, without the slightest doubt that her vision, however transmitted, was correct.

Guidance from a Higher Dimension

There is another possible explanation, which few scientific-minded people will accept. There are those who believe that we have a "guardian angel," as it were, someone who has died, or a deceased person we loved, who watches over us, providing guidance in times of emergency, and who is able to impress our minds with warning visions or urges—or even "direct-voice" admonitions when dangerous or urgent situations arise. A number of men and women who write me of their experiences express the conviction that they were "given help by those on the other side."

Here is one such case, from Mrs. J. F. of Redondo Beach, California:

I have always been a sensitive person. My father died when I was single and working in Chicago. My family lived in East St. Louis, Illinois. About this time, I broke up with a boy I liked. I was home on vacation and missed my father and was unhappy about my romance, so my little-girl heart cried out to my father: "Daddy, if you can help me, please do so. I know you can, and I also know that you can hear me, and that you are with me often."

My last night home, I went to bed in a darkened room, and all at once I felt my father standing by my bed, and heard him say, "I'll bring your boyfriend around, but you will have to do the rest."

The next day I returned to Chicago. I had a close girl

friend who had much education but little faith. I reported this experience to her, and that same evening, as she and I sat in my little apartment living room, the doorbell rang and there stood the young man I had not seen for several months!

I said, "Come in; I've been expecting you." He looked very strange and said, "How could you be expecting me? I didn't know I was coming. It was such a nice evening, I decided to take a walk, so went down Dearborn to North Avenue, to Lake Shore Drive, and as I was coming up the Drive, I passed your place and something just seemed to say, 'Go in and see Jill.' "

He wanted to know why I knew this, but I kept mum, and my nonbelieving friend just sat there in her chair, with her mouth wide open. I saw this fellow afterward, but I wasn't really interested in him, nor he in me, so we finally drifted apart.

That same year, my father returned to me two more times, and told me things which happened exactly as he said they would. Each time, I repeated them to my girl friend, and before the year was over she was beginning to believe. This was the first year after my father died. I suppose I got new interests and probably didn't miss him as much; perhaps I turned my mind away from him. I do not know, but he has not contacted me since.

In so many cases of this nature, if communication has apparently taken place from a seemingly discarnate entity, it has been in the first year or two following death. This would indicate that the emotional bond remains particularly strong for this period of time, until the bereaved relative or friend adjusts to the physical loss of the loved one. When this happens, the emotional call on the one who has died is lessened; he has less "pull" on him, or less reason for continuing to make contact.

Since feeling appears, in one way or another, to generate the power behind thought, we can speculate that, as the intensity of feeling for a departed loved one diminishes, the channel of communication becomes weaker and weaker. Occasionally, when some great emergency arises, even in later years—and this feeling is revived in an overpowering surge of yearning or fear or prayer for help— contact can apparently be made again and a message received, or some kind of guidance manifested, even through an apparitional appearance.

Returning to the case related by Mrs. J. F., you will recall that her boyfriend testified that he had not known he was coming to visit when he started out on his walk, but he was led subconsciously, evidently, past her place, and, as he was passing, "Something just seemed to say, 'Go in and see Jill.'" This would indicate that some directing intelligence had been influencing his actions and, at the proper moment, gave him the conscious urge to drop in on his former girl friend. He did this, not knowing the source of the impulse.

This causes me to speculate about how many times all our minds may be influenced by the thoughts of others, living or dead, under different circumstances and without our realizing it. We usually think, of course, that these urges or impulses and motivations are our own.

We know, as previously stated, that the air around us is permeated with radio and TV waves—vibrations that can be converted into sound and sight. How much more might the "mental ether" be filled with the thought vibrations of untold numbers of people, vibrations to which we are providentially not attuned?

A Powerful Thought Transmission

Given the right conditions, reception of a scene or a happening or a personal message can come through with electrifying certainty. Take the case reported by Mrs. F. M. of Redding, California. (I have collected more cases from this area, in proportion to others, only because I have lectured so often in California and have had contact with so many thousands of people there.) Says Mrs. F. M.:

My most vivid experience happened in 1961. My son had gone rabbit hunting with a friend. Both boys were seventeen, and they had gone in the friend's car. I had taken my daughter, aged twelve, to town to do some shopping. I had made out a long list of errands that were to be done. We had gone into the first store to get a pattern. Kathy wanted some popcorn on the way in, but I didn't want to get it on the way to the dry-goods department, so I told her to wait until we left the store.

I had been looking at the patterns and suddenly realized that I was very rapidly turning the pages of the book and not seeing a thing. I was seized with a sense of great urgency. I noted the number of a pattern, bought it, and grabbed Kathy by the hand and hurried out of the store.

She wanted the popcorn, but I told her that there

wasn't time for it, because Clifford had been hurt and we had to get home.

As I was getting in the car, the police car sped by with its siren screaming. I said, "Kathy, they are going after Clifford!"

I was driving a 1940 Ford and knew it was impossible to keep up with them, so I hurried home. On the way I hit a dog, but the people waved me on, saying that he had run out under my car. I drove as fast as possible.

As I drove into the driveway, I heard the telephone ringing. I said, "Kathy, they are calling about Clifford!" I rushed inside and answered the phone. The lady asked if I was Mrs. F. I said, Yes, and she said that she was calling about my son; he had been in an accident.

I said, "Yes, I know—where is he?" She told me, and the nature of his injuries. I hurried to her house, several miles in the country, and took him to the hospital. She had called several times, but I was on the way home. Even today, when I recount this experience, I get emotionally aroused.

An experience like this does remain unforgettable. If you have had only one in a lifetime, it stands out as something perhaps still inexplicable but of undoubted reality. No one can argue you out of it. You *know* that something exists beyond the reach of the five physical senses that you cannot write off to coincidence or happenstance or imagination.

The emotional line of communication between the mind of Mrs. J. F. and her son was extremely strong. The moment this accident happened, she got a disturbed reaction on "her end of the line." She *knew* that her boy had been hurt as definitely as if she had received a telegram. It was so strongly impressed on her that her conscious mind could not offer any resistance. She was as much with her son as she was with Kathy on that wild ride home, sensing what was taking place, correctly identifying the police car on the way to the scene of the accident, and knowing that a message was awaiting her when she arrived at the house.

Note again the vital part that feeling played in this mind-to-mind communication. Mrs. J. F. was intercepting impressions aimed at her not only from her injured son but also from the lady who was trying to reach her on the phone: "Kathy, they are calling about Clifford. . . . Yes, I know—where is he?"

An Extraordinary Mental Pickup

When your "mental receiver" is open and highly sensitized, it is amazing what it can take in. Quite often, when you are writing a friend or relative and your attention is centered on that person, to the exclusion of everything else, you will tune in on some event or condition.

Here is one such example from Mrs. L. S., who has sent me reports of many remarkable experiences she has had:

This is another one of those things that I can't explain, but I've got the proof of its happening. I am sending you the original letter I wrote my mother's cousin, a lady of eighty-three, about an impression that came to me concerning her, and she has written her confirmation on the back of it. You can put it in your files.

This is what I felt impelled to write her:

Dear Cousin,

Dinner will be announced in a very few minutes, so this will have to be brief.

The other night, and again a little while ago, I got the distinct impression that there is something wrong regarding your nose. Of all things.

The first time, it seemed to be Frank [the cousin's son], and he said you should see about it, but this last time I did not sense him; it was just an impression out of the blue. It seems absolutely idiotic, and if you were not such a close relative and did not understand this sort of thing, I would not even write and let it go. In fact, that is just what I did the other night; I cast it aside. However, this time I decided to write.

These impressions are not infallible. They can and do prove wrong. As my friend Harold Sherman says, "If you hit it right about eighty percent of the time, you are good." I usually hit better than that, but I hope this time is one in which I am wrong.

I can't imagine what in God's world could be wrong with anybody's nose. Yours always looked good to me, and I wish I could see it, and you, right about now. However, we never know—strange things do happen. Take care, dear, and remember, I love you heaps. . . . *Devotedly, L ——.*

This letter to the older cousin was typed, but on the back of it, in the cousin's handwriting, was this note:

Dear L ——,

I received your letter of the thirteenth on March 15, and the evening of March 16 I had a severe flare-up of an old diaphragmatic hernia, which I am sure you had never heard about—and this landed me in the hospital.

Now—listen to this—the first thing they did was to put a tube in my nose! I swallowed two glasses of water so the tube would go into my stomach. It was not painful but most disagreeable. Frank had it done to him once—was probably the reason you thought of him in this connection. He knew how uncomfortable it was, and he evidently knew what was going to happen to me. I was in the hospital one week, with every attention and dozens of X rays. I am fine now . . . and so is my nose!

The amazing feature of this case is that, when the impression came to Mrs. L. S. about something being wrong with her cousin's nose, the event had not yet happened. She felt, however, not once, but twice, on two consecutive days, that the nose of her cousin was involved in some unusual way, and that the condition *then* existed. It was what we call precognition, or a projection of the mind ahead in time. In some manner that still defies explanation, she had foreseen the nose being affected by some occurrence that was yet to take place.

Not only that, but Mrs. L. S. had associated the woman's son, Frank, with this episode. When her first impression was received, and then centered on her cousin's nose the second time she was moved to think about it. Even so, her cousin reported that Frank had had such a nose operation performed on him on a previous occasion and that Frank knew how unpleasant such an ordeal was and sympathized with her at having to have a tube inserted in her nose.

All these feelings, however, on the part of Frank and the cousin were consciously unrelated to the impressions that came to Mrs. L. S., because the cousin was not stricken ill until the day following receipt of the letter, and neither she nor Frank had any thought that a tube would have to be swallowed through the nose.

Some scientists are ready to concede that the mind can communicate with the past and the present, but most of them rule out all possibility of the mind's ability to communicate with the future. This is the point at which the majority of scientists part company with the parapsychologist. I have had some of them say to me: "If I were to accept all aspects of ESP as fact, I would have to throw out all my textbooks and start in all over again, which, at my age, I certainly don't intend to do. What I know about the mind and its functioning is all I need in my work. If you want to play around with these so-called 'higher powers of mind' and waste a lifetime doing it, that's your privilege."

Today, in the face of mounting positive evidence, it is becoming more and more difficult for even the most skeptical scientist to persist in his refusal to admit that telepathy, at least, is a fact. Once having made this much of a concession, he might well decide in time to encourage research designed to explore further the mysterious depths of human consciousness. When this day comes, the study of the higher powers of the mind will become the new science, and many outmoded concepts of mind and emotion will have to be discarded to make way for the discovered functioning of causative forces, both within and without the human body, not yet recognized or taken into account.

How Simple Telepathy Works

What is known at present about how telepathy is performed? I have set forth definite techniques in my book *How to Make ESP Work for You* that have worked for me, and judging from reports I am getting from hundreds of men and women and young people, many of them are getting results.

In that book I explained that, experimenting as a young man in high school, I tried to implant thoughts in the minds of my fellow students while they were asleep, using the theory that their conscious waking minds would not be actively engaged and I could impress them easier. I succeeded in waking up a doubting friend, Homer Coddington, by suggesting mentally that he suddenly come to consciousness, as the town clock was striking two A.M., and think of me. On another occasion I was able to transmit a suggestion to the boyfriend of a young lady, with whom he had had a falling out, that he phone her and ask for a date at seven-thirty on a Sunday night. He was home on leave from the navy and staying with his parents in the country, who had no telephone. The young lady had requested I try to reach him mentally. It worked!

For some reason, these two published illustrations of

telepathic communications have inspired many readers, young and old, to try the technique involved.

I also wrote that I had taken a copy of our high school yearbook, looked up the pictures of Coddington and Yunker, the two chosen subjects, and gazed at each respective photograph until I could close my eyes and see their images in my mind's eye. Then I spoke to them, in the privacy of my own room, both audibly and mentally, as though they were physically present. I repeated my suggestions for ten to fifteen minutes, until I had an inner feeling that these sleeping schoolmates had received my mental suggestions in their subconscious minds. Then I went to bed, in the faith that the thoughts I had been sending had reached their targets.

An avalanche of related testimonial letters has been pouring in on me ever since, especially from teen-agers and college students. But the report I have selected to present now, while typical, is from a Mrs. B. H. of Houston, Texas. I trust that you will agree that her ESP experience was as unusual as it is significant.

She first tried the technique, as she says, by attempting to send a message to a son who lives in California.

At seven in the morning on two occasions, it being five A.M., "sleeping time" in California, I tried to follow your instructions, mentally telling my son to phone me. This was something he seldom if ever did. On the evening of the second try, I received a long-distance call from him and my daughter-in-law. We talked for thirty minutes!

This success quite naturally stimulated Mrs. B. H. to try something else.

Just for the lark of it, I decided to see if I could do something with my husband, Pat. We were dancing on Saturday night when I happened to think of your book, which I was reading for the second time.

I like Pat because he is very well-behaved in public, and it would be very out of the ordinary for him to kiss me. For about one minute I concentrated on his doing just this. It was the only opportunity I had, as he started a conversation and it took my mind off onto something else to such an extent that I forgot all about the "silly" idea. Then the music stopped, and we sat down at our table. They then announced that they would next play "Sugar Blues."

Pat looked at me and said, "When they *do,* I'm going to

get some of your sugar, too." I was so dumbfounded that I said nothing.

We started dancing again, and I said, "What was that you said just after we sat down?" He looked at me and said, "I said I was going to get some of your sugar, too!"

Then he brushed my cheek with about the sweetest kiss I ever got from him. . . .

6
Communication with the Past

WHETHER OR NOT you yet realize it, your mind is, and will always remain, one of the world's greatest computers. Today science is electronically duplicating, to a great degree, man's own amazing filing system of coded information, registered in consciousness from the moment of birth and perhaps beyond that, but science probably can never eclipse the sensitivity of the human organism in its reaction to accumulated experiential data.

Consider the stupendous number of mental images, with their related feelings experienced at the same time, that the tape recorder of your mind has wound up inside the small space bounded by your cranial cavity. You can recall only a minute portion of all that has happened to you, but the electrical circuits of your brain have systematically stored all physical, mental, and emotional reactions to every experience you have ever had, so that you can draw on the specific incident or the knowledge gained at some future time.

This is what man is attempting to do with machines—storing information in photoelectric cells—to speed up the performance of mathematical and logical operations by feeding in figures and data and producing almost instant answers that would require thousands of hours for the human brain to achieve. But, once these answers are attained, they still must be analyzed, evaluated, and interpreted by the mind of man.

Some machines can talk, some can reproduce themselves, some can correct their own mistakes, some can carry out precision assignments—but none of them, thank heaven, has ever been known to *think* or given evidence of what we regard as *self-consciousness*.

As man surveys the animal world, and humbly recognizes that he is an animal among animals, the view from certain angles is not too inspiring. No animal in history has ever been guilty of wanton slaughter of its own kind. With our so-called civilization, greater peace, contentment, and brotherhood between races has not come—often only greater inhumanity to man. Stamped deep into human consciousness are hatreds, lusts, and greeds for power so unrelenting that they now threaten to destroy man himself.

We are still, in other words, communicating, through our minds and what is stored in them, with an unsavory, unholy past. And there remains much of the bestial in us, despite our rise to higher intellectual attainments on the wings of material inventions.

Today we have come, at last, to a dividing of the way. Regardless of our religious beliefs, we must admit that they are not, for the most part, giving us the inner security and guidance we need to solve our present-day problems and the world's crises.

Where now to turn? If the answers are not to be found in the world around us, there is only one other avenue to take—the road that leads into the depths of our own minds and souls. This road is traversed only through the channel of extrasensory perception—the development of our higher mental faculties. Back of them, I predict, we are destined to discover an in-dwelling presence, the awareness of which, when it comes, is so transcendent, so all-satisfying and assuring, that we are compelled to ascribe to this higher power the attributes of a god.

If we do not choose to take this road of self-development, we are traveling on a downward path that can lead, eventually, to demoralization and destruction. Our fears and worries and hates and prejudices can swallow us up, cut us off from any awareness of a god within us or a god about us. Without vision, it has been said, a people perish, and, I might add, without faith.

You must believe in something that is good and constructive to survive, and loss of faith in your fellow man and in your concept of God leaves you—with what? What else do you have to sustain, support, and protect you?

In this book we are embarked on the adventure of trying to understand ourselves, to gain more demonstrable knowledge of the working of our minds, and how we can make better communicative use of our higher mental powers to bring us greater happiness and security in life. But before we can make the progress we desire, we must delve a bit into our past and learn all we evidentially can about what it may be communicating to us that is having a conscious, as well as subconscious, effect on our present and our future.

I am assuming that you want the truth about yourself and the universe, whatever that truth may be. I have had an urge since boyhood to probe these ages-old mysteries of the mind and soul—to seek a knowledge of self that could be supported by demonstrable evidence—to separate my sentiment from my logic, so that I could avoid being influenced by wishful thinking and not believe in something just because I found it appealing, without any real substance for such belief.

Religion has usually spoken with ecclesiastical authority to man about his origin and his past, and has steadfastly reminded him of the punishment or reward that will be meted out to man in accordance with the evil or spiritual nature of his life on earth. Dogmas and creeds of most religious philosophies have grown largely out of "revelations" rather than acquired experiential knowledge. Various spiritual orders and cults have then called upon their followers to accept their admonishments on *faith,* and to conform to certain ethical teachings and principles as a means of saving their souls.

It is not possible to avoid reference to religion as we seek to learn what is knowable about our past existence, since religion, long before science, pronounced concepts of how we came into being, and how God created the earth and the stars and all that could be imagined as a part of His firmament. The answers as well as the records seem to have been lost in the broken continuity of life on this earth—whereon we now have evidence of the many cataclysms that have destroyed great civilizations, beyond our historical and anthropological knowledge. It is possible that, in the long-distant past, life came here from other planets, just as we are now wondering if we are not being visited again by intelligences from outer space.

This much we do know: you and I are the "end results" of a long ancestral line of forebears, the mixture of many races, and quite possibly, colors, if you go back far enough. It is obvious that we have had passed down to us different physical characteristics, as well as mental and emotional ones.

Allowing for the fact that we are distinctly different and

exclusive in personality and identity, we have had physical equipment bequeathed to us, at the moment of the creative act performed by our parents, which we must accept and use to the best of our developed ability. If we have been born crippled in any way, blind or deaf, partially paralyzed or mentally retarded, through unfortunately poor genetic stock, disease, an accident of birth, or some other cause—we have had to struggle against these handicaps in a world not too well organized to care for the unfit. Those who have been so afflicted, if religiously inclined, might be disposed to ask: "How could a supposedly all-merciful God permit such happenings to His own creation?"

Those who believe in reincarnation have a ready explanation. We have committed some foul misdeed in a past life that has imposed upon us a karmic punishment. The laws of cause and effect function inexorably—"as a man sows, so must he reap"—and we are paying the penalty for some sinful thing we have done to another human creature, perhaps a former wife, husband, child, friend, or stranger, for which act or acts we are now being made to suffer, until we have made full atonement. If we do not do so, we will have to return to earth again and again, through rebirth, until our soul has been sufficiently purified to permit us to be freed from the wheel of karma and allowed to go on to higher and more spiritual dimensions.

The theory is that we may already have lived thousands of earth lives. From a scientific standpoint, there is little evidence that reincarnation exists. Countless men and women have had the "feeling" that they have lived before, or have gone through the same experience on earth before, or have been able to recognize a scene or situation in geographical areas that they had never hitherto visited in the flesh. There are, however, other plausible explanations for these feelings, aside from reincarnation.

Dr. Ian Stevenson

The most distinguished and provocative research that is being done today on the subject of reincarnation is that conducted by Dr. Ian Stevenson, former chairman of the Department of Psychiatry, University of Virginia, and now Alumni Professor of Psychiatry in the same department. His book *Twenty Cases Suggestive of Reincarnation,* published by the American Society for Psychical Research (*Proceedings,* vol. 26, 1966), is worthy of study.

C. J. Ducasse, former Chairman of the American Society for Psychical Research Publications Committee, has this to say, in part, in his Foreword:

> Obviously, however, these virtues of the reincarnation hypothesis are not evidence that it is true . . . but if one asks what would constitute genuine evidence of reincarnation, the only answer in sight seems to be the same as to the question how any one of us now knows that he was living some days, months or years before. The answer is that he now remembers having lived at that earlier time, in such and such a place and circumstances, and having done certain things then and had certain experiences.
>
> But does anybody now claim similarly to remember having lived on earth a life earlier than his present one?
>
> Although reports of such a claim are rare, there are some. The person making them is almost always a young child, from whose mind these memories fade after some years. And when he is able to mention detailed facts of the earlier life he asserts he remembers, which eventual investigation verifies but which he had no opportunity to learn in a normal manner in his present life, then the question with which this confronts us is how to account for the veridicality of his memories, if not by supposing that he really did live the earlier life he remembers.
>
> The twenty cases of such apparent and most verified memories which Dr. Stevenson personally investigated, reports on, and discusses . . . are not claimed by him to settle the question; but they do put it before the reader sharply and, because of this, are fully as interesting and important as are the more numerous cases suggesting discarnate survival, to which psychical research has given close and lengthy attention.

The geographical distribution of the roughly six hundred cases that Dr. Stevenson has had called to his attention are a little more than half located in southeastern Asia (i.e., India, Ceylon, Thailand, and Burma). Most of the remainder come from western Asia (i.e., southeastern Turkey, Syria, and Lebanon), Europe, and Brazil. Only a few come from the United States and Canada, apart from Alaska, where numerous cases occur.

In studying the twenty cases set forth in his book, Dr. Stevenson has visited and talked with the children and all concerned, in India, Ceylon, Brazil, Alaska, and Lebanon. He states:

When we think we have identified paranormal elements in the "previous personality" evoked under hypnotic regression, we have still to decide, if we can, whether we can best account for these by our concepts of telepathy or clairvoyance, by an influence of some discarnate personality, or by reincarnation. (These decisions face us also in the spontaneous cases among children.)

I can certainly endorse Dr. Stevenson's further comment about the difficulty in evaluating impressions reported by children with reference to what specific psychic influences and extrasensory sources they may be responding to. It is a well-established fact that a child's mind is highly suggestible, open, and receptive, as well as imitative and imaginative. The parents of these children who appeared to have "recall" of a past life—sufficient to enable them to identify former fathers, mothers, brothers, sisters, other relatives, and friends in a different locality, where they had never been in their present lives—were, for the most part, believers in reincarnation. Thus, brought up in a home where there was parental acceptance of this ability of a deceased person to be reborn and return to earth, the child could be expected to join in this belief.

While a powerful conditioning factor, this alone could not explain the vividness and accuracy of recollections in some cases Dr. Stevenson researched. An experienced psychic investigator might well ask this question too: "Could it be possible that these obviously highly sensitized children, rather than having been reincarnated, were influenced by discarnate entities outside themselves—entities who had actually lived the lives which these children now seemed to remember, and who, by superimposing their memories on those of the children, helped them to recognize scenes and people with which and with whom the discarnate entities had been associated and had known while on earth?"

In a later chapter I will have much to say about cases of "possession," presenting substantial evidence that possession of minds and bodies by discarnate entities appears to be much more prevalent than the medical and psychiatric worlds are yet ready to admit.

A Child's Experience

For the moment, let us consider this case, reported to
me by a remarkable eighty-eight-year-old woman, the
same Mrs. D. L. of Long Beach, California, whose other
unusual experiences are recounted in Chapter 2. She recently sent this story of a childhood psychic adventure,
which she accepted as proving the truth of reincarnation:

> We were on a camping trip, Father, brother George,
> and I. The third night out, long before dark, we came to a
> lovely, shady spot with a spring of cold water. There were
> the remains of a house there, though it had long ago rot-
> ted away. Father said we had better make camp there for
> the night, as we could hardly find a nicer place.
>
> While Father and George were setting up camp, I was
> having a battle with myself. I couldn't have told anyone
> what was the matter with me, but I knew that I had to go
> down the hill.
>
> All of a sudden, I made up my mind and started to run.
> George called to me to stop, but I ran all the faster.
> George told Father, and they both caught me. Father
> scolded and tried to make me go back. He said, "A nine-
> year-old girl should know better than to run off in a
> strange place." I cried, and told him I had to go, that "my
> dishes were hidden there" and "my swing was just under
> the hill."
>
> They said that I had never been there before, but I said
> I had. I cried so hard and begged so hard that Father
> said, "It's early yet, so let's go and let her convince her-
> self."
>
> So we went down the hill to where my swing was. But
> there was no swing there, only the rotted stubs of a grape-
> vine swing, on an old, dead oak tree. I wanted to go on to
> see my dishes, but Father said that was "just a dream,"
> that I couldn't have any dishes there.
>
> George said, "Well, she was right about the swing." Fa-
> ther thought a moment, then said, "Well, come on. Show
> me where your dishes are." So we went to a spot where
> the hill was almost straight up and down. There were
> some good-sized trees there, and a heavy cover of under-
> brush.
>
> I stopped and told them, "They are right in there, bur-
> ied deep in the hillside. We had to hide them."
>
> George started to ask why, but Father stopped him. I
> was feeling very sad. Father looked at me and said,

"What kind of dishes were they, and what color were they?"

"They were Haviland china, white and blue decorations," I told him.

Father carefully removed several shovels of dirt, then stopped and wiped his face, and said in a low voice to George "This is almost too much." Then he reached in and pulled out some of the dishes.

As he did this, he turned very pale. George was also wiping his face, and he too was very pale. But I was dancing with joy. Father held up some of the dishes. They were just as I had described them.

"We dare not tell your mother anything about this," said father. "She would never understand, and I think the shock would kill her."

"Who does understand?" George said. "And now that we have done it, Dad—what does it all mean?"

Father thought a moment. "It's something that I never quite understood and never accepted," he said finally. "It looks like a case of reincarnation."

With that, Father started to put the dirt back. "Does that mean I can't take my dishes home with me?" I asked.

"Yes, dear child, I am afraid it does. Your mother would not believe us. She could not understand. We will have to keep it a secret, a sacred secret, just between us three. This would be too much of a shock for her."

This is the story of my dishes, Mr. Sherman, and up until a year ago, when my brother died, I could verify it. Father, of course, has been dead for years. I don't know what you will think of this, but to my mind, at least, it is a very sacred story, and proof positive of reincarnation.

I was deeply moved as I read this account. I am equally moved as I record it in this book. It rings with the truth of the experience. But to me, it is not proof of reincarnation —it is evidence of possession by a discarnate entity, by one of the persons who lived in the old house that was now rotted away, who had remained there, earthbound, for years with his or her attention and feelings fixed on an emotional moment when it was necessary to hide the prized dishes to keep them, possibly from being stolen by vandals of some sort.

For the first time, perhaps, in all the years since this person had died, a sensitive individual had chanced on the scene—young Dessie, whose entire life history gives evidence of her unusual psychic gifts. Up until that moment, when she testified that she began having a battle with herself (probably the attempt of the discarnate entity to take possession), she had never had a thought about another life. She had not the slightest feeling that this was anything but a lovely, shady spot for a campsite.

All of a sudden, she wrote, she had the impulse to start running—she knew she had to go down the hill, she was almost propelled there, and she then knew that there had been an old swing, and when remnants of it were found, she knew where her dishes had been buried. Of course, she would feel that they were her dishes under the influence of this possessive spirit, acting through her, so that the two were temporarily of one mind.

There is no intent here of challenging Dr. Stevenson's findings and conclusions. I have great respect for him and his work. But I am following his own procedure, when confronted by a touchingly genuine story such as this, in "trying to decide, if we can, whether we can best account for it by our concepts of telepathy or clairvoyance, by an influence of some discarnate personality, or by reincarnation."

Dessie has stated her belief that what happened to her was a sudden recollection of a past life, brought about by her presence in the surroundings of an old house. I have had personal experiences in taking on the environmental conditions of similar places, sensing conditions and activities and even personalities that formerly existed there. I know how real this can feel, especially to a highly sensitized, impressionable child as Dessie was at the time. She would certainly not be in a position to analyze—only to react, to feel very deeply, as the entity felt during the period of the possession.

The influence that caused Dessie to feel as she did, to know and to act, was gone as quickly as it had come, once she departed from the premises. Another psychic, taken into this area, might have walked into the same situation and produced additional verifiable impressions. It is difficult to arrange a follow-up investigation in spontaneous cases of this kind.

Various Ways of Sensing the Past

I have stated my conviction that everything that has ever happened to us is somehow recorded in the very elements or atoms within and without us in some unexplainable vibratory form. Nature apparently has designed more than one method for leaving the imprint of every kind of happening and evolutionary development in the mental ether. There are many ways that a highly sensitized person can communicate with what has taken place anywhere, at any time, if the conditions are right for perception, aside from possible spirit possession.

For example, one possible way this could happen is through the genes, which some scientists believe contain and preserve the genetic history of man's ancestors, stored in the very cells of the latest offspring's body. Some hold that a line of electromagnetic communication appears to have been laid, through which can pass mental and emotional, as well as physical, characteristics. Occasionally, under stress, when a similar experience to that of an ancestor has occurred, this could associatively trigger a sudden flare-up of a genetic memory and give an individual fleeting glimpses of past scenes and persons, which cause him to feel that he has lived before. Great geniuses and child prodigies might then be those who have been born with an intensification of these genetic memories, permitting them to give expression, through their deep subconscious, to inventive mathematical, artistic and other abilities far beyond the comprehension of an average man.

It has long been said that there are sleeping giants in every human consciousness. It might better be said that there are sleeping geniuses, because far back along our ancestral lines each of us has been related to the highest and finest as well as the most bestial of human creatures. Not enough is yet known about the science of genetics, which seeks to account for the resemblances and the differences exhibited among organisms related by descent. The mystery of life itself is herein involved—how the characteristics of parents and offspring are related, and how, going back into unrecorded time, the essence of what has happened in the past may be transmitted at each moment of conception. Obviously, since you did not create life, you possess, as a parent, only the ability to pass life on—to open the door for a new entity, with certain family characteristics, to come upon the scene.

Throughout the centuries men have tried to explain certain related mysteries by the speculation that they have lived before. Today many highly organized, as well as sporadic, efforts are being made to awaken past memories, and various meditative, suggestive, and hypnotic techniques are being designed, so say their proponents, to enable individuals to regress their minds and call forth the recollection of past lives. A cult of past-life "readers" has sprung up, claiming the psychic ability to read mystic records as one would read the pages of a book, and to give authoritative and accurate accountings of selected past existences in different eras of history, when they lived either as males or females. They then purport to point out how these particular life experiences are related to what they are faced with in the present life—that they are undergoing trials and tribulations here as punishment for past misdeeds, and that until they pay the karmic penalty, they are destined to return again and again, suffering what they have inflicted on others.

There is no proof whatsoever that any of these readings are true. They have to be taken on faith. It is easy to establish a similarity to an existing earth situation with something that has been dreamed up as occurring in your past. Some readings may sound quite convincing. If you have had little experience in meditation, and then relax your body and mind, under instruction, while someone takes you suggestively back in your "past" and starts asking you questions, or if you mentally ask yourself questions—you are quite possibly going to get answers from your subconscious, because your imagination can be activated at once by these methods. Most people who have never had the experience of calling on their imagination in any intensified way are usually impressed and astonished at what comes forth. But how do you suppose a science-fiction writer gets his fantastic plots for stories which, in themselves, often seem incredible? He relaxes, fixes his mind on something he wants to create, and lets his imaginative faculty go to work. The mind's capacity to conjure up characters and periods of history, in fragmentary form, and mold them, eventually, into the mosaic of an amazing story is fabulous almost beyond belief.

If you would like to prove how imaginary these past-life readings are, employ the services of a number of the many advertised "readers" and check their readings. You will find that none of them is in agreement, even as to your supposed identity in the *same* past period.

Arthur Ford, acknowledged to be one of the world's greatest living psychic mediums, whom I have known for many years, has made this pertinent observation: "Most of those who purport to give you authentic 'past-life readings' cannot even give you an accurate reading of your present life!"

Certainly, this being true, why should you believe that

names, dates, places, and experiences described to you by these self-proclaimed psychics as being part of your past are anything but imaginary? It is dangerous to permit decisions, attitudes, and actions in this life to be dominated by unsubstantiated claims. It is equally injurious to rely on any feelings or visions which have been induced by suggestive or hypnotic-control methods—which bring, either consciously or subconsciously, impressions of what one may have been told are actual past-life experiences.

An otherwise intelligent friend of mine, carrying out regressive meditative techniques sent to him by a man who claimed he was "master of all life on this planet," wrote me that he had been able to tap his "past-life memory stream" and had relived a scene wherein he had actually "felt" the stab wounds that had been inflicted by his former friend Brutus.

"Yes, Harold—you must believe me. I now know that in a past incarnation I was Julius Caesar!"

A highly spiritual woman stated to me recently, "People make a God out of karma, yet it is nothing but the law of cause and effect, reaping what we sow in this life, as referred to in the Bible. I also have met people who feel that they are the reincarnation of famous persons in history. As to the number of women who believe they once lived as Cleopatra, I am sure there are enough ladies who have been told this, or have imagined it, to form a lodge!"

There is, however, one personality who takes top prize for reincarnative distinction. He must be nameless, although I have a letter in my files from one of his devoted followers, containing his picture and folder, with its "Universal Message." This sincere, well-meaning disciple states that a spiritual master in India claims not only to be "God in human form" in this incarnation but also to have returned to earth in previous times as Christ, Buddha, Krishna, Zoroaster, Rama, and Muhammad.

The most unhappy consequences of this belief in reincarnation have to do with those who feel that they have found soulmates, with whom they consorted in a past life, and who renew this affair, having no qualms of conscience as concerns their present lifemates, because they have known each other long before. They often look upon the present husband and wife with sympathy, even tolerance, when he or she is not inclined to understand or accept this cosmic relationship. This illusory communication with the past is highly disturbing to family relationships in many homes. It is understandably difficult for most people to accept readings of altered sexes as well as relationships in past lives—that, for example, a husband might have been a wife, and a wife a husband, or a child the father or mother of his own father or mother, in some other existence, and so on. This suggests even more confused future-life incarnations, the total destruction of any loving relationship or recognizable personalities and identities now existing—all for the purpose of expiating imagined past sins and wrongs inflicted on others.

If reincarnation should be true—and there is still little evidence, despite widespread belief, that it is—then we must concede that this plan for the evolution of the human soul was established by the creator of this indescribably dimensionless universe. Certainly a force and an intelligence far beyond our human comprehension and capacity would have had to set up this vast scheme; and if such a scheme exists, we are all inescapably a part of it. We must then account for a staggering universal bookkeeping system that mathematically maneuvers each human being into just the right geographical position, and just the right parentage, in company with other members of the environment, each working out karmic penalties in relation to the others. We must believe that six million Jews, for example, were caused to reside in Germany, and, because of past evil lives requiring severe present life penalties, were subjected to fiendish torture and ultimate cremation. I have talked to reincarnationists who actually believe this.

Presiding over this, and other unspeakable atrocities, are "elders" in higher dimensions who are said to be helping us to evolve our souls by counseling a choice of new incarnations that can give us testing experiences designed to free us, eventually, from the wheel of cause and effect known as karma. If you have a child afflicted from birth, whom you dearly love, does it help you to consider the possibility that he may have been an evil person in his past life, and that you are also being punished for past misdeeds of your own, which have caused this child to be born to you, so that you could work out your karmic penalties together? Something is very wrong somewhere in this philosophy—or the universe is a pretty mad place and man is one of the unhappy creatures trapped in it. It seems to me far more likely that we all progress on to another plane of existence after physical life on this earth.

7
Communication with the Earthbound

To RESCUE the mind from the vagaries and superstitions of the past, and to view and understand its many sensitized reactions to experiences that are constantly assailing it from within and without the consciousness of the individual, is a colossal and complicated task. In the preceding chapter I have raised questions about the concept of reincarnation, and in this chapter I wish to present what I consider dramatic and provocative evidence suggesting other possible explanations for the feeling some of us have that we have lived before.

For many years, and increasingly in recent times, because of the widespread interest in Ouija boards, hypnotic regression, meditation, and automatic writing, I have been hearing from men, women, and young people who have suffered an invasion of their minds by thoughts and feelings so foreign to their natures as to cause them great concern and often panic. While many doctors and psychiatrists might dispute my interpretation, it is my conviction, based on years of research and experimentation in extrasensory perception, that quite a number of these distressed people have become unwitting or unwilling victims of obsession or possession.

The late psychologist Dr. Nandor Fodor, one of the outstanding pioneer psychic investigators, whom I knew and admired, had this to say in his valued *Encyclopaedia of Psychic Science* (University Books, New York, 1966) about obsession, which to him was synonymous with possession: "It is an invasion of the living by a discarnate spirit, tending to a complete displacement of normal personality for purposes of selfish gratification."

The cases I am about to present will, I trust, illustrate this—it is communication, starting under the guise of spiritual and philosophic messages, strongly appealing to the sensitive people receiving them, and then either subtly or abruptly changing to profane and obscene writings, or "direct voicings" and sensual feelings of such a revolting nature as to terrorize those so influenced.

I think, again, the best and most convincing way to report these cases is to let the subjects speak for themselves. Obviously, their true identity must be protected, although their complete case histories with their actual names and addresses are in my personal Foundation files. They are all people of character and refinement. They come from intelligent, educated, and cultured backgrounds, so it cannot be charged that this "influence" occurs only to overly unstable personalities who might easily be given to illusions or hallucinations.

You may be revolted by some portions of these case histories, but I think it is important to present them in a fairly uncensored form as a warning to many who may be unknowingly, even trustingly, on the verge of possession, who are delving into psychic matters, and seeking manifestations, without setting up proper mental protection. If you are unacquainted with this type of phenomenon, it may seem so fantastic as to be unbelievable, but before you dismiss its possible reality, consider this statement made by Dr. James Hyslop, professor of logic and ethics from 1889–1902 at Columbia University, one of the most distinguished American psychical researchers:

> If we believe in telepathy, we believe in a process which makes possible the invasion of a personality by someone at a distance. It is not at all likely, therefore, that sane and intelligent spirits are the only ones to exert influence from a transcendental world. If they can act on the living, there is no reason why others cannot do so as well. The process, in either case, would be the same; we should have to possess adequate proof that nature puts more restrictions upon ignorance and evil in the next life than in this, in order to establish the certainty that mischievous personalities do not or cannot perform nefarious deeds.
> I fought against acceptance of the idea of obsession for ten years after I was convinced that survival after death was proved. But several cases of possession forced upon me the consideration of the question.
> The chief interest in such cases is their revolutionary effect in the field of medicine. . . . It is high time for the medical world to wake up and learn something.

"High time," said Dr. Hyslop, early in this present century, and the medical world has still not wakened to the sober significance of the fact of possession—or obsession —a truth that the famed Professor William James acknowledged shortly before his death, when he wrote:

The refusal of modern enlightenment to treat obsession as a hypothesis to be spoken of as even possible, in spite of the massive human tradition based on concrete evidence in its favor, has always seemed to me to be a curious example of the power of fashion in things "scientific." That this theory will have its innings again is, to my mind, absolutely certain. One has to be "scientific" indeed to be blind and ignorant enough not to suspect any such possibility.

It Began with Automatic Writing

Here is Case Number 1, first reported to me on June 12, 1968, by a woman to whom I will give the name of Edna Maynard, from a town in Oregon:

Dear Mr. Sherman: This is not going to be a very pleasant letter to write or for you to read, and if you shock easily, I suggest that you throw it in the wastebasket right now. It is a sordid story that is hard to believe, and if someone told this to me a few years ago, I would not have believed it.

Last summer, through my automatic writing (wherein a subconscious or "spirit" influence controls and directs the arm and hand) I got an "astral tramp" who posed as a spiritual adviser, guardian angel, and guru. He found that he could "turn me on," that is, talk to me . . . and I fell for the whole thing, not knowing that these evil entities existed. He claimed to have been born and died in South Dakota, where he had had a family of three children, two girls and a boy, and little did I realize, at the start, the grief he would cause my loved ones, friends, and members of the community who had become interested in my "developing psychic ability."

As he gained more and more control of me, he said he would break me down, and through me, my husband, too, and told me he wanted me to share his bed and wealth. Ridiculous! But that shows how crazy he is—because I now can't get rid of him. He has followed me, bugged and badgered me for a whole year, keeping me awake nights with his dirty, filthy, smutty, perverted sex talk and mental pictures.

He has begged me to take him into women's public toilets and saunas . . . and said that if I left his side, my ESP would go away. He is along at my bath, all my bodily needs, while I am trying on swimsuits, girdles, and bras, with his dirty filth pouring out day and night.

If I would doze, and I slept light, he would mentally shake me, saying: [obscenities], and "You are losing your mind and need a keeper and Kasha will look after you. [His full name was given.]

I've spent close to two hundred and fifty dollars on pills, doctors, and ads in the papers, trying to get help from this evil thing. My poor husband is drinking too much and trying to run a business just as this evil entity said he would do. He said last night, "Kill the kids, Edna!" over and over again.

How do I get rid of this thing? Shock treatments will not help. Last night he mentally put [himself] on me, saying that the spirits following would know. Isn't that shocking? He is going to take up residence with one of my friends, he says, and I should be full of gratitude that he is going to leave me alone—but shall I warn my friend? He said that her body attracts him.

What kind of a world is the afterworld with such things around as this?

I am a member of the Religious Science Church and have read all your books. I just had to tell someone who knows about spirit communication. Can't this evil entity be reported to the "spirit world" and be taken away from me? I think everyone should be warned about that automatic writing—as this is how I happened to get connected with this awful person. Should I try to find his family in South Dakota? What should I do?

I wrote Mrs. Maynard at once, reminding her that I had warned readers in my book *How to Make ESP Work for You* not to get involved with automatic writing—that there were evil as well as good forces that might make attunement with their minds. I then told her that before I could be of real help, I would require some frank, honest answers to a series of questions.

She answered three weeks later, during which time an incident occurred which could have taken the life of her husband and herself, an accident which she attributed to the evil influence.

Dear Mr. Sherman: Thank you for your nice letter and believing in me, as this story is hard to believe by the average layman.

Since my last writing, we almost had a tragedy . . . we were going to our home in the country three weeks ago, shortly after I wrote you the first time, and the night before, and all the next morning while packing the car, this "Kasha" was on me, really had me unnerved by saying we would have a fatal car accident, and we would be killed.

Well, of course, I knew better, but nevertheless I was upset, and crying, and did not want to go. But about one hundred miles from our destination, a car turned left while we were passing it, at Detroit, Oregon, and threw us into a twenty-five-foot ditch, upside down. We were spared, for some reason, with just bruises and head injuries.

I'm not saying this evil entity caused it, but we were quarreling about this "insane thing" and we were both upset and my husband's reflexes were not at the quickest.

While going to the hospital in an ambulance, this Kasha started in on me something like this: "You dirty [so and so], this is what I wanted, and this is what you get for [denying me]. Next time I hope you get both legs broken so you can't get out!" The hospital was about an hour away, and he never stopped his vicious attack!

Now to answer your questions as best I can. . . .

[There followed detailed answers about where she was born, her family background, church affiliation, schooling, early childhood experiences (no shocking ones) that she recalled, and a report of a happy relationship with her husband, leading into comments of interest and application here.]

. . . my husband was very upset with this whole thing, so upset that he did not understand it at all. It hasn't affected our sexual relations, since I have learned to turn off the dirty pictures that this thing would flash in my mind. I have felt [overwhelmed by him].

My husband thinks this "spirit" has gone. I just couldn't do it to him any longer, as he has a large business with many employees and responsibilities. He cried many times (imagine!), relieved at thinking everything was over.

Yes, I went to a psychiatrist, and he had never heard of automatic writing or the spirits, and did want to give me shock treatments, but my husband wouldn't think of it.

Mr. Sherman, would you go for shock treatments if a ghost came into your house? He claimed [the spirit] he would be right there laughing at me when I came out of the shock. What can be done to get this thing to go away? I have sleeping pills and tranquilizers from the doctor.

In answer to your question, no, I never read anything pornographic of any kind. I prefer to read my *Science of Mind* magazine or study some of the other books on the subject. I put down any novel with filth in it. Believe me, this "character" is very real. Remember, he posed as a guardian angel or guru, at first, and after he found he could talk to me, then came the dirt and filth. Some of it

I had never heard before. I have learned to shut down the perverted and dirty pictures—now all he has going is his voice, which never stops, day or night. He echoes every thought that I have back to me.

The dirt and filth is shocking and repugnant to me. Without my religion, I couldn't have stood it this long. He calls me names like "slut" and every other dirty name he can think of. I had to ask my husband what some of them meant.

I have let my family all think he is gone. I have a spastic daughter so can't worry her any more. My other daughter is in Greece and was with me at Christmastime when I was having a bad time. She believes in spirits, good and bad, but she has her own problems, so my letters to her are cheerful.

I don't think this was a case of "like attracting like," as you inquire. I can't think of any sex feelings in my consciousness he could have latched onto. I just left a door open, through my automatic writing, for him to move in, thinking he was really a spiritual teacher.

He said he was next door and heard the children playing around the pool, and he and another "astral tramp" moved in. He has told me about three or four other town women that he has [plagued], and he claims some of his victims are in sanatoriums . . . but, being Irish, I am not going to give up that easy. It will be a year (perhaps it is already) that he has bugged me.

I feel, as I have said, that I got myself into this by that automatic writing, as he says he has to have the person that he is trying to "turn on" know he is there and talk, by writing first. The only solution is for him to go away and leave me alone . . . and every few minutes he says he is going. This has been going on for many months, but he never leaves my side, day or night, and never stops talking.

Please warn your readers that such evil things do exist, as he says there are many more around just like him.

I think that he is using me as a "whipping boy" for his filth that he pours out . . . and gets enjoyment out of seeing me cringe. He can't do anything physical about sex —just talk evil to innocent victims.

Please keep this in confidence—thank you for your prayers and meditations. I feel they are beginning to help. . . .

In reply to this letter, I sent Edna Maynard instructions for driving this discarnate entity from her consciousness, which has proved effective in many similar cases. I wrote her, in part:

Of course this evil entity enjoys using this kind of language, and feeling that you react to it, because he is attached to your subconscious, and every time you have a sexual experience, he also senses it, even though you may succeed in putting it out of your mind for the time being.

Your car accident could have been caused by the suggestion as well as the tension brought about by the obsessing entity. You are fortunate to have come out of it, you and your husband, with only minor injuries.

I am sure there are many "earthbound entities" of an extremely low character, like him, seeking contact with living mortals, so as to get vicarious sex thrills through them. This is a fact science is going to have to recognize, one of these days.

I am sending you, herewith, this meditation, that I would like you to repeat aloud, as often as you feel the need, day and night, until you develop a conscious awareness of the presence of God within. It has been demonstrated that it is impossible for any evil entity to remain attached to any human consciousness in the presence of this higher power.

> *I am never alone.*
> *God, the Father, is always with me.*
> *My soul, my identity—that something that says, "I am I" to me—is an eternal gift from God, the Great Intelligence.*
> *I can never lose myself because this self is a part of God.*
> *I am part of God, and God has a great purpose in life for me which He is revealing day by day as I grow in strength of body, mind, and spirit.*
> *I am well and strong. I have the power to overcome all things within me.*
> *In God's care, no harm can befall me.*
> *I now give myself over to God's protection and will follow His guidance day by day.*

Following this meditation, I instructed Mrs. Maynard, as I have advised all such possessed or obsessed persons, to issue this order, with all the force at her command:

> GET OUT AND STAY OUT. I WON'T HAVE ANY MORE TO DO WITH YOU ANYTIME, ANYWHERE. I CALL UPON THE GOD PRESENCE IN ME TO THROW YOU OUT. YOU ARE NO MORE.

I then assured Mrs. Maynard that I would do some powerful concentrating each night during my meditation period, and urged her to keep me informed of developments, concluding with this statement: "I feel you are on

the way out of this thing and that the hold this evil influence has had over you will be broken forevermore."

On July 11 came this answer:

> The evil one is gone from my house and consciousness.
> He left, saying that he had used me, abused me, and made
> a big fool out of me, and had all the good that I had, and
> was going on to his next victim.
>
> I can't believe it was any kind of a breakdown for me,
> and still I can't imagine anyone human, having lived and
> died in South Dakota, with a family, doing what he did to
> a fellow man. He claims it was for sex purposes—but what
> sex? Was looking at his lurid, filthy mental sex pictures
> really what he wanted—thinking he could stimulate me?
> Do you suppose he really derived pleasure out of that tor-
> ture? I summed it all up as being just "an old man with
> dirty pictures, a peeping tom."
>
> Thank you for believing in my story. Many, many thanks
> to you and the few others who believed in me and at least
> gave me encouragement in making my fight against this
> frightful thing.
>
> You have no idea what a relief it is to have my own
> thoughts and not have the voice in my head. Thank God,
> as without faith and prayer, I couldn't have stood it. You
> may use my case to help others, but please change the
> name and keep my identity confidential.

If you doubt the reality of this case, there are other
cases just as tragic, many more than can be presented in
this book—psychiatrists and doctors must have thousands
of them which may be being wrongly diagnosed and
treated. Note how promptly, after a year's struggle with
this evil influence, it was compelled to release its hold on
this woman's consciousness, when this method of meditation and call upon God was employed.

Further word from Edna Maynard gives the assurance:

> Yes, he is really gone! To join his buddies, he said, and
> I shudder to think an evil thing like that and others like
> him roam this planet, with their dirty talk and evil sugges-
> tions.
>
> Before he left, he tried everything, as you warned me he
> would. He recited my obituary all night long, droned on
> and on . . . and spewed out his dirty four-letter words
> continuously.
>
> Enough of him now, as I wish to forget this experience
> and pick up the pieces where I left off. I want to thank you
> again and again. It was so important, at the time, just to
> have someone to listen to this weird story . . . but, more
> important, to tell me what to do about it.

There is a woman in Oakland who has also been helpful to me, who does nothing but "treat" people for just this sort of thing. [At this point, Edna gave me her name and address.] She has some hair-raising stories to tell. She gave me courage and told me of others, how they rid themselves, and all about these spirits who roam around close to earth.

The terminology used by this spiritual woman is somewhat different from that which I use, but we were both praying and meditating in our respective ways for the release of Edna Maynard from this evil influence, without being aware of each other at the time. And Edna's own response to the meditations and instructions we gave her did evidently drive this low discarnate entity from her body and mind.

In my last letter from Edna, she says:

I have resumed my old life, which is wonderful. I've never been happier and will never complain about anything again, no matter how adverse things seem. Please warn others that the Ouija board and automatic writing are dangerous. I got into this in the desert with the "gals" down here, and we had a lot of fun with the "spirits." They were playful and gave us a lot of good laughs . . . so I thought the "spirits" were all good. How naïve or innocent I was—or was it just plain dumbness on my part? Anyway, I've learned my lesson, and learned it well. The evil one kept telling me what a gift I had. How dumb can you get? Please let me know if anything like this happens to anyone, as I will pray and give the person comfort just by saying: "You can get free. It can be done."

Edna's helpful intentions are laudable, but if I referred every man or woman who has reported harrowing experiences with obsession or possession to her, she would have to devote almost full time to this assignment. The technique for exorcising these evil spirits, which is herein presented, has been uniformly successful, if faithfully and persistently followed. To convince you further that this psychic phenomenon is alarmingly widespread in today's world, that what is occurring is genuine and not hallucinatory and that great caution should be exercised in exploring this phase of extrasensory perception, I would like to report on a few other cases.

Consider this experience, for example, from a Mrs. Jane Everett (not her real name), who wrote me from a town in Arizona.

A Case of Possession
Involving Automatic Writing

I want you to know I am not subject to hallucinations, and have always regarded myself as a fairly normal person. For a good many years, though, I have had a lot of ESP, such as knowing something would happen before it did, having hunches that proved almost one hundred percent correct, and so on.

About a year and a half ago, my two daughters and I visited London, England, where I was born. While we were there, my younger daughter met and fell in love with a young man. After we were back in the States a few months, we were horrified to hear that the young man had been killed in an auto crash.

My daughter was brokenhearted and expressed a desire to try to contact him by using a Ouija board. I went out and bought one, and the planchette moved right away. After a few tries, a message apparently came from the young man, whose name was Max Reid [not his real name]. We sat down night after night with the board, sometimes using it for hours.

I had the feeling, on and off, that perhaps it was not really Max, just some entity pretending it was him, because some of the messages seemed to take on an evil tone, such as, "I want your daughters," and "Jennie, come here."

We kept on with it, though, and automatic writing was suggested. I sat down one night and started writing in a strange hand, not my own. I remember the first sentence was, "I am a new spirit from hell." It frightened me, but I kept on writing. My daughters asked questions, and I wrote the answers. After it stopped, I tried to write my own name, and it was hard for me to do so. It was as if I was learning to write all over again.

We also found that we were able to make things move, such as ashtrays, plates, knives and forks, many objects, by resting our fingers on them, not pushing; some other force was doing it. Our hands and arms would rise into the air; we were not conscious of doing it; it was some other force.

My daughter told me about her hands and arms starting to move one night after she went to bed. She said she was communicating with some intelligence, presumably Max, by thoughts, and she asked if she would ever hear his voice. If yes, to please move one finger; if no, to move two fingers. She was "informed" she would hear his voice later.

I also noticed my arms and hands moving after I went

to bed. In the meantime, the messages began to frighten me more and more, such as "M. R. is partly in your mind." Whenever we used the board, the spirit identified itself as "M. R."

One night, after some more automatic writing, I thought that I heard a faint voice; as my daughters spoke to me, this voice would answer in my mind. It was so fantastic that I figured that I must have imagined it. Later I was "told" that I could hear the voice all the time, but the entity preferred writing, as I was afraid that I was "going nuts" if I heard the voice.

I was not able to sleep much anymore, as this entity, or "whatever it was," kept communicating all the time, for hours.

The horror got steadily worse . . . but what I couldn't understand, usually requiring at least eight hours sleep a night to feel well, I was never tired or sleepy the next day after a sleepless night. There came a night, however, when I didn't sleep at all, and around five in the morning, the voice became harsh and loud and started to curse. It said that it would force me to return to London with my older daughter, and that when she was at work, I would be at his mercy all day, to do his bidding.

The voice told me of things that I experienced in my childhood and as a young girl. While this was going on, my body was held down with my left hand on my chest, and my right index finger kept circling my lips. Suddenly the voice said, "Hey, what's happening? I'm being pulled out of your body!"

Another voice came in, softer and kindly, and told me that I had many friends who came to my aid. This voice stayed with me for a short while, and then gradually faded out, and I remember hoping it wouldn't go away so I would never hear the other voice or experience the other influence anymore. By this time, I was badly frightened.

One afternoon, as I was driving my husband to the movies, I felt my tongue starting to move, and I knew I was not doing it. I thought to myself, "How could this evil thing possibly come back when I thought and hoped it had been taken away for good?"

I did the only thing I could think of—I prayed—but it did not help. The following day, I knew it was back. This time there were no voices or writing; it was all thoughts. As each word came into my mind, it was emphasized by my tongue pushing against my lower front teeth. I tried to ignore it, but it kept on talking to me in this manner: "Speak to me, please!" it kept repeating. I finally did answer, by thinking in my mind: "What do you want?"

It said something to the effect that I was supposed to make a good spirit out of it, that it was sent back for this reason.

I foolishly believed this, as I couldn't understand why it was allowed to come back. However, I still tried not to communicate with it, and I remember it telling me, "Please don't shut me out of your mind." This went on for about two weeks, and then I found it had not changed, it was still an evil thing, as it said to me, "You are for me."

I was then determined to put forth a supreme effort to shut it out of my mind. I tried chewing gum, to stop it from moving my tongue. I also kept praying, but it did not seem to help. I think that I would have gone mad by now, had I not had a belief in a merciful God, who would not let this thing take over.

The rest of this experience is very hard to relate. After I had shut this thing out of my mind, I went to bed a few nights later and was prevented from sleeping the entire night. I was subjected to the most powerful sexual stimulation that I had ever known, and I could do nothing to stop it.

I started reciting the rosary, to try to get my mind away from it, but it kept on. I am not a practicing Catholic, as I am divorced, but I do say the prayers that I learned in this faith. I prayed all night, until it was time for me to get up and fix breakfast for my family.

The very last communication I received from this thing was just before I got up: "You [obscenity]—I hate you."

I went to my doctor and told him I was having trouble sleeping, and he prescribed tablets. I hated to go to bed at night, but when I took the pill I would fall asleep in about half an hour. I still had the sexual stimulation while I was awake, and in the day time, although I tried hard to ignore it.

Then, one morning as I was applying makeup in the bathroom, I felt as if someone was holding onto me. I felt a presence. I kept thinking to myself, "I must be imagining this; after all that has happened, my mind could be playing tricks." However, I kept sensing this presence. It was there all the time.

Mr. Sherman, I know I am not doing a very good job at getting this all down on paper. It is awfully difficult for me to make it sound plausible. It sounds like the rambling of a sick mind. Please believe me, it all happened exactly as I am writing it.

On Palm Sunday morning, I awakened, and again I was experiencing this sexual stimulation. My body was turning violently from one side to another. Then I was on my back, and it was as if I was being attacked, only there was not anyone there—that I could see.

I started praying again, and it stopped. I did not know what to do to combat this thing. I wrote to a friend of mine, back east, and she, upon hearing my story, told me

to read *Between Two Worlds,* by Nandor Fodor,* saying
that there was an episode in the book of a woman who
had an experience similar to mine. The author referred to
this type of spirit as an "incubus—one who has intercourse with mortal women."

I feel certain now that what I am experiencing is an
obsession—and I am trying, oh so hard, to overcome this.
I have stopped taking sleeping pills, as I realize I can't
keep on taking them forever. I get to sleep by listening to
the radio and praying. Some nights I think it is gone, but
then it seems to come back as strong as ever. There is no
longer any communication of any sort; I guess I have successfully blocked that out.

I agree with you, it must have been my state of mind
that attracted this entity in the first place. I have so deeply
appreciated your letters and your counsel. Looking back, I
recall, at the start, as my daughters and I continued working the Ouija board, the messages became sexier and sexier. I objected to them in the beginning and told my girls
not to pursue this any further, but I guess that I don't
have to tell you the attitudes today are so different from
years ago, and they thought it was all rather fun, and
after a while, I must confess, I was amused by it also. We
thought, at the time, we were in contact with the spirit of
Max Reid, the young man killed in London. We once
asked, "Aren't there any young girls that you could have
fun with where you are?" to which he gave a strange
answer: "I am not like them."

One afternoon a startling thing happened that I must
not forget to report. My daughters and I were using the
Ouija board, supposedly communicating with the spirit of
"M. R." The planchette was moving, and I thought when
I left the house, it would stop, as this entity was moving
my index finger to write messages. But when I returned,
to my astonishment, the girls said the planchette had kept
on moving, without any of their hands touching it, and
messages were spelled out! Curious, I asked "M. R." how
this could be, and the answer was: "Don't ask."

Is it possible there was more than one entity involved?

I am most grateful for all you have done and are doing
for me. I am repeating the words you wrote to me: "No
one can hurt me unless I let them hurt me," and they are
definitely helping to give me a protecting influence.

I was amazed, on receipt of your last letter, when you
told me that during your nightly meditations while concentrating on me, you could feel the hold that this entity
had upon me lessening. That is exactly what happened,
but I had not told you that; I just said the influence was
still around. Although I could feel the power weakening, I

* Prentice-Hall, Englewood Cliffs, N.J., 1964.

was happy to read that you knew it and felt that I was winning the battle.

Mr. Sherman, you don't know (but then, probably, you do) what a fight this is. The entity does not want to give up. I have followed your advice and taken a complete vacation from ESP. However, the sexual disturbance is still a problem. I notice this presence, or influence, mostly when I go to bed. When I feel it increasing, I keep repeating the declaration you gave me: "No one can hurt me unless I let them hurt me." It really works, and I am able to get to sleep.

Since I have been communicating with you and following your advice, I feel so much better and stronger. I have always felt that there was another existence, beyond this, but was completely ignorant of the dangers that were involved in communicating with beings on this plane.

I am very grateful that I have finally been able to get this "off my chest" . . . it is hard to keep it all bottled up, knowing nobody will believe you.

I will keep fighting this influence, and with your and God's help, I know that I will win.

The Experience of a Lady in Wyoming

Recently a prominent woman in a town in Wyoming wrote me about her encounter with an evil entity. She shall be called here Ruth Torrence. At first she had thought this contact with the spirit world, through automatic writing, to be highly spiritual and that one of her communicators was her father, who had passed into the next life an agnostic, and whom she now felt she could help in his soul's advancement. She later stated:

I now realize this idea was ridiculous, but I had read in some metaphysical literature that some entities had been helped, after they had made the transition by those here in this dimension, and as long as I was led to believe I was in touch with my father's spirit, I let myself become deeper and deeper involved.

Gradually, however, what had seemed to be my father's personality faded out, and what appeared to be a high type spiritual guide took over. To gain my confidence, he tried to make me believe that it was my father's spirit undergoing a transformation. Unusual spiritual statements were made, and my curiosity was aroused. Could this be possible? Was my psychic contact with my father's spirit actually having a beneficial influence, after all?

Then, suddenly, it was like having the carpet yanked out from under me—I started getting vile, filthy, and obscene language, insults and threats on my life. I still had no fear of this entity—only anger and frustration took its place. First, I was absolutely shocked into a state of confusion. I put the pencil down and tried to gather my thoughts. Then I began to give him a lecture, telling him I would not stand for this behavior, that I had not spent all this time with this "writing" to end up with such a low-type character who thought he was going to get by with this language or conduct. He knew I was strictly interested in obtaining high information or in helping my father if that could be done. Commanding over and over again, I demanded that he go and let himself be replaced by a God-oriented guide.

It was then that I began to discover that these entities are just as stubborn as anyone can be. Finally, refusing to continue with the writings unless this entity would allow another to step in, I now laid the pencil down. I was thoroughly disgusted. I am a very determined person by nature, once I've set my mind on a goal. I did not regard this entity as one that I would have to contend with for very long. So, for the next couple of days, from time to time, I would pick up the pencil to see if he was still there or if I had gained another in his place. It was immediately obvious he was still there, and I would quickly throw the pencil down on the table, showing great disgust.

Because I resolutely refused to "write," he now began a series of sensations, such as to make me feel I could be melting away, shrinking, losing my mind or equilibrium, rotting away inside, and such other disturbing nonsense.

It was at this time that he gained a *voice*. Since I would not allow him to "write," he was determined to be heard. Once his voice came through, it was constantly heard, both night and day. I could be just as stubborn as he, I thought—and not let him bother me until I could get rid of him. I just simply could not understand, with all the precautions I had taken, and now I was constantly, repeatedly commanding him "out"—but he did not leave. Why? I just did not know. I had certainly made it obvious I didn't want him around. I even used some rather strong language, which is not a usual habit with me. But I hadn't bargained for what was yet to happen.

He would not even let me sleep now. He would continue to "tune in" with his foul language, insults, and suggestions. Since nothing he seemed to say would break me down or make me show fear, he became enraged.

I had by this time written a letter to you, begging for an appointment, and I was greatly relieved to receive a reply that you would be glad to see me, at whatever time I would care to come. God knows I felt I had done everything I knew how to do to get rid of this evil influence.

It took me eleven days before I could arrange to leave home and make the flight to Little Rock—eleven days and ten sleepless nights in which I had to be constantly on guard. Now that this entity knew I was going to get help to drive him out, he tried in every way possible to break me down, to weaken me, to break me mentally. He became even more vile. He did this through making his physical presence known—by attempting physical sexual attacks.

He would wait, being silent now, so that I might think he was gone, and when I would finally fall into a deep enough sleep, he would attack me. I would bolt awake, feeling suffocated from his weight. He would force any sensation he could onto me while I was in the fog of sleep, and when I would awaken violently, obviously letting him know I was disgusted, I could hear him laugh in the evilest manner. He knew he could not accomplish all he had in mind while I was awake. Showing no fear of him only made him rage in a more maniacal way.

I knew that all he could do to me was by sensation, even though he did his best to try to make me feel he had really accomplished his purpose. And because he insisted he had achieved his crude acts, he tried to make me believe I was going to die, so he could completely have me. All he succeeded in doing was to disgust me and cause me loss of sleep and headaches from his ceaseless voice and laughter.

The day finally arrived when I would fly to Little Rock. I felt positive you would see what I was, or perhaps wasn't, doing properly in order to get this *thing* out of my life. I had reached a point by now that I would have hitchiked anywhere you might have been at that moment, for I knew that I could not spend too many more sleepless nights without collapsing. This was just what this entity was hoping for—to wear me down to the right moment, and then jump in and overtake me completely. My "inner guidance" had told me this was what he had in mind, and I wasn't about to let him have his way any more than I could help.

When I finally reached you, you had me relax physically and mentally and talked to me easily and frankly about my life. You didn't ask me questions—you told me what had happened to me, how I had suffered a shock from having been sexually molested when a child, from which I had never recovered. You explained that this was one way an evil entity could gain entrance to a mortal's consciousness—by tuning in on a sexual frequency of mind that was still existent, and amplifying and playing upon it by its own sexual cravings and former lifetime practices.

You pointed out that "Like always attracts like in the realm of mind," and that each of us has had a variety of experiences throughout life that we may consider good or evil, and that these are all stored in the subconscious, and unless we release them, if we still permit guilt complexes or these wrong images to disturb us, that discarnate entities having like experiences or desires, can sometimes attach themselves, as in my case.

I made it plain that I wanted absolute frankness, for you to withhold nothing that you felt would be helpful to me, and you surprised me with the intimate knowledge of the experiences I had had in life. Then you revealed to me a simple little mistake I had made in trying to rid myself of this evil entity.

I had overlooked it, because it had been a lifetime thoughtless habit. My use of a common little word, which has been highly underestimated by many others than just myself. A word that had become fixed in my mind as a child, a word often used by my elders because of their doubtful or negative feelings about everything. The word: "If."

When I subconsciously became obsessed with the idea that I could still help my father, even after death, and with the hope of losing this evil entity for a higher guide, I became so engrossed that I thoughtlessly used the word "If," saying, "If you (meaning the evil entity) are not God- or Christ-oriented, then be gone from me forever."

The "If" left the door open for this entity to hold himself within reach of me. Once you showed me what I had done, I could very well see what had happened. After enlightening me further as to the many ways or reasons an evil entity can gain a recognition with an individual, I felt so relieved to know that all I had to do was to eliminate that one simple word, "If"! Later that day I followed through on your directions, to command properly, and it was as if this evil thing was jolted instantly into the distance.

This would not be a complete and true report if I did not add a little more detail here about what occurred after leaving you that day. It was July 28, 1968. The evening of that same day, after I had settled into a motel room, I gave the proper command again. This entity, having been jolted to some distance, did not seem to go any further away. You had warned me that they do not give up easily.

After my command, there was absolute silence. The evil voice and his presence seemed suddenly to be gone. I felt so relieved to know the exact cause for all this and what to do about it that I now felt I could finally really get a good night's sleep. To add further safeguard for myself, I gave my subconscious orders to automatically send out the identical command, each time, should this *thing* attempt to enter again.

On two occasions before 1:30 A.M. the entity tried to talk to me. I remember faintly waking and the command given, and silence came immediately, and I would fall right back into sound sleep. The third time awakened me, and before "he" could say anything, I had jumped out of bed to a standing position, pointed outside, and repeated the command, adding, "Now I mean it—Out, Now, Go!"

I got back into bed and slept the remainder of the night.

For the rest of the trip home, all was calm and quiet. After I arrived home, I began to feel the distinct presence of a pair of eyes watching me. Only now, instead of the leering appearance—the eyes seemed to register disbelief, and shock, as one who might suddenly exclaim: "You really did mean it! Didn't you? And I didn't believe you!"

There has been no further conversation from this evil thing—but his eyes remained. I have refrained from doing any automatic writing. I've also watched very carefully, not only my behavior, but my words or thoughts used in meditation, so that there is nothing that could give "him" reason to get back.

As of August 2, 1968, I have had no further sign of the evil entity being around at all. Even the eyes are gone. I sense nothing of evil nature anywhere near me now.

I would like to say here that I felt your thoughts accompany me from the moment I left you, and that I sensed they were with me all the way home, and even after I arrived, offering added protection.

During the time I spent so many sleepless nights, I was so engrossed in keeping the entity at a distance as best I could that I had not noticed the strain my husband was under also. He is a very quiet person. I became aware of his concern and how much he was really aware of what was going on only after I returned from Little Rock. After I told him the whole story, which I thought I had managed to keep pretty much to myself so as not to upset him, he admitted knowing what was going on. His relief was so great to know it was all over. He said that knowing I had an appointment with you made him feel he didn't have to mention anything, as he felt it would all be taken care of when I got to Little Rock. Besides, he didn't know what to do about it, anyway.

This is my story, every word of it true and not exaggerated in the least. You have my permission to publish any part of it you wish, protecting, of course, my identity. May what I have gone through be of some help to others who have delved into automatic writing and found more than they had bargained for.

                                        Sincerely,
                                        RUTH TORRENCE.

There you have it—those are graphic cases that should indicate to anyone but the most closed-minded of persons that possession can be a very real phenomenon. This being true, it raises a profound question that must be laid at the door of those who believe in reincarnation: If reincarnation is a fact, and if it is part of a universal plan for evolution of the soul, then it would seem that proper controls should be exercised by higher intelligences in charge, to prevent those who die and who are destined, in time, for rebirth on earth, from attaching themselves to the minds of living mortals. Why should discarnate entities even have the urge to return to earth in any other way than through reincarnation if this is the established cosmic scheme? If, however, people who die, conditioned by a belief in reincarnation and expecting to be returned to earth through entrance again into the womb of a child-bearing woman, find that rebirth is impossible—isn't it logical to presume that a certain percentage of the carnally minded would attempt to occupy the bodies of others who are still living in order to experience, even partially, the sensations of the flesh?

There are many more questions than answers when we dare to face, head-on, the mysteries of our own minds. However, it is clear to me that possession can take place and that faith in God alone can overcome it.

8
Communication
with the Future

SCIENTISTS STILL SAY that it cannot be done—that it is impossible for anyone to predict the future accurately. Some of them may grudgingly admit that telepathy may be a proved fact, but they can find no scientific ground for proving any way by which the human mind can project itself ahead in time and foresee an act of nature or of man that has not yet taken place.

If anyone just happens to guess something that later happens, it is labeled pure coincidence. This has been the general attitude of science before every great breakthrough. There was a time when there was no such thing as microbes or bacteria. You couldn't send a voice over a wire or through the air, or an image. The things that were proclaimed impossible were legion. It is a fact that many of man's greatest inventions were not the original work of scientists. They came through the minds of men and women who were never told or trained to believe that "it couldn't be done."

Scientists scoffed at the reported prophecies of Nostradamus, at the works of Tennyson, Jules Verne, H. G. Wells, and many others who pictured in their writings visions of things to come, sometimes hundreds of years before the events arrived on the earthly scene. Where did these flashes of precognitive perception originate? How could Nostradamus, the French astronomer (1518–1566), for example, accurately forecast names and dates of kings and other rulers who were destined to live some centuries hence, and predict quite recognizably our World War I, among many other happenings, clothing these predictions in different languages and puzzling quatrains to avoid condemnation by the Church of his day?

But we do not have to go back in time and study the misty and often inaccurate or exaggerated records of the past to produce evidence in substantiation of precognition —the ability of some sensitive-minded men and women to foresee a forthcoming event of world or individual significance. These impressions, later confirmed in many instances, may have come to them through the medium of dreams or waking visions, or under hypnotic influence, in a trance state, gazing at a crystal ball, or by contact with a spiritual presence.

Jeane Dixon

One of the most highly publicized and discussed prophetesses of our time is, of course, the Washington seeress Jeane Dixon, whose phenomenal lifetime predictions are recounted in the book *A Gift of Prophecy* by Ruth Montgomery (William Morrow & Company, New York, 1965). Among her documented predictions are: the assassination of President John F. Kennedy and the name of his killer, Edward Kennedy's plane accident, the assassination of Mahatma Gandhi, the deaths by plane of Dag Hammarskjöld and Carole Lombard, Marilyn Monroe's suicide, the partition of India, the adoption of communism by China, the Soviet Sputnik, and DeGaulle's competitive France.

I know Jeane Dixon personally, and we have exchanged views on our different ESP experiences. I agree with her, when she says that "you cannot turn this power on and off like a water spigot." Nor can any genuine sensitive, as I have previously emphasized, guarantee always to produce one-hundred-percent-accurate impressions.

Of all the predictions that Jeane Dixon has made that have come true, none has caused such worldwide interest as a sudden vision that came to her first in 1956, while being interviewed by two reporters from *Parade* magazine, when she said: "A blue-eyed Democratic President elected in 1960 will be assassinated." This prognostication was published in the March 11 issue of *Parade*, and when John F. Kennedy won the upset victory of 1960, friends remembered her description of the man in the vision which so strongly resembled the new President. Asked if she still felt the same about her original feeling of four years ago, Jeane said, "Yes, I continue to see a black cloud hovering above the White House." She persisted in this conviction and tried to get friends to warn Kennedy not to go to Dallas, but to no avail. At noon on the day of the assassination, she sensed what was about to happen and repeated again her overpowering feeling that the President was going to be shot.

I have deliberately repeated this persistent pre-vision of Jeane Dixon's because at least a hundred men and women have written me from all over the country, testifying that they, too, had received similar impressions. I myself had written a high official in Washington expressing my own concern that President Kennedy was in great danger, but I had not made public this feeling.

There is an old saying that "coming events cast their shadows before," and I believe there is substance to this statement. Events of great potential magnitude—in some way beyond our present explanations—send out vibrations that reach the consciousness of sensitive persons and cause them to have visions and feelings about a happening that is going to have a profound effect on humanity, while this happening is still forming in some still timeless dimension. This is a most difficult concept to put into words. Expressed in another way, I believe that: The future is a projection of the causative forces of the past, which are in the constant process of materializing in our present moments in the form of an act of nature or an act of man.

It is evident that we are ruled on every level of our existence, within and without ourselves, by the infallible functioning of the universal laws of cause and effect. We are constantly setting up causes by the nature of our thoughts and acts which transform themselves into effects in our outer world, in due course of time—unless we change our thinking, which, when we do, instantly brings about a change in the causes, and subsequently the effects growing out of them.

This is why people who have established prophetic ability sometimes miss the mark. They sense, at the time of a prediction, conditions existing in a mind or minds which could lead to a certain event, if the conditions remain as they then are. After this, if mental attitudes and objectives are altered in any material way, the predicted events of course do not occur. You must realize that, concurrent with changes taking place in the mass mind, there are also changes of a vast character taking place throughout all nature, including the earth, the atmosphere around us, and all planets and heavenly bodies existent in the unlimited universe.

The average human being is fortunately unaware of what is taking place continuously in and around him, or his body and mind could not endure the vibratory pressures. This is why nature has wisely limited man's senses for normal functioning in this three-dimensional plane of existence.

Unless you open the door by conscious development of your extrasensory faculties, you ordinarily are not bothered by impressions other than those brought to you by and through your five physical senses. If something is about to happen, of a possibly harmful nature, to you or anyone you love, you are seldom warned of it by any advance feelings of apprehension or concern. If, in some cases, you are warned, you usually argue yourself out of the impression and realize, only after the happening, that some power or influence had been trying to guide you and protect you.

No one yet knows how the mind is able to foresee the future, but it is evident that a sensitive-minded person not only can pick up the thoughts and feelings of others but also can sense in vibratory form the conditions and activities of objects and forces in nature. We do not have the proper words to describe this precognitive phenomenon when it occurs, but we can testify to the effect that it has on us. During my pioneering experiments in long-distance telepathy with Sir Hubert Wilkins, for example, I sensed and accurately delineated the only two accidents that were to befall his plane, days before the events took place.

The Power of Emotion in ESP

As I reported in *Thoughts Through Space:*

After I had received the "previsions" of accidents which I felt were going to happen to Wilkins' plane, the human side of me was affected. I was personally fond of Wilkins as a friend, and my emotions tried to tell me that he might meet with some serious physical injury, or even death.

This brought on a real battle with myself each appointed time that I sought to telepathically communicate with him. I found instilled in me an emotional apprehension that I might "tune in" at any sitting and receive impressions of a possible fatal crash. This apprehension had been brought about through the intensity of the conviction in my inner mind that what I had foreseen would really come to pass. I had no doubt of it. I could not determine the exact time when my premonitory impressions would materialize, but I felt they were imminent in the "very atmosphere"—a fact which proved to be true.

The effect on me was almost nerve-shattering. On each night of a sitting, it required a strong effort of will to put my own emotions out of the equation, and to "blank my consciousness" so that I might receive, "uncolored" by my own fears, impressions of what was actually happening.

Obviously, to have permitted these apprehensions to have dominated my consciousness would have prevented the reception of any genuine impressions at all.

I experienced a tight, tense sensation in my solar-plexus region, with occasional shortness of breath, and nervous indigestion, followed by stomach cramps. This condition, despite all efforts to throw it off, became chronic.

I walked the floor many nights with severe stomach pain and "gas pressure" which defied relief. It seemed that my entire stomach and central nerve area were in a knot.

I could not and would not abandon the experiments, and simply made a note of my physical reactions for the records, while keeping on with the tests.

I consulted my physician during this period, and he told me that my condition could not be alleviated until I was able to get out from under the mental load I was carrying. I was "highly keyed up," ordinary happenings—such as a slammed door or the sudden backfire of a car in the street—striking me like a knife in the solar plexus. My entire nervous system was greatly "oversensitized" and reacted involuntarily to conditions which normally scarcely influenced it at all. Yet all that I was experiencing was of profound value to me, and of marked significance, although not fully realized at the time.

When the five and one-half months of tests were concluded, the relief from strain was almost too much to endure. I had to let myself down easily and gradually like a horse that has run a furious race, and must now be walked about and cooled off by degrees before being returned to the stable.

I continued, at times, to receive unsought impressions from the minds of others when I fixed my attention upon them.

This serves to indicate that when you develop additional faculties of mind, and set them methodically in motion, you will have difficulty in subduing them—once the intensive work is over.

In my case, due to this prolonged nervous strain, I had developed ulcers of the stomach, which, in turn, produced several hemorrhages. My life itself was threatened before I was able to regain proper control of my nervous system.

This knowledge that our thought processes are so definitely tied up with our emotions should cause us to consider the continuous effect upon our lives—physically and mentally—of wrong emotional reactions. Many of us have had nervous breakdowns, or have been on the verge of them, through letting our emotions get out of control. A well-ordered body is the product of a disciplined mind. We must have both if we are to realize our fullest degree of mental and physical efficiency.

In the years following the long-distance telepathic experiments with Sir Hubert Wilkins, as I have continued my studies and research on various phases of extrasensory perception, hundreds of men and women have reported to me on how they have been affected by the reception of thoughts and feelings, particularly having to do with the approach of a forthcoming personal happening or event.

Prophecy in Alaska

One of the most outstanding and representative cases is that of Vernon L. Wheeler, geologist and engineer, who wrote me this account of his experiences from Anchorage, Alaska:

I would like an explanation of why I have what I have, and am continually in hopes that I may hear of someone, somewhere, who has had a similar reaction. [Mr. Wheeler has been assured by me that he has plenty of company with many others who have shared his physical and emotional reactions.]

For years I have been blessed or cursed with an odd warning system. I would like to be able to say that I have been given a clue to what danger lies ahead—a vision, a thought, a vague hunch—but in all of these incidents I am about to relate, I have never been able to even guess what it is that the "warning" tells me is about to happen.

Further, the warning is not for me, that is, it always concerns someone that I am associated with. My immediate family, or friends. Also, this "warning signal" always stays in my immediate area. That is, I have yet to receive a warning that extended for a period of miles, say, for someone in another state.

Also, since my arrival in Alaska, ten years ago, the warning has definitely strengthened. I mean, it has not increased in frequency, but when it arrives, I am more aware of it. This may be due to location, or it could be due to my having given greater recognition to it—I would not know.

The warning system I experience is a definite, uncomfortable tightness in the abdomen or stomach area.

When these experiences first occurred, many years ago, I naturally thought of upset stomach, gas pains, and tried bicarbonate of soda. Finally a light suddenly dawned on me, so to speak, and I realized that this tightness was due to coming incidents. It did not interfere with my eating or sleeping—and ended immediately when some incident occurred.

Rather than report all the times and places, I will limit my description to the shortest and longest periods that I have experienced these "warning sensations."

The Shortest

It is a winter morning in our second-floor apartment in the Anchorage area. I sit at the kitchen table studying a law course, my stepdaughter is at the kitchen sink washing dishes, and my wife has just put a leash on our small dog to take him outside. A typical morning scene, a replay of many past mornings.

All of a sudden, for no reason, a severe tightness grips my abdomen. From years past, I know something is about to happen. I tell my wife not to take the dog out, but she disregards me. I literally scream at her to be careful. She goes down the long flight of stairs without incident.

Then, a few steps on the icy ground—she slips, falls, and breaks an ankle—a break that will keep her in bed in a cast for twelve weeks.

My tightness is gone when I hear her cries for help, as she cannot get up off the ground.

I could not tell what was about to happen. I could only tell that something was about to take place.

Now, don't try to tell me that yelling at my wife caused her to be nervous and fall. I have had enough past experiences of a warning nature to know it didn't. The causative forces must have been already forming to bring about this event when I somehow "tuned in" and got this solar-plexus reaction.

The period for this "tightness" feeling, from its beginning to the time of the accident, could not have been more than three minutes—my shortest on record.

The Longest

January, 1964—shortly after the holidays. A light tightness developed—or appeared. I say "light" because it did not have the same intensity as others. I became cautious and advised friends and associates to be careful.

February, 1964. The tightness has not left. It's still there, morning and night. To say the least, I'm uneasy. Also wondering if I'm not "off base" in believing it to be my old "warning system." Nothing happens to anybody around me.

March, 1964—the tightness has stayed with me and is increasing. I get to the point where I become irritable—extremely uneasy. I have tried all stomach remedies. There is nothing wrong with my stomach. It is definitely the "old warning tightness." I can eat well and sleep well —but the tightness never leaves.

My line of work causes me to be out of town. As I start to prepare for a trip to Soldotna, my wife asks if she can go too. I say yes. This is the first time she accompanies me. Usually I always go alone on a bush trip.

The tightness does not go away even though she is by my side.

It Finally Happens

March 27, 1964. My wife and I get in our car at 5:30 P.M. to drive to Kenai to meet a plane. A friend of ours has promised to bring us one of Alaska's king crabs, and we are looking forward to a wonderful evening of the best the sea has to offer. I have been so continually uneasy with my tightness, I wonder if I'll enjoy the dinner.

5:34 P.M. Our car pulls onto the highway and we head for Kenai.

With a thunderlike roar, waves rolling toward us in the earth, as though it were an ocean; cracks in the ground around us opening and slamming shut with a spray of dirt; trees whipping to hit the rocky terrain on one side, and then the other; our car bouncing up and down as the visible waves approach and pass under us—THE GREAT ALASKAN EARTHQUAKE OF 8.6 MAGNITUDE OF THE RICHTER SCALE HAS JUST TAKEN PLACE!

The car is still vibrating, the earth seems to have an elliptical roll to it! My wife is crying. I tell her: "Everything is all right—my tightness is gone." Now I knew.

We had left my stepdaughter in Anchorage. My wife was extremely worried about her, but I told her she was all right. My tightness works both ways. When I don't have it, those near me (my immediate family and my associates) are not in danger.

All communications were dead. A ham-radio message a few days later that my stepdaughter was well and not injured verified my feeling.

Truly, Mr. Sherman, I have something—but I don't know what. I would like to hear of others so "afflicted." I can't believe I'm the only one.

In my reply to Mr. Wheeler, I said, in part:

You possess an unusual sensitivity, a faculty in you which projects itself ahead in time and gives you flashes or continued feelings of apprehension until you get evidence of what has brought about your precognitive feeling. Then you get instant relief, and so do I, when the event has finally materialized.

I have had what you call "warning sensations" since early in life, although I usually get a *specific* feeling concerning the nature of the forthcoming event.

It is easy to explain the difference in degree of this solar-plexus reaction. The further away the event that is coming toward you, or your family, friends, or the world—in time—the lighter the feeling in your solar plexus. The closer the event gets to you, as to actual happening, the more intense the feeling.

As you well know, you cannot force this extrasensory power to work for you—or you activate your imagination.

Should you wish to have revealed to you the nature of a forthcoming event, the next time you get this tight feeling in your stomach or solar-plexus region, simply suggest to yourself each night before retiring that this knowledge will accompany the "forewarning sensation" when it comes. I think, up to now, you have, subconsciously, not really wanted to know—and so this awareness of the specific happening could not get through to your conscious mind.

In the uncertainties of today's world, many are deeply concerned about the future, and fortunetellers and astrologers and psychics of one kind and another are doing a big commercial business. A high percentage are fraudulent or self-deluded, and many who trustingly follow their prognostications become mentally and emotionally confused and disillusioned. You can learn to sense quite accurately what is coming toward you in time, both as concerns your private life and world events, if you will remember and apply one universal mental law: LIKE ALWAYS ATTRACTS LIKE IN THE REALM OF MIND.

Gauge your future by this. Analyze your thoughts and feelings with respect to whatever goal you may have in life. If you have permitted fear and hatred and other destructive emotions to occupy a dominant position in your consciousness, you can expect, in time, to attract experiences of like nature—the products of such thinking. If you accurately observe the minds of other people in the world to be filled with this same hate and fear, you can reliably predict that these thoughts and feelings will lead to destructive ends for them.

In two lectures presented at McFarlin Auditorium on the SMU campus in Dallas, I was asked to predict what I felt was about to happen on the world scene. I am always reluctant to do this because, as I have stated, existing causative forces on which precognitive forecasts are made can always change, so that prophesied events may not happen. However, I stated that, as I sensed the present mood of humanity, especially in certain hate and power-lusting groups, I felt that more assassinations of black and white leaders would take place. It was not long before Martin Luther King and Robert Kennedy were shot.

As in the case of Vernon Wheeler, you may get an unshakable feeling that a tragic event is going to occur—the assassination of a public figure, possibly—without being able to name the person. Again, many people have written me declaring that they had either dreamed or had a powerful presentiment that either King or Kennedy, or both, would be assassinated. The intent to kill both of these men was "in the air."

Several years ago I conducted a private experiment to see if my mind could picture for me, in a dream or a waking state, important developments that were coming toward us in time on the national and international fronts. In my meditation period each night, before entering sleep, I gave myself this suggestion: "Determine what needs to be known to protect our country and her leaders in this time of crisis."

Nothing happened for a few nights, and then this suggestion began to take hold. I have reported some of the precognitive impressions that came to me in *How to Make ESP Work for You*. These impressions were passed on to a confidential source in Washington for whatever service they might prove to be, and a number were confirmed. I have continued, at intervals, to follow this procedure.

It is baffling enough to accept that some sensitives are able to foresee, at times, what influential human creatures and/or their governments are going to do; but for the mind to have the power to foretell an earthquake or some one of nature's catastrophes, where no other mind is involved, is really too much for science to accept. Apparently, however, disturbances in nature (as in the case of earth tremors) must set up a vibratory reaction, too, much as a disturbance in a human mind, and these vibrations do register in the consciousness and in the solar-plexus and stomach regions of the Vernon Wheelers of the world.

Today, at last, world leaders are beginning to wonder what man may be doing to himself and his fellow man through his thinking that brings on tragic national and international events, in addition to all manner of personal disturbances. In a television interview recently I heard Senator Philip Hart of Michigan express the hope that the members of President Johnson's newly appointed Crime Commission could determine "what makes us tick . . . a way for a better understanding of ourselves . . . and how to curb our animal instincts. . . ."

He could not have put the problem more succinctly. It is man's individual lack of knowledge, as Senator Hart has suggested, as to what makes him tick, of a way better to understand himself, and how to curb his animal instincts that is accountable for his mad acts of violence and destruction.

This is the crux of it all, and every other contributing factor having to do with man's savage attacks on society, his growing disrespect for law and order, his unrestrained outbursts of hate, prejudice, and resentment, and his lust for power and vengeance are *secondary*. Poverty-stricken conditions, racial conflicts, the widening gulf between the rich and the poor and between youth and their elders, unemployment, starvation, the present war in Vietnam and the threat of World War III—these, as well as individual economic, sexual, and other personal difficulties are only the triggers that activate mental and emotional tensions beyond the breaking point.

Thus far, in seeking to meet this steadily worsening crisis, nations and governments of the world have been trying to remedy the effects rather than the basic cause. The basic cause is obviously erroneous thinking—wrong mental and emotional reactions of an increasingly larger segment of people at home and abroad to what is happening to them.

To find a cure for this situation, we must face the inescapable fact that, as I have previously emphasized, man is an animal. Built into his lower nature is the bestiality of all animals, supposedly beneath him; but contained in his higher nature is the potentiality of a God.

Mark Twain said it all in one sentence: "The only trouble with human nature is human nature."

A Precognitive Film

In 1933 I wrote an original screenplay which was produced by an independent Hollywood company. It was entitled *Are We Civilized?* Using newsreel clips and scenes from old historical feature pictures, I depicted man's inhumanity to man throughout the ages, from the days of primitive man on. The story illustrated that, as man has become more civilized, he has not become less savage—he has only improved his weapons of self-annihilation. I showed pictures of various nations conducting military maneuvers—testing new explosives, new and more destructive means of warfare—and I asked the question: "Do nations prepare in this manner, who are preparing for peace?"

Are We Civilized? opened at the Rivoli Theatre in New York and drew rave reviews. Walter Winchell called it "the most stirring plea for peace ever produced." It was booked for distribution throughout the United States, and then the booking was mysteriously canceled. We learned later that Hitler, through the German Embassy, had threatened to cancel all American-made showings of pictures abroad if *Are We Civilized?* was released.

In this story I had pictured the coming of World War II, and the shoe had fit too tightly.

How was I able to create such a story and so accurately predict, if man did not change his thinking, what was going to happen? I had rediscovered and proved to myself the existence of a great and infallible mental law—a law known to ancient wise men—which deserves repetition: "As a man thinketh in his mind and in his heart, so is he."

You can think of *nothing* without first *picturing* it in your mind. Every thought you think, with feeling behind it, is an act of creation. It seeks to materialize itself in your outer life, in the form of an experience, taking after the character of the thought or mental picture.

How is this done? Through the agency of the creative power in you which exists, as I have stated, as a part of your subconscious. This creative power doesn't reason. It produces for you what you order in the form of a mental picture, with strong feelings of fear or desire behind it. If your thinking is constructive, you will eventually get constructive results; if destructive, you will ultimately get destructive results.

This is the way your creative power, and the creative power possessed by every individual on the face of the earth, has been serving you, and them. The kind of results obtained have depended, in every instance, on the kinds of mental pictures that have been presented to this creative power by you. Hate, then, always breeds hate; force leads to more force; and love attracts love in return.

It is therefore obvious that if great masses of people have their minds filled with hate and prejudice and resentment, as well as loss of respect for law and order, combined with feelings of depression and frustration and other destructive thoughts, including desires for vengeance, violence and destruction will inevitably result. If you know this, you can predict in advance what is going to happen—unless a GREAT CHANGE IN THOUGHT can be brought about through new leadership and understanding.

Because we think basically in mental pictures, we are influenced not only by the mental images that our minds record of whatever we think or do or feel but also by what we read and hear and see on radio and television, and through other media of communication. It is worth repeating: What a man can picture in his mind, he can, one day, do or attain in life—good or bad. Thoughts are things; they are the world of tomorrow, in creation—NOW.

Recently a minister and his wife with two children, a boy and a girl aged five and three respectively, visited us. The children picked up some sticks and ran around pointing them at the adults, shouting: "Bang! Bang! You're dead!" Then the little three-year-old girl ran up to me and hit me across the back of the neck with the side of her hand. "What are you doing?" I asked. "Karate," she said.

Those who desire to influence and control the thinking of great masses of people know the power of picturization, know how to arouse strong feelings for or against a situation or an issue, or a world or community leader—how to make individuals think what they want them to think. We have a classic example in our time. How many people either in Germany or around the world took Hitler and his *Mein Kampf* seriously at the start? In this book he outlined his political philosophy, set forth his plans for German domination, PICTURED what he was going to do, fired the emotions of the German people, played on their hates and prejudices and resentments, aroused their lust for power, and brought about World War II.

Don't think something like this can't happen again. Today is the age of PICTURIZATION. The peoples of the world, especially in the United States at present, are being bombarded with images of violence, of war, of destruction. Weak minds of men and women who lack mental and emotional stability and who are highly suggestible are being influenced consciously or unconsciously to commit acts that they would not ordinarily commit.

There are conspirators, as we know, who are plotting to destroy or intimidate world leaders and to employ dissolute individuals to perform acts of sabotage or assassination and to so disrupt law and order as to produce widespread fear and chaos. Then there are misguided religious fanatics, radicals, racial haters, and social misfits who are motivated by their own distorted or insane desires to wreak vengeance against society for real or imaginary wrongs. The innocent and the idealistic are often caught up and made a part of this turmoil. These acts, whether by design or spontaneous eruption of feelings, are all, nevertheless, due to the products of man's mind. It cannot be stated too often that a destructive thought planted in a mind will always result in a destructive act in some future moment of time, unless counteracted by a constructive thought.

In facing the fact of "what makes us tick," we must realize that we, and we alone, are responsible for what we think and how we feel about things. Having done this, we must recognize that what we think and feel—multiplied by what everyone else on this planet thinks and feels—is going to determine not only our future but also theirs.

On the personal level there are countless examples wherein a person's mind has tuned in on the future intentions of someone close to him and then receives an urge to respond in a protective or helpful way, in time to prevent a tragedy or a contemplated unwise act from being carried out. One of the most touching and illustrative of these ESP experiences was sent to me by Mrs. Margaret Dutton of Cleveland, Ohio.

A Sister Foresees Trouble

This personal story, Mr. Sherman, involves my older sister and myself, and even at a distance of some twenty-odd years still has a haunting and memorable quality.

The time was 1943, a war year. I was married to a serviceman stationed in Texas, and I had gone there to be near him prior to his going overseas. My sister, Sally, was living in Washington, D.C., boarding there with a family who was seldom at home. Because of the displacement caused by the war, all of my sister's friends had left Washington for the service or elsewhere.

One Saturday morning I received a letter from my sister, and her naturally cheerful personality was now revealed in the letter to be depressed and unsettled. I was disturbed somewhat by the tone of the letter and decided to answer her later in the day.

Throughout that day, some vague sense of uneasiness gripped me and would not let me be. Suddenly, almost like a command, the thought came: "Send her flowers."

This was an extremely odd impression for several reasons: I had very little money to spend for such an extravagance, and I had never in my life wired my sister flowers —so this was a most unnatural thing for me to get the impulse to do. Not only that, but I lived outside of town and had no means of transportation, so this entailed a long walk over hot, dusty roads, which did not have much appeal at the time.

Nevertheless, that "inner voice" was absolutely persistent, so I obeyed the unspoken command and walked into town to the only florist for miles around.

I ordered red roses to be wired to my sister in Washington, and when the clerk asked what words I would like on the card enclosure, I said without thinking, "Somebody cares."

What followed, I learned from my sister when later we met again. That Saturday night Sally was in a terribly distraught state. She felt completely and unutterably alone; she was ill and could see no reason to go on living. She began to contemplate suicide. She walked the floor, wringing her hands and repeated to herself: "Nobody cares . . . nobody cares. . . ."

She had reached the point where she cried out from the depths of her soul: "Oh, God, if somebody cares whether I live or die, send me a sign."

At that moment the doorbell rang. She composed herself and opened the door to discover a messenger with a long floral box. With trembling hands she opened the box, picked out the card, and read, "Somebody cares."

This may all have been coincidence [consider the mathematical chances against this], but no "coincidence" ever had happier results. Sally immediately recovered from her depression and is convinced, to this day, that a "higher power" was at work behind the scene.

Higher powers of our own, of which we so little dream, until and unless we have had experiences such as this, do exist. Mrs. Dutton, whose life has been filled with "coincidences" of this type, ended her report to me with a most meaningful and significant commentary:

I did not intend to be so personal in this letter, Mr. Sherman, but I did want to express to you my very deep feeling that the world is at a crossroads in human evolution. Our civilization, for all its sophisticated "hardware," seems to have cast off the concept of man as a spiritual being. It regards him now only as an intellectualized animal-machine. The products of a scientifically oriented culture refuse to accept any philosophy on faith and will give credence only to that which can be "proved," and proved apparently by the "scientific method."

I believe, but it is not enough for me to believe; sufficient numbers of people must believe to effect the change in direction which humanity demands if the "noble experiment that is man" is not to fail.

For the past two years the ESP Research Associates Foundation has been serviced by a battery of sensitive-minded men and women who have established track records on having correctly predicted a wide variety of national and international happenings. They have volunteered to dispatch to the Foundation, independently of each other, whatever impressions come to them, so the Foundation can act as a clearing house, as well as a check, on the prophecies made.

The subjects covered are too extensive to be herein presented, but since all of the sensitives have been unanimous in their earthquake predictions, I have chosen to let them serve as a fundamental illustration of the power of precognition.

An Earthquake Prediction Is Confirmed

When I made my first trip to the Philippines in January, 1966, to study the work of faith healers who were purportedly performing major operations with their bare hands, I spent considerable time observing Tony Agpaoa, most controversial of all psychic surgeons. He claimed that the Holy Spirit, or power of God, using his body and mind as a channel, enabled him to do these operations and that he was guided by a spiritual presence whom he referred to as "my protector."

On page 167 of my *Wonder Healers of the Philippines* (DeVorss & Company, Los Angeles, 1967) there is contained a prediction made by Tony during an interview:

Q: Tony, does this power of God, your protector, give you any feeling about the future?
A: Yes, sir.
Q: Any idea or suggestion of what is going to happen to the peoples of this earth in the next two to three years?
A: Yes, two or three—perhaps seven.
Q: What does your protector say or indicate is coming?
A: Big trouble.
Q: Where—here in the Philippines?
A: Here—in your country—Japan—everywhere.
Q: What kind of "big trouble"?
A: Maybe big earthquakes—maybe big war—maybe both.
Q: Where will *you* be, when and if this happens?
A: Here, with my people.
Q: What can we do, where *we* may be, if "big trouble" comes?
A: The best you can. Do not worry. Trust in the power of God, like I trust in my protector.

Approximately two and one-half years after Tony's prediction, earthquakes hit both Japan and the Philippines, specifically mentioned by him, and greater earthquake activity has occurred in many diverse places throughout the world, including the United States. Note these news items:

QUAKES JOLT JAPAN

Tokyo, May 16, 1968 (AP). Two massive earthquakes, striking 10 hours apart, roiled the western Pacific and jolted 600 miles of Japan's eastern seaboard today. The first quake, in mid-morning, killed at least 25 persons, and caused tidal waves and widespread damage. . . . The second, of similar size, and from the same direction at sea, was recorded in Tokyo at 7:42 P.M. . . .

WORST QUAKE IN 12 YEARS HITS TOKYO

Tokyo, July 2, 1968 (UPI). An earthquake described as the worst of its type in 12 years hit Tokyo Monday night. . . . The tremblor, registering 6.4 on the Richter scale, swayed tall buildings, broke dishes and brought transportation to a halt. . . .

SEVERE QUAKE ROCKS MANILA

Manila, August 2, 1968 (UPI). A severe earthquake struck Manila early Thursday, disrupting electric power and telephone service throughout most of the city. Over two hundred persons were killed and many injured.

The earthquake shook the entire length of the main island of Luzon from Aparri in the north down to the island of Samar off the southern tip. Many buildings were badly damaged. The earthquake snapped power lines and radio stations and telephones went dead.

When word came of the Philippines earthquake I immediately wrote friends there, including Tony, to inquire as to their safety.

Tony replied: "Thanks to the All Omnipotent, we were not hard hit where we live. We had an intensity of four in Baguio City, but damages were not great here, and no lives were taken."

Professor Guillermo Tolentino, famed Filipino sculptor, head of the Spiritist organization to which most of the faith healers belong, gave me this report: "Thank God that nothing happened with us except that the heroic statue I was making of Manuel Quezon, first president of the Commonwealth of the Philippines, toppled down and was completely destroyed. You are very right that you feel it is man's wrong thinking that is bringing many disasters upon himself—both nature-made and man-made. Big cities are no place to be in such a disturbed civilization."

While these quakes are said to have been the most severe in some years, I do not think they represent the "big trouble" that Tony felt was coming. I am listing now impressions independently sent me by four outstanding sensitives over the past year, who, understandably, do not wish their identities revealed. I am, therefore, referring to them by their initials.

A. D. is a prominent woman in her community, B. E. the administrator of a large hospital, C. W. a geologist and gem specialist, and J. S. an astronomer and electronic scientist. Their impressions are herewith presented according to dates, as they have been received.

A. D. (December 1, 1967). Most of California will be destroyed, but many people will be saved, even out of this terrible earthquake.

A. D. (December 14, 1967). I now feel that 1968 is going to be a dangerous year for California. Before the year is finished, I feel the next tremor will be felt all the way to Texas.

A. D. (March 13, 1968). I continue to feel . . . a great disturbance is about to happen to this country and the world at large. . . . I feel it will affect millions, and I fear for all in the California area.

B. E. (February 8, 1968). I see a tremendous earthquake starting in the northern continental area of Canada and Alaska, with simultaneous effect on the West Coast of the United States. The cause of this earthquake will be a subterranean, volcanic type eruption which will break the crust of the earth quite severely in the northern area, with less damage in the Washington and Oregon sectors, due to the continental geography. This huge quake will follow the coastal faults and cause severe damage in California and Lower California, down through the west coast of Mexico.

C. W. (June 22, 1967). I don't see these continental upheavals for another five years, and I hope, Sherman, you are wrong about 1967 and 1968.

C. W. (January 1, 1968). My impressions are changing. Increasingly, as we enter 1968, I feel it could be a year of impending doom. I do not know, or get the feeling yet, as to just what the difficulty will prove to be. Someone told me the other day that Edgar Cayce predicted that part of California would "flop into the ocean." I do not "see" this happening yet.

C. W. (March 25, 1968). I reported to you on January 1 that I did not "see" any serious natural catastrophe, but this is changed now. I have had two "visions." In the first "vision," about six weeks ago, I "saw" the state of Kansas becoming one giant "receiving center" for refugees from disastrous earthquakes. People were pouring into that state, and many were dying from hunger or killing one another over available food. The second "vision" concerned "seeing" in "the twinkling of an eye" a gigantic tidal wave—between two and three hundred feet in height. Entire landmasses submerged within this country. This latter "vision" was particularly vivid—but, of course, "visions" do not usually carry with them a date.

J. S. (March 10, 1968). There will occur a major earth disturbance in California and New York. They will vanish beneath the oceans in what would be considered the "near future." The Pacific coastline will exist along the mountains of Arizona. It is well known by some scientists that the oceans have scooped out huge caverns under New York, California, Boston, and Argentina, as well as other coastal cities around the earth. Any severe motions of the earth's crust will cause these caverns to collapse, and these cities will be lost.

The reader will observe that all of these predictions were made in advance of April 8, 1968, when the strongest earthquake to hit Southern California in thirty-five years occurred.

My friend John Hefferlin, pastor of the Church of Religious Science in Palm Springs, California, wrote me, under the date of April 10, 1968, as follows:

The day before yesterday, we had an earthquake. It was the most severe quake I can remember in thirty-five years. No visible damage was done to our home that we can see, but everything shook and rolled. All the pictures on the walls were tipped to one side or another. Dishes rattled, and the dining-room chandelier, hanging from the ceiling, swayed like a swing fastened on a tree limb. You could see the floor actually move up and down. The glass sliding doors swayed back and forth, almost coming off their hangers.

Considerable damage was done to one of the large chain stores (Von's) when the roof opened up and hundreds of items were knocked off the shelves. This earthquake covered a larger area than any I've heard about before—practically all Southern California, parts of Arizona, Nevada, and even the most northern parts of Mexico. I wouldn't be at all surprised if we have a number of quakes this year.

Following this quake, I received a communication from J. S., who said:

As you are well aware, the first shock has struck the West Coast. This is the warning shock and should not be taken as a major quake. The magnitude (area) of the warning shock tells only the scope of things that may come soon. There may or may not be a major quake on the East Coast at this time . . . but seawater is now working into the San Andreas fault. This will create a very serious situation, in time.

On August 3, 1968, newspaper headlines announced:

MEXICO CITY EARTHQUAKE KILLS FOUR, SEVERELY DAMAGES OFFICE BUILDINGS

Mexico City (UP). An earthquake hit Mexico City at the morning rush hour Friday, badly damaging buildings, and killing at least four persons. . . .

There were breakdowns in the water systems, and telephones were knocked out. The 72-second shock was felt over an area from 300 miles south of Mexico City on the Pacific Ocean to the state of Veracruz on the Gulf of Mexico, about 200 miles east of the capital. . . .

It is significant that the impressions of reputable sensitives are supported by top scientists, geophysicists, geologists, and seismologists. C. F. Richter, professor of seismology at the California Institute of Technology, stated in a lecture on March 21, 1968, that "there are many minor quakes which can cause a great deal of damage without causing a widespread disaster." He warned, however, that "nobody living in California is really safe."

Science and Mechanics magazine, September, 1968, in "Danger in California" has this to say on its contents page:

It could have already happened by the time you read this. Or it may not happen for another decade. But, according to the best available scientific information, it will happen—a California earthquake of such magnitude that the disastrous San Francisco quake of 1906 will seem like a ripple in comparison. . . .

My files contain many letters with impressions like this from Mrs. M. B. of El Centro, California:

Tuesday, around 1 A.M. April 23, I dreamed, and suddenly awoke in a wild state of panic, sure that the earth would soon open (figuratively speaking) and swallow me up. My fear—it was sheer terror—stayed with me until daylight. I was positive that this meant a major and disastrous earthquake in the future—possibly during the summer of 1968 or 1969.

The increasing prevalence and persistence of all these earthquake predictions compels serious consideration. They are even more numerous than the many who reported their feelings that John F. Kennedy, Martin Luther King, and Robert Kennedy would be assassinated. Certainly, should a major quake strike any highly populated area, such as New York City or Los Angeles, or any other in any country, the destructive consequences would be beyond imagination.

There are those who believe that they can, through meditation, project such love that the slippages of the San Andreas fault can be controlled, thus easing the mounting stresses and strains so that only minor quakes will result. I believe profoundly in the higher powers of the mind. But I believe also in the wisdom of balancing faith with logic. There are laws of nature as well as laws of mind. Both are equally influenced by the laws of cause and effect. Psychokinesis can be defined as the alleged power of controlling the behavior of physical objects, cards, dice, etc., by the direct influence of emotional states, strong desire, or extrasensory factors. The mass mind, in my opinion, could have an effect on everything physical; a great disturbance in the mass mind could bring about, eventually, a great disturbance in the earth, coupled with structural changes in the earth itself. Realistically, though, it will require more than the love of a single individual or a group, however spiritual, to control or mend a San Andreas fault.

What *can* be done is this: an individual, through meditation, visualization, and prayer can provide guidance and protection for himself and those he loves to a great degree. There are many, of course, who are afraid to face the future; who would rather not know what may be coming toward them in time—even if this knowledge could quite possibly save them from illness or injury or death. In any event, it should be reassuring to them to know that no seer or seeress—however accurate their prognostications in the past may have been—can specify the *time* that a happening of any great magnitude, such as a major earthquake, may occur. We can be warned, however, it now seems clear, by those who possess genuine prophetic gifts.

9
Healing Power

"HEAL ME!" is the cry of all humanity at one time or another. When we become ill in body or in mind, we for the most part disregard the admonition "Physician, heal thyself."

A headache, high tension, indigestion, and similar physical disturbances usually respond to drugs without recourse to doctors. We make little or no effort to remove the causes of our minor afflictions, preferring instead to treat the effects. When we have sufficiently mistreated our bodies by excessive appetites and unwise conduct, and the drugs begin to lose their effectiveness, we finally seek medical attention. Even then we do not want to give up smoking or drinking, or whatever we have enjoyed doing, to bring about a cure. It is up to the doctor to put us back in shape and still permit us to continue living as before.

I met a prominent businessman friend recently who was suffering from emphysema and had been given less than a year to live. He was still getting around, after a fashion, but was wheezing and gasping for breath. With all this obvious discomfort, I was amazed to see him puffing on a cigarette.

"Hasn't your doctor ordered you to stop smoking?" I asked.

"Hell, yes!" said my friend. "But it's one of the few things I've got left that give me pleasure. So, if I die a few weeks sooner, so what?"

This fatalistic type of thinking is characteristic of many people today. They would rather give up their lives than give up harmful habits and appetites. Only when an affliction, after sufficient warning symptoms, has reached dangerous and highly painful stages are they moved to do something drastic about it, and then it is often too late.

The natural re-creative healing power contained in the body since birth, and actually since the moment of conception, is prevented from performing its normal repair job because of man's erroneous thinking and his continuous abuse and mistreatment of the wonderful organism that he occupies. In this present materialistic world, with man's massive resort to drugs, all kinds of painkilling and digestive-upset medicines, his constant visits to doctors, psychiatrists, and surgeons, he is pursued by ill health into old age, seeking always outside help for his ailments, hoping desperately for a miraculous healing, without giving much if any thought to what he might do to change his own body chemistry by a change in his thinking.

The Rise of Faith Healing

Despite the great and continuing advances of medical science, there are many illnesses that have not yielded to treatment or surgery, and countless people, so afflicted, have turned away from their medical practitioners and sought healing aid in the unorthodox, unlicensed, often medically condemned area of faith healing. Various Protestant and other religious spiritual leaders, seeking to meet this need, have set up organizations like the Spiritual Frontiers Fellowship and prayer groups to study the part that modern extrasensory perception may play in the healing of bodies and minds. The contention is that Christ may have employed the same healing methods now accredited to some of these faith healers who claim that it is the "Power of God," or "Holy Spirit," working through them, that performs the "miracles."

Undoubtedly, with all the healing ministries that are being carried on in the United States by such individuals as A. A. Allen, Willard Fuller, Billy Graham, Kathryn Kuhlman, Oral Roberts, and Ambrose and Olga Worrall —to mention only a few—the faith healers in recent years who have caught the biggest headlines and aroused greatest world interest have been the so-called "psychic surgeons" of the Philippines. The first report of this purported spiritual phenomenon was brought to me by William Henry Belk, head of the Belk Psychic Research

Foundation, in 1965, who returned from the Philippines with color motion pictures of fantastic-appearing operations performed by a Filipino native, one Tony Agpaoa, twenty-seven, a young man with no medical knowledge or training, who apparently performed major operations by entering the patients' bodies with his bare hands. Mr. Belk said he couldn't believe his eyes, but there it was on film, so he couldn't have been hypnotized, and unless it was the most remarkable Houdini-like magic, something extraordinary was happening that merited unbiased scientific and medical research.

While I am not a scientist, doctor, or psychiatrist, my fifty years of research into the higher powers of the mind might at least qualify me as a lay authority on the mind, emotions, and extrasensory perception. In this period of time I have witnessed all kinds of psychic phenomena, and in addition to observations of genuine manifestations unexplainable on any physical basis. I have also detected fraud, self-deception, and self-hallucination.

After witnessing the films on psychic surgery and learning that there were perhaps as many as ten to twenty native healers who professed ability to operate in this fashion, I agreed with Mr. Belk that a study should be made of them and their work. As a consequence, Mr. Belk made it possible for me, as head of the ESP Research Associates Foundation, Little Rock, Arkansas, to return with him to the Philippines in January, 1966, accompanied by Dr. Hiroshi Motoyama of Tokyo, Japan; Dr. Seymour S. Wanderman of New York; and other competent observers. We spent approximately three weeks, devoting much of our time to a study of Tony Agpaoa, who then had a home in Quezon City, near Manila, and was more regularly accessible, as he was operating every day.

Tony was not a member of the Union Espiritista Cristiana de Filipinas, Inc., the large spiritualist organization, to which most faith healers belonged. This devout membership was headed by the venerable Professor Guillermo Tolentino, widely known sculptor, heralded as "the Michelangelo of the Philippines."

The spiritual healers, under his supervision, were often on the move, performing operations on hundreds of patients throughout the provinces, making no charge for their services but accepting donations for the organization —for the most part exceedingly small, if made at all. Most of these abjectly poor people could not afford hospital care or medical surgery and depended on either magnetic treatments or psychic surgery, both of which were administered by the healers, according to the patients' spiritually diagnosed needs.

I watched Tony Agpaoa at close range, under spotlighted conditions, and with still and movie cameras photographing his movements from almost every angle; he apparently, when ready to exercise this "Power of God," or invisible psychic energy, opened the body at any point required. Keeping his left hand in the opening for retracting purposes, he would perform the operation, such as the removal of a tumor, with his right hand. The moment the hands were withdrawn from the place where the "incision" had been made, the opening closed and healed instantly, leaving no scar. Operations took from five to ten minutes, the patients fully conscious throughout, feeling no pain. Nor was any effort made at employing sanitation measures, yet no cases of infection had ever been reported. The patients, however serious their complaints or afflictions, would get up from the table following the operation and walk off, without ordinarily requiring a convalescent period.

"Wonder" Healers of the Philippines

On my return to the States, I wrote a volume titled: *"Wonder" Healers of the Philippines* (DeVorss & Company, Los Angeles, 1967). What I and other observers had witnessed had been so unbelievable, so contrary to any accepted concepts of what could and could not be done physically that we could not be expected to be in agreement. I therefore decided to report as truthfully and completely as possible everything that had happened, as I had seen it, so that each reader might feel he was experiencing this research adventure and do his own evaluating.

Personally I am convinced that genuine psychic surgery does take place, but I have also detected some fraud and trickery among native healers. I am supported in these observations by a number of doctors and surgeons who have gone to the Philippines to investigate on their own, but because of the widespread charges of fraud and condemnation, they understandably do not wish their names made public. In my book I warned people NOT to go to the Philippines, however remarkable some of the apparent heal-

ings that have been reported. I stated that the risks are far
too great and phenomena that might be adjudged genuine
are too surrounded with alleged fraud to warrant such a
health gamble. Despite these warnings, and I was by no
means the only American eyewitness publicly reporting on
psychic surgery, many desperately ill men and women,
knowing that a percentage of patients visiting Tony and
other healers claimed to have been helped, made the long,
expensive, ten-thousand-mile flight to the Philippines in
the hope that they, too, would be healed.

In the fall of 1967 I learned that Joseph Ruffner, a former steel-plant inspector from Wyandotte, Michigan, who
had been healed of a crippling back injury by Tony on
November 5, 1966, was taking a specially chartered plane-
load of 116 patients, classified as hopeless cases by their
respective doctors, to be operated on by Tony at his new
home in Gabuio City. I had met Ruffner, I have a copy of
his medical case history in my files, and I was convinced
that his healing had been genuine. Ruffner had complete
faith, as a result of his own experience, that the Power of
God, working through the instrumentality of Tony's mind
and hands, could bring about miraculous cures in the bodies of fellow humans.

In a consultation with Henry Belk, he suggested that I
return to the Philippines to observe Tony's work on these
patients, since all of them possessed "undeniable medical
case histories" and would provide a good "laboratory test"
of the genuineness and effectiveness of psychic surgery
should a significant percentage of them be "healed." When
I advised Mr. Ruffner of my decision to make the trip, he
expressed pleasure and indicated that I would be permitted
to have eventual access to case histories of the patients, as
well as to observe and photograph the operations and to
give an objective report on whatever occurred. I was en-
couraged to purchase camera supplies and financially
aided Mr. Ruffner in securing additional supplies of his
own. J. F. Liddon, a prominent Jackson, Mississippi, businessman who had long been interested in extrasensory perception, volunteered to make the trip with me.

We left by a commercial airline a few days ahead of the
departure of the "hospital plane," stopping off in Tokyo,
where we visited with Dr. Motoyama and discussed the
electroencephalographic examinations he had made of Tony
during my first trip to the Philippines. These tests had produced positive results, indicating the existence of some ex-

tra-energy source which functions through Tony at the time of his operations.

We arrived in the Philippines in time to meet the chartered plane containing the 116 patients, who disembarked on the afternoon of October 5, 1967. At the airport they were besieged by an army of reporters and cameramen, as well as by officials representing the Philippines Medical Association, and also by members of the NBI (resembling our FBI), who were seeking the arrest of Tony Agpaoa on charges of "practicing medicine without a license."

Fortunately for Tony, he had been forewarned and was not in evidence. He had dispatched twenty-three passenger cars with drivers from Baguio City to transport the patients to the vicinity where they were to be treated. Baguio City is a resort town, situated some two hundred and fifty miles from Manila in rugged mountains where Tony's new home and clinic was now located. The police and medical examiners were told that the patients were to be taken to Baguio City, but they were actually taken over rough highways, to Cresta Ola Beach, a large resort motel some sixty miles from Baguio City on the South China Sea. This maneuver threw pursuing officials off the patients' trail for at least twenty-four hours, as was true for the local and foreign press representatives.

The unloading of the patients from their plane and loading them into cars with their baggage, collapsible wheel chairs, and other physical aids beggars description. This was done with Mr. Liddon and our group aiding all we could, in the face of a threatening electrical storm, which finally broke as the last cars pulled away from the air terminal. How some of the extremely ill patients managed to withstand the rigorous automobile ride, packed in the cars as they were and bounced over dangerous mountain roads in the dead of night to this far-out location, can almost in itself be attributed to divine protection.

There followed a tortuous week of attempts on the part of Joseph Ruffner, Joe Plaza, his home-town friend and assistant, and James Osberg, a newspaperman from Chicago (who had been healed of a fibrous growth in the bladder by Tony earlier in 1967) to keep the NBI authorities from finding and arresting Tony and other healers whom Tony had brought in to administer to the desperate needs of the patients. As a result of these high pressures, Ruffner decreed that I would not be permitted to interview or fraternize with the patients, that they were not to talk to me or any of the reporters, and that I was not to witness any of the operations, as previously promised.

Some of the patients did seek me out and reported behind-the-scenes happenings. There was, however, much confusion and apprehension, in what might be called a cloak-and-dagger atmosphere, with patients being whisked away into the night to secret hideaways where operations were performed, or healers brought into certain motel rooms where operations were conducted in the early-morning hours without the knowledge of police and medical authorities.

To expect uniform success or any substantial success at all under the clandestine conditions in which Tony was compelled to operate would have been asking too much of any medical doctor or surgeon, who I feel certain would not have attempted to perform any operations if faced with similar obstacles and tensions. James Osberg, acting as spokesman for the Ruffner group of patients, sought to bring about a truce between the contesting medical examiners and the NBI authorities, who had been harassing the healers and trying to "protect American patients" from the "fraudulent" practices of Tony and other healers. A conference was called, which I attended, wherein Osberg volunteered to submit himself as a subject for a psychic-surgery operation on an old back affliction. Osberg made this gesture so that the press and the members of the medical examiners board, headed by Dr. José G. Molano, might see a healer actually open and close a human body with his bare hands, without leaving a scar.

"In staging this public demonstration," said Osberg, "to prove to all concerned the genuineness of psychic surgery, I only ask that a written guarantee of immunity from arrest be furnished, not only for the healer involved, but for all healers now treating the American patients. This guarantee of immunity is to be in effect only until Ruffner and his group leave the Philippines."

Dr. Molano replied that such immunity could not and would not be granted, as it was against the law to compromise with "the illegal practice of medicine without a license."

A Dr. Padua suggested that a better test of the genuineness of healers would be for the doctors to supply the patients. He said that he had two patients, one with a stone in the bladder, another with a bullet in the head, both difficult operative cases. Would Osberg furnish a psychic surgeon to operate on them?

Osberg immediately accepted, stating that he had offered himself only to spare the American patients this public showing of themselves. Dr. Padua, a bit taken aback, said he would have to gain permission of the patients to be operated on in this manner. Osberg told him to go after such permission at once, and he would have a healer standing by who could open and close the bodies. This proposal fell through when Dr. Molano stated that even if a healer should successfully perform these two operations, he would still be arrested for operating illegally —an incredible admission that even if psychic surgery were proved beyond any doubt, medical authorities would prosecute and do everything possible to prevent its practice.

Before we left the Philippines, announcement had been made to the press, and photographs had been permitted, of three patients for whom healings had been claimed. Other invalids refused to give their names or the details of their treatment, nor were the names of the healers given out. However, the assumption was that Tony Agpaoa had worked on the most difficult cases, perhaps almost all of them.

Although every effort was made to keep Tony in concealment, and even from my seeing him, he finally sent for me, and Jerry Montáñez, Tony's private driver, took me with my associate, Flint Liddon, to his hideout. We spent more than an hour talking with Tony. He was resting after four hours of the hardest kind of work on difficult cases and was trying to throw off the effects on him of their different physical conditions. He said there were far too many patients to be adequately cared for in the short space of time allotted and under the brutal pressures being exerted.

Even so, Tony seemed to feel that quite a number of the patients had been helped. He emphasized, however, that removal of basic causes of bodily afflictions has often required follow-up "magnetic" and other treatment procedures not possible in these cases.

Regardless of charges of fraud and many still unanswered questions with respect to psychic surgery, I could not help but sympathize with Tony in the supreme effort he was obviously making to be of service. I had talked with some patients who had declared to me that Tony had actually performed operations on them and that they felt better. One, the wife of the only medical doctor who had made the trip, had been a complete invalid for three years, with two deteriorated discs in her back, after a number

of major surgical operations. She was now walking without pain and reported to me in July, 1968, that she was
now recovered, still free of pain, and had returned to her
profession of nursing.

William Kernosek, fourteen, was a ninth-grade pupil
and the nephew of Father Joseph Francis Kernosek, a
Roman Catholic priest. The boy had been invalided since
the age of four with muscular dystrophy and was able to
walk after Tony operated on him. Recent word from Father Kernosek, almost ten months later, states that his
nephew, taking physical therapy to strengthen long-dor-
mant muscles, is continuing to gain strength and mobility.

Most patients are naturally reluctant to let their names
be known, as they do not wish notoriety or to be inun-
dated with mail and other demands on them. I have, however, reports of a number in my files, in substantiation of
these statements.

There are patients who have had blood stains analyzed
and received pathological reports of "animal and not
human blood." It is charged that Tony and other healers
"palm" animal tissue, parts of chickens and pigs, to make
it appear that organs have been removed. Subsequently,
some patients have returned to the States and had surgical
operations for removal of diseased or afflicted areas that
psychic healers were supposed to have removed. This has
not been true in all cases, and there is also evidence of
genuine recovery from undoubted afflictions supported by
pathology and medical examination. (See the description
of cases in *"Wonder" Healers of the Philippines*.) Unhappily, however, the healing pilgrimage, which promised so
much in providing knowledge and evidence relative to the
truth as well as the falsity of psychic surgery, was so beset
with medical and police pressures that no organized collec-
tion of medical case histories or reports could be made by
me or any others concerned.

Half a day on my second trip to the Philippines was
spent, in company with my associate, J. Flint Liddon, in
the modest home of Juan Blanche, some hour and forty
minutes by *jeepney* from Manila. Blanche was a respected
member of the Unión Espirita Cristiana de Filipinas, Inc.,
one of their most noted psychic surgeons.

We saw him operate on at least fifty patients. He invited
us to extend our right arms with hands clenched and index
fingers extended. He pointed our fingers, individually, at
the area of the patient's body he wished to open; then he
made a swishing motion some six to eight inches above the

body. The body beneath our fingers opened up—without contact. Blanche then pressed open the incision line, from which blood extruded, and performed the required operation. Then, pressing the opening together, it adhered, leaving a faint red line, and we were told it would heal rapidly —in a few days' time—and leave no scar. We took motion pictures in a brightly lighted little room, packed with patients waiting their turn to be operated on.

Reputable medical doctors, friends of mine, have witnessed this phenomenon, have photographed it, and still can offer no scientific explanation.

Just as this book was going to press, I received word from the Director of the Institute of Religious Psychology in Tokyo, Japan. Dr. Hiroshi Motoyama, a scientist who was with me on the first trip to the Philippines in January, 1966, studied and tested Tony Agpaoa and other "psychic surgeons" at that time, and has made the following report:

"We made a second visit to the Philippines, extending two weeks from the end of September to the beginning of October, 1968, for a further investigation of psychic surgery. Through the cooperation of Blanche—the healer Mr. Liddon and I witnessed—Dr. Ramon and Dr. Leon (the latter the chief professor of Pathology of Far Eastern), found their psychic operations to be genuine."

Dr. Motoyama was disturbed because Tony Agpaoa had come to the States and been arrested on a charge of fraud. He went on to state:

"The film of Tony's operations was displayed in Japan before Tony went to America. It caused a sensation in Japan as to whether psychic surgery was true or not, producing much recent discussion in newspapers and magazines. But since the testimony of a patient who had been operated on by Tony and relieved from his illness, and the result of my parapsychological experiment carried out with Tony was published, the matter became tentatively settled."

These events demonstrate how difficult it is to gain acceptance for anything new or revolutionary, even when it is true. Open-mindedness, unhappily, is not a virtue possessed by too many scientists. But Dr. Motoyama concludes his letter to me with these encouraging words: "In Japan, some professors of anatomy and surgery at a national university in Tokyo are willing to cooperate with us in the study of psychic surgery."

In the light of such developing scientific interest, it

would be most regrettable, even tragic, if charges of fraud and commercialism against any of these "spirit healers" should prevent continued unbiased and open-minded research. In time, exploration of the unknown may produce significant discoveries of great possible medical and humanitarian value.

A Provocative Scientific Theory

The purpose of this chapter is to cast some useful and usable light on the remarkable healing powers that quite evidentially exist and can be manifested in and through the consciousness of man. When I returned from my first trip to the Philippines and reported what I had witnessed on radio and television programs and in lectures, before the book *"Wonder" Healers of the Philippines* was written, I was questioned increasingly by medical doctors, psychiatrists, physicists, chemical and electronic engineers, and laymen, as they viewed color motion pictures of Tony's purported psychic surgery: "Granted this is true—how does he do it? What energies or forces are involved? What intelligence? From what sources do these come?"

I was at a loss even to attempt to answer these questions, freely admitting that I was as baffled as anyone else. My job, primarily, was to report as frankly and truthfully as possible what I had seen and experienced.

In the course of my travels across the country, I was brought in touch with a Swiss scientist of international standing, with doctorates in physics, chemistry, medicine, and electronics (math), who is engaged exclusively in advanced research, and with whom I became friends. He expressed no astonishment after viewing the films of the Antonio Agpaoa phenomenon.

"Accepting these operations I have just witnessed as genuine," the doctor said to me, "I am not at all perplexed. I believe it has a scientific basis in fact, and, in time, will be done by instrumentation. I can offer an explanation which, if it does not silence some of your skeptics and detractors, will at least give them pause for thought."

On my promise not to reveal his name or professional affiliations for the time being, because of the controversial nature of the subject and his not having had opportunity to investigate psychic surgery personally, the doctor prepared a detailed statement which he permitted me to include in *"Wonder" Healers of the Philippines,* the essence of which is as follows:

Mr. Sherman, I am not ready at this time to announce this to the scientific world as an accomplished fact, but it might interest you to know that I have, in the laboratory, through developed electromagnetic instrumentation, been separating and reuniting plant-cell structures and animal-cell structures from rats and mice.

It is the same magnetic cohesive energy that holds the cells of our bodies together. This means that if Tony is actually performing this phenomenon, he has to be absorbing, converting, and using, in my opinion, the same electromagnetic energy from the terrestrial energy field. If he is doing this, he is not cutting the cellular tissues, he is simply separating them through a form of unipolarization, and mere separation does not injure the cells as happens with a surgeon's knife, so cells do not have to repair themselves before healing. Once the separated cellular tissue which has been parted and is in a unipolar state is released, the opposite magnetic polarities pull them quickly together again, and they fuse and appear exactly as they were before.

This presents a vast field for speculation, because if it is possible to separate and reunite cell structures in vitro in the laboratory, then it seems logical that the same can be done in vivo, as Tony and other healers seem to do it.

You tell me that Tony says the Power of God functions through him. If he uses the expression "Power of God" as a synonym for "Creative Power," to that which was "at the beginning of the beginning"—then he is perfectly correct, since everything in existence represents this power, is made of it, and exists through it. But this same power, call it "Power of God" if you wish, also operates the telephone, lights the electric lights, propels the rockets, gives life, and kills. It is not a power *who* is, but a power *which* is, always was, is now, and always will be! It is free for the taking by him who bothers to find out *how;* it is man's birthright.

Man's birthright—free for the taking. This from one of the world's top scientists. A man who told me he had known Albert Einstein throughout most of his life, recalled that Einstein had once shown him the files of letters, newspapers, magazines, scientific journals, and papers all bitterly attacking, ridiculing, and vilifying him for his concepts of the universe.

"Of course," said my new doctor friend who had come to my defense, "before he died, Einstein and his theories received great acclaim—but he was fortunate. Many of the great minds of the past never lived to see their ideas and inventions vindicated."

The fact that this man had already created an instrument to duplicate a phenomenon claimed by healers like Tony Agpaoa indicated that it was within the realm of possibility and that, one day, when perfected, such an instrument might enable surgeons all over the world to perform surgery not by slicing through tissue cells but by *separating* them. This would shorten or eliminate the lengthy recuperative period, eliminate or reduce post operative shock, and remove the danger of infection.

Reports have come to me, from many sources and countries, of faith or spirit healers who have local, national, or world reputations and who employ different healing techniques from individualized forms of psychic surgery, to laying-on of hands, to prayerful meditations, to magnetic treatments, to suggestive and hypnotic practices, to telepathic transmission of healing powers, to the exercise of spirit controls. There are accredited accounts, for example, of discarnate spirit doctors and surgeons who diagnose physical ailments, prescribe medicines, and perform operations through taking over the minds and bodies of mediumistic healers.

An entire book could be written on this phase of extrasensory perception alone. What has herein been reported has been done for the purpose of giving you the assurance that genuine healing energies do exist and that you can, through the proper exercise of meditation, prayer, and faith, experience healings in and through your own mind and body. You can also be helpful in the healing of friends and family. There is no question but that faith plays a vital part in whatever healings take place, whether the healing power comes from an inner or outer source.

A Spiritual Healing

I am indebted to Clara M. Dodd of Delray Beach, Florida, for an enlightening account of a healing she received. Let her tell it in her own words:

A friend advised me about spiritual healing (no mention of surgery). She said she had received healings. I became interested in all things of a psychic nature and subscribed to some magazines and papers dealing with the subject. In one I found an advertisement from Dr. Doreal of Sedalia, Colorado. Also, about this time, I met a psychically gifted person who knew Dr. Doreal personally. His stories of Dr. Doreal's healings were fantastic, and I never doubted their truth. I was new to this field and thought any psychic must be a very devout and Godly soul to be awarded these spiritual powers. I knew nothing of fake or fraud in this work, so I was as a little child in faith.

I answered an ad of Dr. Doreal's for literature about his school and retreat at Sedalia. He sent me a booklet which contained specific instructions for "sitting to receive healing" at a specified time, when he was sending out this power to absent ones—along with a timetable of our time zones—so we could sit at the exact time he was transmitting.

To me this was wonderful. There was no mention of money, no request for anything in return. I did not even know enough to write and thank him.

At the specified time, I sat according to his instructions, made my mind receptive, let my mind assume an expectant attitude. In a few moments I actually felt the "spirit hands" working on my fistula area in the colon, as I sat on a chair! When the time was up, I went into the bathroom and expelled about a quart of bloody material, and my hemorrhoids and fistula were completely cleaned out.

This did not seem extraordinary to me at the time. That was the extent of my faith. Since then I have developed healing powers of my own. How I wish everyone could know and have faith in the powers of the spirit, and the powers they possess in their own minds.

I have heard of Dr. Doreal and his work but I do not know him. I can accept Clara Dodd's account of her healing because I have had so many authentic reports of healings of a like nature.

Olga and Ambrose Worrall

There is a book that anyone interested in healing should read. It is *The Gift of Healing* (Harper & Row, New York, 1965) by Ambrose A. Worrall and Olga N. Worrall, an extraordinary husband and wife healing team. Ambrose is consultant to a major industrial corporation in Baltimore, and Olga is director of the Healing Clinic at Mt. Washington Methodist Church in Baltimore. They are both sensitives, persons subject in unusual degree to the influence of psychic forces, particularly, in their case, forces associated with spiritual healing.

When I visited them in their home and attended their clinic for an entire day not long ago, I was able to observe their spiritual therapy. Prayer is the most important factor in their treatments. They make it very clear that God alone can heal and that they can only cultivate a worshipful state so that others may commune with God. I saw a church full of men and women, with all kinds of afflictions, treated by the Rev. Robert C. Kirkley, who is associated with Olga Worrall in the Healing Clinic. Individual attention is given to each, often a laying-on of hands and a quietly voiced prayer, and if proper communication is established between the healer, the patient, and God, something happens.

Mrs. Worrall makes this point clear, however: "Instantaneous healings are extremely rare, so don't expect them. And above all, don't be disturbed if nothing happens for weeks or months . . . remember that healing takes place in God's time and not man's time. . . ."

The thousands of grateful letters received from men and women and children who have visited the Worralls, or who have been healed through their "healing hour" established at a regular time, once a week, to which anyone seeking a healing may "tune in," testify to the phenomenal healings that have resulted. The Worralls refuse to resort to gimmicks of any kind, and one of the rules they have made is that they will not give a consultation to anyone who has not first been examined by a doctor.

"We do not ask for or accept remuneration," state the Worralls. "We do not seek to pry into the individual's personal business or his religious affiliation. We do not seek to instill distrust of his physician or discourage medical treatment. We do not tell the patient he must believe in us or in our theories. And we do not, in any way, shape, or form, practice hypnosis.

"In the silence, we seek attunement with the patient. His spirit and our spirits are part of the universal, and we seek to harmonize them, to merge them completely. Spiritual being reaches out to spiritual being. The patient is relaxed; his whole physical, mental, and emotional state is at ease, restful, receptive; he is breathing lightly, easily, all problems and all difficulties for a moment being in a state of hiatus.

"In such a state the spirit also transmits to us information we must have regarding treatment, placing hands, massage, whatever is required. We must be, like the patient, receptive to these forces and facts and ready to act knowingly and certainly."

This is not too unlike the procedure that Tony Agpaoa and other healers have described to me; all of them, without exception, credit God or the "Spirit Realm" with the healings that take place.

There is great, often unrealized magnetic power in the human touch, associated with the exercise of faith and the placing of a mental image in mind of a person restored to health. This power is not limited alone to humans in its reception, since we have a kinship, on subconscious levels, with all life. Consider this poignant, true story related to me by Theresa Di Sirco Conway, who entertains by singing and playing piano and organ in a restaurant and cocktail bar.

Healing by Prayer

I am and always have been an old-fashioned girl despite the night life. I believe, had I not tasted the bitter side of life and had I not depended on God through faith, these experiences may not have come to me.

A very wonderful man from Paris, a French doctor, told me that he was sure I had a healing power if I would only start using it.

My little girl had been suffering from agonizing leg pains in back of her left knee, which she had had for several years. She had been X-rayed, examined, and treated by big specialists and doctors, and nothing wrong could be found. I decided to try prayer, and applied gentle stroking of the leg. To my amazement and gratitude, the pain disappeared and she hasn't complained since.

After that, I have helped two dogs, a cat, and a bird, somehow, by stroking them gently . . . and saying a little prayer. I don't really understand it, but it works.

A little dog, all his legs crippled by a hit-and-run driver, began to walk, got up immediately after I stroked him and said a prayer. He had not walked since the day of the accident, a week and a half before, and he had been bleeding internally. The dog's owners had been carrying him around in their arms. They were stunned.

Could this all be coincidence? I have read several of your books, and perhaps you can explain. The other day, I took my two children to the beach at Hyannis, Cape Cod, and left our two birds—one a parakeet, and one a baby bird we had found that couldn't fly, as well as our two cats—in the house.

Before we returned, I had the horrible thought that the cage might have sprung open and the little bird gotten out. Sure enough, we arrived home to find the little bird outside, bleeding. The cat had carried it out in its mouth. It was running frightenedly through the bushes, and we finally caught it. The feathers were gone about its neck, and a wing had been nipped, and there was blood over her.

As soon as I stroked her gently over her wound, for a little while, holding her in the palm of my hand, she seemed so content. I didn't do anything else. The blood or wound just dried up. I never washed her or applied anything. She's happy and healthy so far, and back in the cage with my parakeet—back home again.

Only two nights ago my niece had been complaining, like she had for the past four months, about a pain in the right side of her stomach. We were at a drive-in this night, and she felt like vomiting and sick. I rubbed her right side gently, said a prayer, and she has been okay since. But I suggested to her mother that she have an X ray anyway, which they had already planned to do. She had been to a regular physician.

One night, before this, I had terrific pains myself, and I said, "If what I have been doing is good for others, including dogs and cats and birds, why not me?" I slightly rubbed over the ache—and it disappeared!"

What Theresa Conway is doing for herself and others, you should be able to do. We are all surrounded by this creative terrestrial energy. All we need to do is to personalize and apply it through communicating by faith with this healing power.

The Worralls instruct those they cannot contact physically to practice a laying-on of hands and the use of prayer, supported by faith. Try "gentle stroking." Feeling is extremely important—the feeling that healing is taking place.

In my book *How to Use the Power of Prayer* (Master Publications, New York, 1959) there is a prayer for re-creation that has helped many activate this God-given healing power within. This prayer contains the technique of thinking that will enable you to visualize a return to health for yourself or someone you love.

Our Father,
Designer and Creator of the body in which I dwell,
In and through which I live and move and have my being,

Help me to realize
That the perfect pattern of my body is contained in my
mind . . .
That anything less than perfect which has manifested
Or does manifest in this body,
Has been the result of wrong thinking and wrong
Operation of Your universal laws.
Should my body have been imperfect at birth,
It has still been the result of human causations
And not by any divine decree.
Help me to realize
That Your Creative Power, which fashioned this body,
Is still resident in my mind, ready to serve me
At any time of need;
That I, as a creature of free will, now have control
Of this creative power,
And may direct it for my own good or ill,
Dependent upon the nature and character of my thoughts
And feelings.
In full realization of this,
I now call upon Your Creative Power within me
To correct and eliminate any and all body imperfections.
As I do so,
I know that re-creation is taking place,
In every cell and nerve and gland and tissue and organ,
In direct accordance with the degree of my vision
And my faith.

AMEN

10
Out-of-Body Travel

SLEEP HAS BEEN described, by men and women who have been able to leave the physical body and travel about, as the little sister of death. This is because, in order for the soul or entity to depart from the flesh house in which it resides during life on earth, it must leave the physical form in a deep cataleptic state closely resembling death.

Typical comments from those who have experienced out-of-body travel, or "astral projection," all attest to similar and characteristic sensations.

Mr. L. A. M., to whom I shall refer later, tells us of what he describes as "four satisfactory astral-projection trips" he made from his apartment when he lived in Great Neck, Long Island, New York, to the home of his in-laws in Mt. Rainier, Maryland, which is adjacent to the northeast corner of Washington, D.C.

Being well familiar with the area, I concentrated on their house in Mt. Rainier—not strenuously or with overly eager anticipation, but by assuming a rather calm rapport.

On the original projection trip (also on each of the following trips) I visualized myself leisurely leaving my physical body. As I did so in this completely relaxed state, the approximately 240-mile distance was accomplished without the slightest sense of movement or duration of time. It was instantaneous, or at least I had no consciousness of transition. Likewise, on each occasion of arriving over the house in Mt. Rainier, and pausing there briefly, there was no "descending" on into the house; I would simply, almost simultaneously, "be there" among the in-laws.

I found myself viewing their three-story frame house in Mt. Rainier from an altitude of seemingly a hundred or so feet. I observed the area for a long moment, then I was in their kitchen, perfectly seeing and hearing my wife, her mother, and sister. Mother-in-law was finishing drying some utensils at the kitchen sink and placing them in their storage spaces; sister-in-law Hazel and my wife were seated opposite each other at the large table in the oversized breakfast nook, which was the east portion of the large kitchen. Hazel suggested making up another batch of scrapple; my wife enthusiastically agreed to the project; mother-in-law concurred. Then they began busying themselves with utensils and condiments.

Within two minutes or less, I realized my condition of tiredness or strain from tenseness, and the following instant I was making leisurely reentry into my physical body in Great Neck, with the knowledge that the folks in Mt. Rainier were in good spirits. During the trip I had not even considered trying to leave any sort of thought impression with them, but was merely concerned regarding their well-being. Furthermore, I hadn't considered my being there as anything unusual.

When I drove to Mt. Rainier the following weekend, mother-in-law mentioned that she had very strongly felt my presence among them at the time of my projection trip. My wife and Hazel had not been aware, nor did they seem at all interested in my prior knowledge of the scrapple-making.

During succeeding months I made three more "projection trips" to their home, each time arriving above the house with full awareness before emerging into their midst; once they were relaxing in the dimly lit parlor, the other two times in the dining room listening to Arthur Godfrey on Washington's local radio station. These visitations took place in the year 1934.

Mr. P. E. B. of Buffalo, New York

After studying literature on "Astral Projection and How to Accomplish It," I decided to try it. I waited until late at night when everything was quiet. Then I put into practice what I had read. I lost track of time. Suddenly I felt myself rocking back and forth, but I knew my body wasn't moving. Then I heard a small pop in my ear. I opened my eyes to see what had happened. To put it mildly, I was shocked. I saw my body lying on the bed. For a couple of seconds, I thought that I was dead. Was I relieved to see that my body was still breathing! Then I remembered what I had read in a book, that "thought is creative."

So I concentrated my mind on a place that I knew well. In a few seconds (I can't be sure, because, as I have said, had lost consciousness of time) I was there. At that point I must have done something wrong or gotten too excited, because I felt a tugging (the silver cord attaching me to the physical body, probably), and I was flying through the air. The next thing I knew, I was back in my physical body.

The Experience of a Mother of Three

Like you, Mr. Sherman, I have had innumerable personal experiences with psychic phenomena, and I would undoubtedly be considered something of a "sensitive." I am, however, the mother of three active and demanding youngsters, and I would have neither the time nor the opportunity to go off the deep end—even were I so inclined.

My adventures started about a year and a half ago when I bought the Sylvan Muldoon and Dr. Hereward Carrington book *The Projection of the Astral Body* (Rider & Company, London, 1950). After reading this book, I planned one afternoon to experiment. I followed Muldoon's instructions carefully, and to my utter amazement, they worked exactly as he had described. Within minutes after I began, I was standing in front of the mirror, gazing at the reflection of my body, which was, of course, lying on the bed.

During the few days that I conducted these experiments, I never at any time tried to appear before anyone. I was afraid of the consequences. Nor did I ever "will" myself to any particular place. I wish now that I had done so, but at the time I was interested only in the phenomenon itself.

Soon I decided that I had had enough. The ease with which I had accomplished my projections was disconcerting, and I considered the whole thing eerie and frightening. It was, however, almost a year before I was able to free myself completely from the forces that I had inadvertently unleashed.

To anyone who didn't realize what was taking place, the sensations in leaving the body would be terrifying. A numbness gradually spreads over the body, the jaws lock (at least mine did!), and, at the moment the projection is occurring, the natural body is in a state of catalepsy. Once the projection is complete, of course, all unpleasantness ceases.

An experience I had sixteen years ago may explain, in part, why the sensations involved in astral projection were so repellent to me. It happened about two weeks after my first child was born. I was lying in bed beside my husband

and I was wide awake. The baby was in her bassinet, just a few feet from our bed, and I was expecting her to awaken at any moment for a feeding.

Suddenly, without any warning, and without feeling ill in any way, I found myself in a state of complete catalepsy. This was long before I had started delving into psychic matters, and I knew nothing whatsoever about catalepsy. All I knew was that my body had suddenly turned to stone, and I was terrified; I wanted desperately to call out to my husband, but I couldn't move a muscle or utter a sound.

Then, from outside the window (where there was a deep drop-off, since the house sat on a high bank) I heard celestial music and voices that sounded like (don't laugh) angels singing; I thought I was dying.

I don't know how long this state lasted, probably not more than a few minutes, but all the time I was struggling frantically to regain control of my body. Finally I was able to move one big toe, and then gradually feeling began to return to the rest of my body.

Needless to say, this was a traumatic experience, and I buried it deep in my mind. I hadn't thought of it in years, until my first experiment with astral projection.

What I have related will probably sound unbelievable to the uninitiated, but I found an "astral projection" as easy to accomplish as flicking on a light switch. This, of course, was after I had familiarized myself with the techniques involved. Once activated, however, trying to put a stop to this ability—this force, or whatever one would call it—was like trying to put the proverbial genie back in the bottle. The astral body seems to have a will of its own.

—Mrs. T. B.
Portland, Oregon

He Couldn't Believe It—at First

Mr. R. J. M. of Manchester, Tennessee, was deeply concerned about the strange experiences he was undergoing, until he read about astral projection in my book *How to Make ESP Work for You.*

Now I am beginning to understand some of the things that have been going on in and around me, which have been causing me considerable difficulty. I have been examined very thoroughly and am physically as well as mentally sound (though sometimes I doubt my own senses).

It all started in 1949, when I was eighteen years old. I'd

had a good night's sleep and a good breakfast, and I was feeling quite well.

I sat down in a chair to wait for a friend. I got up and walked across the room to look out of the door to see if he was coming, and felt quite normal. When I turned around to go back, I got the scare of my life, because I saw myself sitting in the chair. I hadn't moved. I guess the shock brought me out of it. There was a flash and a smothering sensation, and I was back in my body on the chair again.

Since then, this has happened again at different times, but I have lost most of my fear of it. It doesn't seem to affect my senses. I can see, hear, and feel, and generally am quite comfortable, although I have had a couple of bad moments, possibly from trying to fight it, which I still do at times.

Out-of-Body Visits to Definite Locations

"Autoscopy" is a term dating from the age of Mesmer, used to describe people who testified that they were able to see their internal organs or have visions of their "double" in what were called "morbid states of consciousness." Mr. L. A. M. reporting to me from Canon City, Colorado, used the word "autoscopy" as applied to his out-of-body adventures.

My original experience occurred during a condition of physical exhaustion, not as a result of any prior arcane preparation for the event. Without recollection of any willful intent to do so, I knew that I was leaving my body —firstly by head and shoulders, then midsection, and lastly, with a slight hesitancy, disengaging from my ankles and feet. This phase seemed to have taken at least ten seconds. Then, from a position approximately ten feet out from the side, and slightly above, I was seeing my body lying in somber stillness on the middle of the three-tier berth assigned to me as a radio-transmitter-room technician during the shakedown cruise of the original navy cruiser, U.S.S. *Houston,* in late summer of 1930.

My body was resting at full length, slightly onto my left side, with the crook of my left arm inserted through the noose of a quarter-inch line fashioned into a bowline knot. I had been using this method of securing myself in preference to the more elaborate and less comfortable routine of tying or strapping oneself into the berth during the preceding five days and nights of storm-tossed weather. By now, though, the rough seas had moderated and the violent rolling and pitching of the vessel had subsided to more leisurely contortions, so that the accessory loop was no longer needed.

As I watched over my body, there in supine repose, I realized the feeling of deep tiredness. In fact, the "deeptiredness feeling" permeated the entire compartment. Looking about me and above my physical body, I could see and feel the other crew members, also in their berths, in various positions of relaxation, some occasionally twisting around in search of new comfort.

What I wish to determine now, Mr. Sherman, in detailing the following points of my autoscopy, is whether or not they may be in common with or comparable to other persons':

(1) The conscious realization of leaving the body.

(2) I became aware of total, or omni-vision. I could simultaneously observe above, below, in every direction —without being aware of having a "head" to turn. "I" was simply an immaterial conscious presence.

(3) After observing my "body" in the total environs of the living quarters for several moments, I reached out and touched my body on the right shoulder; then, after a very brief hesitation, I exclaimed, "Why, it's still warm!" Very specifically, I "reached out," without being conscious of a limb to reach with, and my exclamation consisted of, "It's still warm!"

(4) Without pausing to ponder this phenomenon, I leisurely accomplished reentry into my body by the reverse manner whereby I had departed from it—feet first. Then, without a moment's lapse of consciousness in the process, I was awake in the berth with full realization of the autoscopy.

Evidence to Support Mr. L. A. M.

The files of the ESP Research Associates Foundation contain hundreds of case histories comparable to the experience Mr. L. A. M. has related. This one from Mr. R. A. S. should suffice:

My first experience was when I was seventeen years old. Since then, until now, I have had these strange conditions come over me at least once weekly. Until I read in your book about astral projection, I always thought of them as bad dreams. But now I realize what they really may be.

I joined the Navy when I was eighteen. These bad dreams kept getting more frequent. Always during these dreams I am completely paralyzed and cannot speak. I have a feeling that my body is vibrating. There have been times when I can open my eyes. But things appear to be very distorted. You must remember that I always thought I was dreaming when this was happening.

At times I was in fear that I was dying, so I would try to move a hand or a leg. At one time I succeeded in moving my hand, which went directly through the mattress of the bed. I now believe I was putting my astral hand through the mattress.

One time I had the sensation that I was floating above a group of lockers. (This was in the service.) I was looking down at myself and people in other bunks. [Observe the similarity with the experience of Mr. L. A. M. in this instance.]

Thinking I was having hallucinations, I went to see a navy psychiatrist, and I was soon admitted to a psychiatry ward for observation. [This, unhappily, is the usual procedure in cases of this kind.]

I kept having these dreams there. During this stay is when I had the big one. I was very tired and lay down in the afternoon to take a nap. Before dozing off, I was thinking of these dreams and wondering what the doctor might diagnose was causing them. I had no sooner dozed off than I experienced the coming of one of these dreams.

All of a sudden, I was standing in my doctor's office. He was alone. I talked to him, but I received no answer. Then I woke up, as quickly as it had happened. Within five minutes he called me to his office. I told him of the "dream" (and it had seemed like a vivid dream, as real as life). He did not acknowledge my being in the room before, so he probably was not conscious of it, though he must have thought of me at the time or shortly after.

He looked at me strangely and said that I was just experiencing something caused by my subconscious, which he could not explain. He informed me that I would receive no further treatment from the navy, because the problem dreams did not first start happening when I was in the service. He told me then that he was having me discharged.

I was a medic, and he said he was afraid that I would worry about the dreams, and it would interfere with my work if I went back to duty. So I was discharged.

Please do not think I am insane. . . .

No, Mr. R. A. S., I do not think you are insane. You are simply one of those human creatures who possess a higher degree of sensitivity and awareness than the average person, so that your mental and emotional nature occasionally triggers these out-of-body experiences.

There is growing evidence for an astral world, as real as

the three-dimensional world we live in, which exists in a higher vibratory plane about the earth. Those who have learned how to leave the physical body not only can visit various places and people on this planet, but also can apparently project themselves into the astral or spirit world and make contact, on occasion, with friends and loved ones whose physical bodies are no more.

A Swami's Testimony

Swami Panchadasi, in an article in *Chimes Magazine*, December, 1967 (excerpted from his book *The Astral World*), describes the reality of this higher existence in these words:

Just as steam is actually as real as water, or even as ice, so is the astral just as real as the world of physical senses. For that matter, if we could see our world of matter placed under a sufficiently strong magnifying glass, we should perceive it not as a great body of solid fixed matter, but rather as an aggregation of an infinite number of tiniest particles, themselves built into atoms; these built into molecules; and these built into solid masses.

The space between the ions of the material atom is as comparatively great as the space between the planets of our solar system. And every ion, atom, and molecule is in constant and intense motion. Under a glass of sufficient power, even the ions would melt into seething nothingness, and there would be nothing left but the ether, which has no weight and which is imperceptible to the senses even when aided by the strongest instruments of the laboratory. So you see, the solidity of things is merely relative and comparative. The vibration of substance on the astral is higher than those of the material plane; but even the astral vibrations are far slower than those of the next higher plane, and so on.

To the traveler on the astral, scenery, and everything connected therewith, seems as solid as the most solid material does to the physical eye. It really is just as solid as is the astral body in which you visit it, for that matter. As for its reality, the astral is just as real as the material in every way.

The forces of nature are not perceptible to the physical eye, except as manifesting through matter—but they are very real, as all of us know by experience. You cannot see electricity, but when you receive its shock you realize its reality. You cannot see the force of gravity, but you become painfully aware of its reality when it drops an apple on your head, or causes you to fall suddenly when you make a misstep on the curb of the street. So, never permit yourself to think of the astral as something comparatively unreal, as only relatively existent.

The astral senses are not one whit less real, reliable, and important than those of the physical body. Each class of sense perception has its own proper field in which it is king. Each is master in its own realm. And there should be no attempt to draw distinctions of reality between them. They are all but the mechanism of consciousness, or awareness, each adapted to its own peculiar requirements.

The astral has its scenery, geography, and things just as the material world. These things are just as real as are England, the Vatican, St. Paul's, the Capitol at Washington, Broadway, Piccadilly, or the Rue de la Paix; the great redwood trees of California, the Grand Canyon, the Alps, or the Black Forest.

Its inhabitants are just as real as any of the great men of the country, whose names I hesitate to call lest they pass from this material plane and thus become unreal even before these printed words pass before your eyes, so impermanent are the inhabitants and things of this real material world. The law of constant change operates on the astral just as on the material plane. The difference between things on the two planes is like that between red and blue—simply a difference of rates of vibration. . . .

An English Author Attests to Out-of-Body Travel and Survival

Robert Crookall, an English writer who has done monumental research work in astral projection and survival after death, quotes Sylvan Muldoon, of Darlington, Wisconsin, in his book *The Techniques of Astral Projection* (Aquarian Press, London, 1964) as saying:

Once you experience the projection of your astral body, as I have many times, you will no longer doubt that the individual can exist apart from his physical body. No longer will you be forced to accept theories. No longer will you be forced to base your belief in immortality upon the word of the medium, the pastor, the Holy Books, for you will have proof for yourself—as sure and as self-evident as the fact that you are physically alive.

An Out-of-Body Travel Authority

Certainly one of the foremost adventurers into dimensions and realms beyond the physical body is a prominent businessman in an eastern state, who shall be known here as Robert Penn for personal as well as professional reasons. At my urging, Mr. Penn has written a book, not yet published, titled *You Are Two*. In it he details, with documentary evidence, many out-of-body trips he has taken to different people known and unknown to him on earth, and to higher planes of existence where he feels he has communicated with loved ones and friends who have departed this life. I predict that this book, when published, will be an instant best-seller, both because of its fantastic nature and the conviction it carries that the experiences recounted are not dreams or hallucinations but are actual astral projections.

When scientists are ready to accept that a second body actually exists, possessing a higher rate and character of vibration and functioning under the direction of the soul or ego (and that this form, utilizing a type of electromagnetic or extraterrestrial energy, can apparently travel through or around the earth in seconds of time, or to worlds now beyond ordinary comprehension), present existing concepts of the physical universe will have to be drastically altered as well as expanded.

Through the kindness of Mr. Penn who has responded with specific answers to a series of questions propounded by me, I am herewith able to provide information on many phases of this out-of-body phenomenon from an authority who has made more than five hundred such projections in the last ten years.

Q: What was your first experience of an out-of-body nature, and how did it come about?

A: I had been experimenting with meditation in my bedroom for some eight to nine weeks. I experienced vibratory sensations, and one night, while I was waiting for them to subside, my thoughts idling, I must have triggered the phenomenon, because I suddenly found myself bumping against the ceiling. I had been visualizing the taking of an actual gliding flight the following day, and this may have done it, for here I was floating in the air above the bed. When I saw my physical body about seven feet below me, it gave me quite a fright, and I dived back into it.

Q: What convinced you that this experience was not a vivid dream or hallucination?

A: In thinking it over, I concluded it could have been a dream or a hallucination, but I wasn't sure. I decided I wouldn't be satisfied until I had conducted a test, so I got in touch with a psychologist friend and told him I would like him to observe me and my physical body while I tried to duplicate the experience. I repeated the same meditation, instructing myself to go to this friend's house, some four miles distant, should I get out. Well, it happened again, and what I saw and experienced on this trip and was able to return to my physical body and report—not at all what I had expected—convinced me as well as the psychologist that this had certainly not been a dream or a hallucination, nor did I have a brain tumor or any other organic or nervous affliction that a doctor had suggested might be the cause.

Q: How were you able to reproduce this experience?

A: By trial and error. Once I knew that I was actually leaving my physical body, I tried to develop and to improve on the techniques for getting out and into it. Gradually, after some unpleasant sensations and experiences, I was able to gain a fairly dependable measure of control.

Q: Have you now worked out a method by which you can leave your physical body more or less at will?

A: Yes; it is too detailed to answer here, but I have described the technique in detail in the book *You Are Two*.

Q: Can you, on occasion, direct your entity to go to a specific place on earth and to return to your physical body with a conscious memory or recollection of what you have observed and experienced there?

A: This is difficult. I cannot always direct where I go. I am often taken somewhere. I seem to be drawn to people more than places. Sometimes I have a memory, sometimes not.

Q: If your tendency is to go to people rather than places, when you have apparently made contact with a living person, are you then conscious of the place or surroundings he or she is in?

A: Part of the time; I would say—a third of the time. The surroundings—when I take the trouble to notice them.

Q: Does your second body appear to be as real and substantial, when you are in it, as the physical?

A: Yes; it's a different form. I would say "highly plastic," but none the less real and substantial. I have found you can make it become what you want it to be; it seems to be controlled by your thoughts and desires. It can be a humanoid form, or even a tear-drop, or a snake shape, or an arm a thousand feet long. I have reached out for something a long way off, and my "spirit" arm has elongated and made contact at this distance.

Q: Is the second form the same shape and size and general appearance as the physical, and can this shape and size and appearance be changed?

A: Generally speaking, yes. Unless you "will" it to be different, as I have indicated.

Q: Have you found that you can pass through what you have always regarded to be material objects?

A: Yes, very easily.

Q: Is there any sensation while passing through a door or wall, or penetrating the ground, if this is possible? Are you aware of structure, color, and so on?

A: Yes; when I pass through a wall, for example, I can feel the whole texture. If there is a cable in the wall, I go through it and even feel what I suppose would be the molecules. I have learned to go through solid objects of the physical world slowly. I have given up doing it rapidly. Diving at a brick wall, seeing it rushing at you, and feeling you may splatter against it is not a pleasant sensation. I usually stop "seeing" until I am through it.

Q: Is the feeling of being out of the physical body ordinarily a pleasant, even exhilarating one?

A: Very much so. There is an inexpressible sense of freedom, release, lack of restriction. You are not limited by a sense of gravity, glued to the ground or the earth. These limited feelings are gone.

Q: How long have you been able to remain out of the physical body, and how long do you think a developed "projectionist" could remain out?

A: I was out once for four hours and twenty minutes. Never again. They say adepts in India can remain out indefinitely. I prefer a much shorter time—five minutes or less.

Q: How far do you feel a person could go in the non-physical body?

A: How far? No limitation, apparently, in the physical world. You can go *through* the earth as well as around it, impossible as this may seem.

Q: Is there any way to judge distance when you seemingly leave the physical dimension and find yourself on a different plane of being, in contact with entities who have apparently died?

A: Distance doesn't seem to exist, as we know it, in higher dimensions. Ten miles, here to there—who knows? There is a swishing motion—and you're there. Measurement? No.

Q: Do you feel you have actually communicated with any of your friends or relatives who have "gone on"?

A: Yes; two close friends, one young, one old. My father died at eighty-three. Paradoxically, my mother, who was a medical doctor, died a little more than a year ago. We were very close spiritually. I have made no great attempt, except at the moment of her death, to contact her. Surprisingly, perhaps, with all this feeling of closeness, I sense that she has many things to do where she is. She read my book manuscript, describing all my "out-of-body" experiences, and died knowingly and peacefully. I am sure there were a thousand friends waiting to greet her. She doesn't need to communicate with me. I'll be seeing her some comparatively few years from now, anyway.

Q: If you have contacted a father or any other relative or friend, have they looked the same as they did on earth, at the time of death?

A: Very real. But, going to find them, I was unexpectedly surprised. My father, who died, as I have said, at eighty-three, looked fifty-five when I saw him. A doctor friend, who died at seventy, looked about twenty-three. I didn't recognize him until I had returned to the physical body and later saw a picture of him at the age of twenty-three; then I realized. A friend who had died in an airplane crash, his body cremated —I didn't recognize him by form, yet his personality was unmistakable. Visual acceptance was not good in this case.

Q: Then you would say that "personality" survives?

A: Definitely, in all three cases, and others I have observed.

Q: Has communication been verbal or mental, or both, seemingly?

A: Mental, not verbal. Largely feelings and emotions. I could sense every emotion in them, and I felt they could sense every emotion in me. I translated these feelings into words when I returned to my physical body with a memory of the experience.

Q: When you have left your physical body, experimentally, have you felt at any time that you have had to get a "booster shot" of energy from some escort or guiding intelligence, aware of your desires and objectives?

A: I don't know as you would exactly call it a "booster shot," but "assistance" certainly. Some intelligent being seems to be aware of my desires and objectives, and I am dimly aware of aid extended to me, like "a little child that is led."

Q: Have you been able to see such entities, or just feel their presence and their assistance to you?

A: I can see, I would say, about fifty percent of the time —often people unknown to me. Six or seven times they have looked tremendously familiar, but not parents or relatives. My memory seems to have been blocked off. I may have had experiences with them before, somewhere, but I cannot recall.

Q: Do you at times sense that you are a part of a vast, organized plan of progression, beyond comprehension, when you are out of the physical body?

A: Very much indeed. I am often preoccupied, doing something in association with others, and I feel this is no happenstance, but the progress I and others seem to be making is only partially visible or vaguely knowable.

Q: Is there awe or fear associated with such out-of-body projection?

A: In the beginning, very much fear. This is the big problem—fear. Until you get accustomed to it, the experience of leaving the body is so much like dying. This is, of course, the basic fear of mankind, death. As for awe—it still exists; it is a "little miracle" each time I find I can leave the body, and the immensity of life and what lies beyond makes me—I am sure it would anyone—feel very humble.

Q: Have you had to pass through areas wherein you made contact with "earthbound entities," for want of any better words to describe lowly developed, carnally minded "spirits" close to our physical existence?

A: Yes; I have had to pass through these areas, at times, inadvertently—and, I'm telling you, I go through them in a hell of a hurry! Or, better said—in a hurry through hell.

Q: Have you had any unpleasant encounters with such entities, trying to attach themselves to you, in any sexual or other way?

A: Yes, many. I soon learned that if I did not violently resist, they did not try to cling. *Nonviolence* seems to be a spiritual law. This, and *understanding*. When such low entities tried to attack me, I showed compassion, and they no longer seemed attracted.

Q: Even so, have such experiences been frightening and horrifying?

A: Those are good words to describe my reactions, at times. I had no guidelines to go by. I had to learn to deal with such entities only by experience. When I found that allowing myself to be horrified didn't solve the problem, I stopped letting myself get so upset.

Q: Do you feel there is any connection between your

own life experiences, sexually or otherwise, which—
"like attracting like"—occasionally brings you into
the area of such entities and makes you temporarily
susceptible to their influence?

A: Psychologists have thought this might be so—internal
repressions, suppressions, not on the surface, possibly
setting up an attraction. I was bothered considerably
seven or eight years ago but have gotten past this
now. It may have been true in the beginning.

Q: Would you conjecture that it is possible for "earthbound entities" to take over the physical body and
mind of living mortals who become mentally and
emotionally disturbed for one of a number of reasons
—alcoholism, drugs, and so on?

A: Yes, quite possible to take over, for the reasons mentioned. But I feel there would have to be some weak-
ness beyond the drugs or alcohol. However, I can see
how this could happen, definitely.

Q: Have you ever had an experience wherein you temporarily found yourself in the body of another person,
living or dead? Could you describe such an experience, if so?

A: Temporarily, unknowingly, one time I entered the
body of a man who had just died. He was in a hospital, and I was able to prove this out by checking with
doctors and describing to them what had taken place
in the patient's room at the time of his demise, and
my finding myself in his body. You can be sure I got
out of it as quickly as possible, and back into my
own body, in my home, several miles away! Two
other times I entered the body of a person who
seemed to be in a nightclub, possibly under the effect
of drugs. I found myself smoking. I was not conscious of the personality or identity; it may have
been temporarily off somewhere.

Q: Have you been conscious of the so-called "silver-
cord" attachment of the second body to the physical
body? Does its connection apparently keep you from
passing into the next plane of existence, and are you
willing to believe that its severance would not enable
you to return to the physical?

A: I had read a lot about the "silver cord" but had not
paid much attention to it, so I went "out" especially
one time to take a look. I saw that it seemed to grow
out of my shoulderblades and entered into my chest.
I assume it *does* keep me from entering the next dimension. I am willing to believe it, at any rate, and
I'm not ready to try to find out. I've got too much to
do yet in this life.

Q: How much risk do you feel is related to experiments

in out-of-body projection in depth, and what might these risks be?

A: I don't have the answer to this one. I suppose there is a calculated risk. I've been out of the physical body so many times, and I've always gotten back all right. I have confidence I will make it again. Once you have become adept at leaving your body, you often do it in your sleep, and have little choice. I suppose if you stayed out overlong, something might happen to your physical body. It could get too cold, aching in the joints. The body slows up physiologically when you are away from it. I sleep with something over me, even in summer, so if a separation occurs, my body will be kept reasonably warm. Sometimes there is a lack of total integration with the physical when I return. I feel like I'm not quite here—"out of focus" is a better description. During my earlier experiments I felt there might be danger of some other entity taking over my body while I was out. There was a debilitation risk. Now an out-of-body experience is quite refreshing. I become so engrossed with the bigger reality where I am, I'm sometimes tempted to stay— to become a "mental dropout"—and I have to watch that.

Q: Have you at times found yourself attending classes, as quite a number of out-of-body projectionists have reported, and have you been able to retain much of a memory of what you were taught and have experienced?

A: Class, yes. This occurs on the average of once a week. Much that takes place is beyond my conscious comprehension. I may be using what I am being taught without knowing. I am aware of training periods, when I'm taught how to do things not necessarily related to this life, not knowing for what purpose.

Q: Have you seen your instructors and other students attending, and have you been able to communicate in any way?

A: Yes. I see and communicate in a different way than here. There is a sense of unity and common purpose. For example, I was waiting around one time for the class to start, when the instructor brought up a newcomer, a neophyte, and directed me to show him to the classrooms and around the place. I was astonished, but I accepted the assignment, and was surprised to discover that I apparently knew where we do this and that. This was a shock to me, proving that I had been attending and knew more than I had normally been able to recall.

Q: Have the instructors been aware of your presence and shown any personal interest in you?

A: No more than professors in any classroom on earth. The classes have never been large, not more than ten to fifteen students.

Q: What do you think is behind these "instructional sessions"? Do you think that many living humans are being taught in their sleep, even though they ordinarily have no conscious recollection when they awaken on earth?

A: I do not know what is behind all this, but I feel it has to be a great purpose. The how and why of it, you'll have to ask God. Yes, I am sure a significant number of humankind, many more than meet the eye, are being taught and guided, to a degree, while they sleep.

Q: Where, from the standpoint of location, would you presume these classes are being held?

A: I do not know—it might be heaven. Who has a word for it? It's not in the physical plane. The structure, I have observed, does not lend itself to description. You cannot float or walk there; you *go,* maybe quite a distance, maybe just one hundred and eighty degrees out of phase with the earth. All I know is, I am there, and after a time I am back here.

Q: Have you experienced sensations of travel, going somewhere at great speed, on any of your astral journeys, and do you have any visual remembrance of such travels?

A: Travel is like moving through a fluid—heavier than air and lighter than water. Sometimes so fast that you are here, and in the next instant you are there— wherever "there" is, or wherever you set out to go.

Q: Have you seen your physical body in its sleeping state many times when you have left it on such trips?

A: Yes, many times. But I usually don't turn back and take a look. I don't like what I see—the slob or slab of my physical form. I'm always surprised at how my face looks, seen from this other perspective. It's not too inviting to me.

Q: How do you usually leave the physical body, from what point, and how do you reenter, and usually at what point?

A: I back away from the body, using what I call a "peeling-off" technique. Like separating the leaves of a book, unfolding one from the other. I reenter the same way, come up from behind, remold into the physical from the back. I use a diving method, and sometimes wriggle around, and in, beginning with the feet, until I have shoved up to where my head is. Sounds funny, but that's it.

Q: Have you ever been able to see a second arm or leg outside the physical body, while half in and half out?

A: Yes, it looks transparent—I can see through it; it's like electrical fire—sparks often emanating from it.

Q: Does it take you a few moments or minutes to take over control and activate the physical body when you return to it?

A: Yes; I'm very careful about not leaping up the moment I am conscious back in the body. I take a few deep breaths. I could get up, but I am likely to feel lightheaded if I move too fast.

Q: Is the physical body in a paralyzed state, so-called, before you leave it, and when you first return and re-animate it?

A: At the start and for the first year or two it was, but not now. I have no sense of paralysis on returning or leaving.

Q: What new concepts of life and existence have your experiments in a second-body projection given you?

A: Harold, that's why I have written 125,000 words in a book, in an attempt to express those very items.

Q: Do you now believe in survival after death, and has all fear of death, as a consequence, disappeared?

A: I do better than believe that we survive death—I *know* it now. But, despite this knowing, all fear has not disappeared. I like to be here on earth; I am not ready to go on yet. I still have work to do. But it is a *knowing* fear—not overwhelming.

Q: Do you look forward to your adventure in the spirit, or second, body when the time for physical death does occur?

A: I still have evolving to do here. I have no death wish. I am glad of the increasing awareness I am getting of the life to come, but I am perfectly content to wait until my time for departure.

Q: Most projectionists report that, as they are about to leave the physical body, they find themselves unable to move; they are conscious of a violent vibration or even of convulsive reactions, and sounds, not always pleasant, followed by an explosion of some sort; then a blackout and a sudden awareness that they are in the second form, looking down on the physical body, or are in some other place. Can you please comment on such experiences? The feelings?

A: I used to get what you term "violent vibrations," but no more. I never had a convulsive reaction, or sounds. When people try to hold to a consciousness and proceed with no loss of continuity, it is never unpleasant.

Q: In physical tests that have been made, what is the difference, as detected by instrumentation, between the reactions in a physical body, when a person is dreaming, and when he is out of the body?

A: This is under study. Tests have been made on me by scientists using modern technology. This will be reported in the Appendix of my forthcoming book.

Q: Could you describe the results of E.E.G. tests conducted on you by a noted parapsychologist, and what you experienced, as you recall, while out of the body, during these tests?

A: They have been published in one of the psychiatric journals. They will be reproduced as a part of the Appendix in my book.

Q: Is there any danger of a physical body being occupied by a discarnate entity while the "soul" is on a journey?

A: In the early stages of development, this seems possible. As a person evolves, something of a protective nature builds up, and this possibly is eliminated. (I hope!)

Q: What do you suppose happens to the soul of a person who is possessed during the time a discarnate entity has taken over? Is it still resident, on subconscious levels, in the body? Is its consciousness sometimes fused with the indwelling alien consciousness, so we get a distorted—what psychiatrists might describe as a schizophrenic—effect?

A. I don't know what happens. I don't believe what you term a "fusing" takes place. I would call it more a "displacement." I have studied catatonic cases in mental wards. I believe that in many of these cases the "soul" has gone someplace and hasn't come back. The body is left running on "automatic pilot." When I look at many types of schizophrenia, I often feel that the entity is out on a trip and hasn't returned.

Q: Little has been actually proved, as yet, with respect to reincarnation, despite the great interest in it. It is evident that there are different planes of "being" in consciousness; and in most regression experiments it is evident that the mind has simply activated the imagination, producing seeming memories that cannot be proved. What have your experiences and observations indicated?

A: Life to me is like fingers reaching down from a hand, which comes from the oversoul, and we may be living other lives or experiencing on more than one plane of being simultaneously, which may account for confusion in our concepts as to what is real and unreal. This is not original with me—it is simply the most acceptable theory I have encountered.

Q: I believe no research today can approximate the potential of what you can do in the astral realm as related to the question of life after death, possible possession, different planes of being, etc., and I would like your summarizing comments on this, and any other observations that have been activated by my questions.

A: To really know, those who investigate these phenomena must explore and experience the techniques available. They can develop the ability to have out-of-body experiences without too much trouble. Most people find this experimentation, however, too disconcerting; they are too fearful. Their imprint for survival is so strong. The fact that man can leave the physical body and actually travel in higher realms, as well as about the earth and in space, is against mass knowledge—contradictory to the concepts of the present world of science. Few scientists are yet willing to discard a great part of their life training and experience. People are reluctant to admit the existence of anything contrary to their environment. It's too profound a transition, however true. They will think twice before making a change. It is easier for them to oppose, without investigation, rather than to accept.

If out-of-body experiences were put on a scientific level for examination, communication on other planes of existence and with entities who have "died" could be established. A deeper, more understanding relationship with the Creator we call God would take place. I don't feel that humanity is quite geared for this great realization of the immensity of life and the unlimited potential of each human soul. I believe that great spiritual leaders who have gone into higher realms in the past, who have glimpsed the wonders of them, and the promise of soul development, must have found it difficult to retain their interest and objectivity when returning to earth. Suppose everyone might produce body separation, visit the higher realms, and come back with total conscious recall. Could they stand it? Could they continue to exist in this world and face the trials we are called upon to meet here on this disturbed planet?

Most of us still hang on to our little self-important egos here, to what we think we possess; we still participate in the marketplace. If a spiritual leader tries to reveal to us a better way of life that threatens to take away many of the things we have come to prize more than our own souls, we tend to make martyrs of them, or even to assassinate them. Crucifixion, I suppose, is the real word. Sooner or later, however, I believe, from the experiences I have had, that each human creature must become involved spiritually and start his evolvement, because life is continuous, and there is no eventual escape.

11
Communication with Intelligence in Outer Space

A Science-Fiction Novel

WHEN I WROTE a science-fiction novel, *The Green Man*, published in the October, 1946, issue of *Amazing Stories Magazine*, which told of the visit to this planet of Numar, a being from another galaxy, I did not realize that I was contributing to the legend of "little green men" associated with flying-saucer sightings. But what I thought I had *imagined*—a "spaceship that caused car motors to stop, fouled radio and electrical systems, and traveled at fantastic speeds," has now been provocatively reported time and again, enough times at least to have established me as a seer of sorts in this area.

Other writers of science fiction have experienced the same fate of having their supposed figments of the imagination converted into nonfiction realities. It is now becoming increasingly difficult to conceive of anything that man cannot ultimately accomplish. This is because man has discovered that what he can picture in his mind, an amazing creative power related to his subconscious can eventually produce for him in external life.

Nevertheless, the fact that I was able to dream up a story of space people visiting this planet about a year before Kenneth Arnold, in his private plane, sighted nine glowing objects over the mountains of California and dubbed them "flying saucers" is, possibly, evidence that I might have been given a forevision of the future. To my knowledge, I was the first one who mentioned the power of spaceships to stop car motors and cause electrical blackouts. It is possible that many science-fiction writers not only possess vivid imaginations but also, when they concentrate on speculations of the future, actually project themselves ahead in time and sense events and inventions that are forming in some higher dimension.

The Green Man story caused such a sensation in its day that readers demanded I write a sequel, which I did, under the title *The Green Man Returns*. It was published in the December, 1947, issue of *Amazing Stories*. I have not had occasion to reread it in all these years, until now, and I am somewhat startled at its contents. I could have been predicting the future in the opening of this story:

Nineteen hundred and seventy-five will be known forever to the inhabitants of this earth as the Year of the Great Light.

It was seen first by the frightened people of the Eastern Hemisphere. Word of this tremendous illumination, which turned night into day, spread quickly by radio and television to the millions of humans on the other side of the globe. They awaited its manifestation with growing feelings of terror, as continued reports and descriptions of this heavenly phenomenon gave rise to the fear that the end of the world was at hand.

This light was appearing in the east as the sun was setting in the west. Observers said it started first in what seemed to be a new and brilliant early evening star, the luminosity of which rapidly and vastly expanded while yet one looked. Shadows left by the departing sun were swept away by the onrush of this tremendous beam of light, which lit up the countryside with an awesome glow. No other stars could be seen, not even the moon. The heavens themselves were invisible. As one looked upward, all he saw was dazzling brightness. Strangest of all, the light was without heat.

In the capitals of Moscow, Chunking, Berlin, Paris, Rome, London, and Washington, there was wild consternation, for it was in these capitals that the Third World War was being plotted. At secret army air bases and rocket atomic bomb sites, orders were even now being awaited to launch undeclared warfare. Mighty Russia and her satellites against the United States, Great Britain and their allies, in an intended final test of power to determine the destiny of all humans for all future time!

And now—the great light! What could be its cause? What its meaning? What its foreboding? Until these questions could be answered, there could be no further thought of war. Mankind was being threatened by a possible cosmic catastrophe so colossal as to strike fear into the hearts of rulers and common people alike. . . .

My original *Green Man* story had been written in a humorous vein, depicting how Numar had landed his spaceship beside a highway leading up the mountain toward the Wilson Observatory in California, after first electromagnetically stopping the car of the astronomer Professor William Roscoe Bailey. He emerged, a handsome white-robed figure, but with an unmistakable green skin, to astound the professor by calling him by name, introducing himself as "Numar, from the Planet Talamaya, a trillion or so miles in space"; and he announced that he had chosen the professor to be his "host" during his visit to the planet earth.

It took some convincing to make a believer out of the professor, who thought Numar to be a Hollywood stunt man exploiting a new feature picture about to be released. When he found that Numar had no stomach, needed only pure water, and had organs that generated electrical energies that sustained life, and that when he shook hands with Numar he received a powerful shock, the professor decided he was actually in the presence of a being from a race vastly superior to the human creature.

Of course, as the story unfolded and Numar drew world headlines, scientists and most people denounced him as a gigantic hoax. He was laughed at when he declared:

I, Numar, the awakener, am here! I have been sent to speak a prophesy to you . . . a great light is soon to appear in the heavens . . . it will cast an illumination over the entire earth. It will mark the beginning of a great change to take place on your planet. It will awaken all humans to the realization that there is a Power far greater than themselves. . . .

The presence of this great phenomenon in the heavens will cause the greatest spiritual revival known to man . . . awe-struck millions will search their souls as never before . . . and when this great light appears, a host of higher intelligences will arrive—sent here to work with your leaders . . . Man will then commence to grope from threatened chaos toward a new harmony with all things.

The finale of *The Green Man Returns* saw the peoples of earth now cooperative, under direction of their rulers, with the new plan of living that had been brought to our planet by Numar and his hosts from outer space.

How strange that a number of scientists, researchers, and many laymen, concerned at the mess our world is now in, and impressed by increasing evidence of extraterrestrial activity, are voicing the possibility that inhabitants from other planets may be planning to descend on earth in a vast fleet of spaceships—for what they hope will be friendly rather than hostile intentions! Could I have somehow foreseen and pictured such a coming occurrence in these two science-fiction novels? Only time will tell, but there are parallels.

Today we read these headlines and news stories:

STANFORD ASTRONOMERS WONDER—
ARE SPACE SIGNALS FROM NEW CIVILIZATION?
By George Getze
Los Angeles Times Science Editor

Mysteriously regular and powerful signals from outer space have been picked up by Stanford University's 150-foot dish radio antenna, it was reported Thursday.

The signals are making Stanford radio astronomers wonder if they've begun monitoring the communications network of another civilization far out in the galaxy. . . . [The article appeared in the Los Angeles Times, April 5, 1968.]

SOMEBODY IN SPACE MAY BE
EXPLORING US, SAYS SCIENTIST
By Frank Carey

Charlottesville, Va., April 3, 1968. A government space scientist says it's remotely possible newly detected mysterious signals from outer space may represent "galactic navigational beacons" being employed by an advanced civilization to guide their manned spaceships along the Milky Way.

Another admittedly far-out possibility, said Dr. Kenneth Kellerman, is that the radio wave signals may represent communications signals between four inhabited planets, as well as attempts by each to contact still other planets such as Earth. . . .

Evidence of UFOs

Various new investigations, both official and unofficial, related to the mystery of unidentified flying objects have been taking place since around the time that my first science-fiction novel was published. There have been countless sightings, attributed by skeptics to optical illusions, hallucinations, temperature and light refractions, weather balloons, conventional aircraft, ice particles in the upper atmosphere, and one or another of the planets—as well as to meteors, the fiery reentry of a Russian or American space rocket, flashing beacon lights, and all kinds of earthly explanations, including "swamp gas." But still flying saucers cannot be explained away, because more and more thousands of men and women, among them scientists and experienced airmen, continue to testify to their observation and even purported contacts with them and the space people involved.

A vast literature about flying saucers and their spiritual as well as scientific implications is now in existence. There are those who claim to have communicated either verbally or telepathically with space people; who have been given rides in spacecraft controlled from outside the earth's atmosphere; who declare that "our space brothers" have told them that they have been visiting and studying the earth for a great many years, and are now concerned that we are on the verge of destroying ourselves with the new atomic weaponry we have created, because our spiritual development has lagged far behind our material progress.

Numerous photographs have now been taken, some faked by self-exploiters and sensation-seekers, but many by scientific, military, and astronomical observers. These present undeniable evidence of "something going on upstairs" that is far from illusory.

Knowing of my extensive experience with telepathy, many have asked me if I have been contacted by any space people as yet or have tried to communicate with them. I must truthfully answer no. But, allowing for the existence of higher intelligences on and about this earth, I would not rule out eventual telepathic communications as a possibility, if it has not already occurred in some instances. Apparently, however, this may not be necessary, as these "visitors" may have monitored and mastered some of our major languages.

I have long been convinced that something is going on. Dr. James E. McDonald, senior physicist at the University of Arizona's Institute of Atmospheric Physics, has recently declared, "We may well be under surveillance by a far more advanced civilization than we on earth. In my opinion, the UFO problem should be given first priority by Congress with the aid of the United Nations, since a large number of foreign sightings demand attention, together with those viewed throughout the United States and Canada."

A Personal Sighting

My belief in the reality of UFOs is based not only on a most impressive quantity of authoritative sightings of strange and alien objects in our skies but also on the fact that Mrs. Sherman and I, in company with some hundreds of other persons, were recently witnesses on two successive nights to the appearance of a pulsating red ball-like craft, which remained in a stationary position at an undetermined height above Los Angeles. It looked to be about one-quarter the size of the full moon and did not move for some twenty minutes, then began to rise slowly and soundlessly, getting smaller and smaller, finally changing into a dazzling white glow drifting off to the southeast, and then shooting straight up into the stratosphere in a burst of unbelievable speed and disappearing.

An exhaustive investigation proved that no planes, no weather balloons, nothing manmade had been even remotely in the area on either of the two nights. On the second night the "red ball" seemed to explode with a great flash of light and a sonic boom; then it vanished from sight, only to reappear a few seconds later, again a red, throbbing orb, at a considerable height above its former motionless position.

No satisfactory explanation has ever been made of these two astounding sightings. Their appearance on two successive nights at almost exactly the same time (11:30 P.M.) in the same identical spot above Los Angeles certainly is indicative of intelligent control and motivation.

There is no point here in detailing other sightings or reports made to me by eyewitnesses to similar phenomena, since such a vast amount of evidence has been published. What has been presented is designed only as speculative background for the possible development of a telepathic means of communication for all who travel in outer space, whether it be astronauts seeking to maintain mind-to-mind contact with trained human transmitters and receivers on earth, or the acquired ability of these same astronauts and other sensitized humans to communicate mentally with the consciousness of intelligences alien to our planet.

A Basic Technique
for Transmitting and Receiving

In *How to Make ESP Work for You* I discuss at length the factors involved in transmitting and receiving thought impressions. There is much that remains to be researched and discovered about mind-to-mind communication, but I have been reasonably successful in the exercise of this method, and I am convinced that new techniques yet to be evolved must still follow some of the fundamentals related to relaxation of the physical body and making the conscious mind passive and its attention turned inward in order to concentrate on a visualized focalizing point in the subconscious—in which area mental images and strong feelings are either sent or received.

The ability to let go completely of the physical body with the conscious mind must first be achieved. This means divorcing the conscious mind from any awareness of the outside world or body sensations furnished by one or more of the five physical senses.

You have to be able to cut off the constant stream of impressions that are pouring into your subconscious from your senses of sight, hearing, taste, touch, and smell. Your extrasensory faculties possess duplicates of these sensory powers that function beyond the physical limitations of time and space. When you have made conscious contact with your extrasensory powers, you can then "see" with your mind's eye, "hear" with mind's ear, "taste, touch, and smell" on higher levels of awareness. Once you have done this, in connection with any other person, experience, event, or source of knowledge, you must be able to translate these impressions into words and either write them or speak them into a tape recorder or dictate them to a friend or scientific observer while they are still fresh in consciousness. If you do not do this, you will not be able to hold your attention on the extrasensory level, and your conscious mind will become aware again of the outside world and your limited five physical senses, as well as your sense of logic; it will try to argue you out of whatever you have received. There is a sensitized dividing line between the conscious mind's awareness of what is communicated to it by the five physical senses and its ability to recognize and become aware of impressions from beyond the reach of these same senses. If the two levels of conscious awareness become superimposed one on the other, you get an immediate distortion of whatever impressions you may be receiving.

We actually appear to be existing in two worlds of awareness at the same time, capable of slipping from one into the other, often without realizing it, so that extrasensory impressions fuse so naturally with information coming to you from your five physical senses that you cannot distinguish between the two. You are benefited, nevertheless, by hunches or feelings from your higher powers of the mind that enable you to make decisions and act on them with more surety.

After you have developed the necessary physical and mental receptivity, your extrasensory faculties, without any conscious effort on your part, apparently set up the *frequency* required to make attunement with whatever other intelligence or information you wish to contact. Once you suggest to your subconscious that you desire to communicate with a certain party or secure certain knowledge beyond the capacity of your five physical senses, if you are properly sensitized, mental wheels are set in motion—a circuit seems to be closed—and mental images and feelings start to flow.

When you act as the sender, however, you do not hold this visualized, focalizing point in your mind *blank;* you fill it, as on a motion-picture screen, with the picture or feeling of what you wish to transmit. Without forcing it, you exercise the quiet but genuine faith that your message has reached its target in the mind of your receiver.

This, in essence, is the way to control and direct your extrasensory faculties. Quite often your thoughts may be received on subconscious levels but do not reach the surface of the person receiving because his conscious mind may be too occupied with other experiences demanding attention. In some such cases there may be a delayed pickup, when your thoughts, still resident in the receiver's subconscious, finally break through later, causing him to think of you and to have either a vague or vivid feeling of what you wanted to convey.

Telepathic Training for Astronauts

I have discussed with Everett Dagle, research officer for the U.S. Air Force Cambridge Research Laboratories, at

Bedford, Massachusetts, the possibility of eventual development of mind-to-mind communication between astronauts and trained human transmitters and receivers on earth.

He has conducted instrumentation tests of telepathy that have not proved too conclusive. In my opinion, we may be able to record changes in the bodies and minds of sensitives when in the process of sending or receiving thought impressions, but telepathy itself is beyond reproduction by manmade devices or electronic simulation. There have been reports that Soviet researchers have experimented with the possibility of, first, discovering the wavelengths or frequencies on which human minds operate; secondly, of trying to amplify the intensity of these mental emanations to such a point that thought impressions could be beamed into the minds of millions. We know now that people can be hypnotized or put to sleep by electrical means. We also know that all kinds of attempts are being made to control the minds of the masses, by suggestion, hypnotism, and electronic methods. There are inherent dangers present in all of these approaches. For the unwary there are hazards enough in the possible influence that living or discarnate entities can exert over minds left open and unprotected by a variety of causes.

Astronauts, by the very nature of the outer-space adventures awaiting them (including contemplated trips to other planets), have to be among the most highly trained human beings from the standpoint of developed physical, mental, and emotional controls.

This, in my judgment, automatically qualifies them as excellent candidates for the coming age of mind-to-mind communication. I would like to see tests wherein they are placed in isolation for a week or more, cut off from all sensory contact with what is taking place in the outside world, and compelled to depend only on what impressions they may receive from human senders transmitting information to them at regular intervals.

I would also like to see tests of the degree of accuracy with which these human sensitives might receive impressions from the minds of astronauts confined in simulated spaceships in order to learn to perceive what is happening to the astronauts. The latter could imagine that certain mechanical defects have developed, with all radio communication cut off, and then try to transmit in mental pictures and through feeling the nature of specific envisioned dilemmas. If the majority of the sensitives could independently receive the same impressions, the chances are that a check, when the experiments were concluded, would prove their validity.

There are many refinements that would have to be made in a series of tests such as these proposed, but they could prove of great practical value, should it be found that a percentage of accurate impressions could be sent and received.

All life possesses a degree of conscious awareness. The higher the intelligence, quite obviously, the greater the awareness. As humans we assume that we possess, for the time being, the highest intelligence of any known life on this planet.

If we have been or are now being visited by people from other planets, we are compelled to concede that their intelligence must considerably exceed ours for them to be able to create the power and the vehicles necessary to traverse the heavens, and possibly to communicate with life in many parts of the limitless universe.

I have talked with individuals who claim they have been in touch with these space people, through either telepathy or verbal contact. Some of them are quite apparently self-deluded, however sincere. Some believe they have taken actual trips in flying saucers, out beyond the moon and back, from Los Angeles to New York in half an hour, and so on. On close questioning, some of them admit that the trip was not physical, that they made an out-of-body journey in these spaceships, or were taken in sleep out of their physical bodies and given this psychic experience.

Why these particular persons should have been chosen for contact by these higher intelligences, or should have been visited by a space being in the flesh and given certain information, is difficult to conjecture. Few of them as yet have sufficient authoritative backgrounds to command serious consideration, however difficult it may be to explain some of their stories.

It would seem, however, high time for scientists and governmental leaders to be exploring possible means of communication with alien intelligent beings, not necessarily of human origin, who might any day arrive in sizable numbers, to command our attention for purposes not yet spelled out. Certainly those who have recognized the ability to perform telepathy, or to be sensitively aware of things beyond the limitation of the five physical senses, should be utilized to attempt a solution of the mystery which could quite possibly confront all mankind should a sudden crisis and threat of invasion from outer space develop.

This is not said in any alarmist sense; it is simply a logical procedure that would be called for by such a possible development. Unhappily, skepticism in high places of government is still so prevalent that the reaction to any sudden global appearance of innumerable spaceships might cause government to respond with an attempted exercise of force—such as aiming atomic missiles at the incoming spacecraft.

My intuition tells me that we are on the verge of great changes (not necessarily unlike those my science-fiction character Numar predicted) beyond the capacity of the average human to conceive. I am certain that we should be preparing ourselves now, today, to face and to adjust ourselves to these changes. This adjustment can take place only inside ourselves, and it will lead, perhaps quickly, to an almost unbelievable expansion of our understanding.

12
Communication with the Dead

Frauds

THE FACT THAT some magicians can apparently duplicate various psychic phenomena—such as the faking of a trumpet séance, a materialization, a "direct-voice" communication, the delivery of an "apport" through space, the performance of levitation, moving objects mentally, and reading minds—is no proof that genuine extrasensory perception does not exist, any more than the production of counterfeit money refutes the existence of genuine currency. It is an unhappily established fact that there is much trickery and chicanery here and that there are many fraudulent practices in the name of the psychic generally and of psychic healing. It is even possible, due to the suggestibility of the human mind, for an out-and-out faker to aid in the healing of many of his followers. This is not due to any occult powers resident in the "master," "spiritual leader," or "healer" in such cases, but due to the faith individuals place in him, which activates the healing powers inherent in their own minds and brings about a "miraculous" return to health.

For this reason it has become easy for millions of gullible, trusting men and women, desperately searching for answers to physical, mental, emotional, and economic problems, to be preyed upon by those who promise a change in their fortunes as well as their health. The psychic, in its multiple forms, has become almost a billion-dollar business per year. Because the basic truth of ESP has been established—and public acceptance of it has vastly increased—the door is now wide open for shameless, outright fraudulent practitioners to jump in, proclaiming their psychic ability to read mystic records and reveal your past life; to tell you how to overcome your karmic penalties; to put you in touch, for a fee or the price of a book, with "spirit helpers" who are "experts" on money, health, affairs of the heart, locating lost articles and hidden treasures, and predicting your future. They can even provide you with an "invisible bodyguard," day and night, and "spirit helpers" assigned to you by a spiritual brotherhood, "spirits" who can travel with the speed of light to do things for you that you could never accomplish alone.

This, for the most part, is bunk and hokum of the worst kind. It is understandable that some inexperienced men and women, unfamiliar with genuine psychic phenomena, would respond to publicized assurances such as, "your spirit helpers can bring you great streams of money, gold, diamonds, and jewels; can help bring you health, glowing new strength, and vitality; can bring you love and power beyond belief, if you will only make contact in the right way. . . . Some may whisper in your ear, others may touch you with an electric vibration or the feeling of a gentle breeze on your cheek, or an exotic scent such as oriental herb incense. . . . When you see each new symbol, or otherwise sense a new presence . . . ask for the name. Then address your spirit friend just as you would another being in a physical body. You may have occasional visits from relatives, but your most important contacts will come from those entities who are assigned to work with you."

There is perhaps no subject closer to the minds and hearts of a fair percentage of mankind today than extrasensory perception and the implications that its developed powers of consciousness hold for the spiritual evolution of the individual soul. Because of this, those associated with the psychic, professional, or religious exercise of ESP should be called upon to be utterly responsible and employ the utmost integrity.

Unfortunately this is not generally the case. Rather, representations are made and practices are conducted that are either self-deluded or palpably false, and countless people of all persuasions are often misinformed, misled, deceived, or misguided.

In a spiritualist camp, for example, infrared motion pictures, aided by a U.S. Army "Snooperscope" lens, were taken of a purported materialization séance by Dr. Andrija

Puharich, noted psychic investigator, and Tom O'Neil, editor of *Psychic Observer* (one of the foremost psychic publications in the world). These pictures, when developed, revealed the séance to have been entirely fraudulent. Fellow mediums were posing as spirits, entering and leaving the "spirit cabinet" through a hidden doorway. Two veteran, internationally known mediums were involved, among others, who enacted the materialized spirits, clad in "pink ectoplasm," brilliant headgear, and flowing robes that shone in the darkness.

The masthead of the July 10, 1960, *Psychic Observer* which discussed this carried the standing imprint of a motto, in capital letters, "TRUTH FOR AUTHORITY— NOT AUTHORITY FOR TRUTH," and to Tom O'Neil's everlasting credit, he published a full account of this photographic exposé. He placed a black printer's band around the front-page story, which contained the heading:

We Are in Mourning
THE TRAGIC DECEPTION OF MATERIALIZATION
Or
WHY SPARE THE "ANGELS"?

Diehard spiritualist believers even then charged that "mischievous spirits" had played a prank on the "true mediums" and had impersonated them, taking on their likeness, which had shown up unmistakably in the film, thus causing profound embarrassment and the "apparent evidence" of fraud.

Years before this (in 1949), when my book *You Live After Death* was first published, I had warned those interested in psychic phenomena against being taken in by fraudulent mediums in trick séances. At the same time, I declared my conviction that genuine mediums existed.

My published comments were attacked by spiritualists and others who felt that I was too harsh in my criticism. When the above exposé appeared, however, apologies were extended to me by some of the leaders of the criticism, and I was invited by Tom O'Neil to submit an article for his publication, with excerpts from the book that had formerly been unacceptable. As a matter of fact, I had visited this camp thirty years before and had met some mediums on the grounds whom I felt to be genuine and others who seemed not genuine—which had caused me to be wary of each, and to test them carefully before crediting any with real psychic powers.

A portion of *You Live After Death* (Master Publications, New York) follows:

. . . the afterlife contains every type of human soul from the lowest to the highest, just as we have on earth. When you open the higher centers of your mind to make contact with intelligences without, and have not developed the proper self-conscious, directional, protective control, it is just as though you were living on a busy thoroughfare and opened the door of your house to whatever types of humans might be passing, including the worst possible riff-raff. But, because these intelligences are now invisible to you, and beyond detection and examination by your five physical senses, unless you are a "trained sensitive," you have no developed power of discrimination and may permit the wrong influences to enter and take possession of your consciousness.

For this reason, those who dabble innocently in the field of the psychic should beware. They do not know with what tremendous forces of good and evil they are playing. Nor should these inexperienced investigators permit themselves to be hypnotized or attempt to develop trance states or take on any condition which would open up the possibility of making their ego or entity subservient to any other intelligence, either within or without the physical body.

Each human soul is protected and insulated against the direct trespass upon, or imposition of, the will of any other soul, unless this protection and insulation is surrendered by that soul, either of its own volition or through the subtle influence and suggestion of a designing mind in which trust has been placed.

It is imperative that you retain, at all times, your own free-will control of your ego in all of its manifestations, dealings, and associations with others. Only in this way can you be certain of maintaining your absolute integrity and your contact with unperverted and undistorted truth which exists within your own soul through its relationship to God, the great intelligence.

Try to conceive, if you can, the boundless ocean of intelligence in which you exist. Each thought of every human has a rate and character of vibration and is being transmitted unconsciously into space. The mental ether about you is thus filled with vibratory thoughts of mankind, high and low. Add to this the vibratory thought of discarnate intelligence existing in the in-between world, close to earth, and you have some small idea of the colossal activity of ever-changing and intermingling thought forms, many of which are charged with the destructive emotions of fear, greed, hate, prejudice, and lust.

Have you seen a great city such as Chicago in the grip of a smoke-fog which blots out the upper stories of skyscrapers and so blankets the town as to turn day into night? Wrong thinking can and does produce what might be termed low-flying clouds of thought forms, which you must break through in order to reach the higher, finer thought vibrations of developed souls on the plane called heaven, beyond this borderland or in-between world of confused and disturbed entities.

This is one of the basic reasons why true spirit communication has been so difficult and fraught with a certain amount of mental and physical peril to the uninitiated. You have evidence of many unprincipled charlatans and impostors on earth. Sadly enough, there are just as many in the in-between world of the afterlife, and there always will be until mankind reaches a higher degree of spiritual development and enlightenment here.

The Path of Spiritual Confusion

When you begin to perceive the true picture of life existing simultaneously in many dimensions and on countless planets, on a vast scale beyond human comprehension, your reason and logic should tell you that spirit helpers, as advertised, are not supplied on a wholesale, commercial basis, in return for perhaps the purchase of a book, through a method of meditation, or through the offices of a reputed "master" teacher.

That there is a great God-given creative power within you that functions impersonally and impartially in helping you to solve your personal problems and in attracting right conditions, circumstances, resources, and people to you can be demonstrated. But this power responds always to your meditations and prayers in accordance with the character and quality of your own thoughts and desires. It is not dependent on a waiting spirit world of entities, slaves to your bidding, prepared to serve you whether you merit help and protection or not, to bring you riches and all kinds of material things, merely for the asking or the repeating of magic or secret words. There are two profound statements that you have heard time and again that are eternally true: "God helps those who help themselves" and "Faith without works is dead."

For anyone to make a blanket promise of anything you want, made possible through spirit helpers under your command, is contrary to all laws of merit. We know in this life that we must earn the right to possess good things, that we must qualify through effort and education and often sacrifice to reach worthwhile objectives. It is no more right for an adult to be given everything he wants just because he wants it than it is for a child to be handed everything he requests. We might like to have someone wave a wand and produce whatever we desire, or to have spirits to take over and supply our needs, but there is no soul development achieved by such a process—and the universe is obviously operating on the irrefutable laws of cause and effect. In due course of time, as has been stated, like always attracts like in the realm of the mind, and what you picture in your mind, supported by faith and work, is ultimately materialized in your life, in whole or in part. This does not mean that you are without the guidance and, occasionally, the help of discarnate friends or people you love, or beings that might be characterized as guardian angels, but this response to you is usually in answer to a definite need expressed through prayer and meditation or a deep yearning.

In the next dimension, or world, friends and people you love have duties and activities just as real to them there as the demands on us here. They are not always at our beck and call any more than they would be if they were away from home on a trip or had located in another part of the country. Genuine psychic mediums cannot produce messages from loved ones or friends on order, any time you wish to contact them.

There are times, however, as testified to by thousands of case histories, when the dead have managed to manifest their presence to those on earth, by the moving of physical objects, direct voice, a reproduction of their physical likeness (an appearance in astral or spirit form), through a vision or dream, a telepathic communication, or the instrumentation of a trance medium.

Arthur Ford and Bishop Pike

Arthur Ford, perhaps the greatest psychic medium living today, recently drew headlines throughout the world when he got messages from the late son of Bishop James A. Pike during a television interview with Allen Spraggett of the *Toronto Star*.

Arthur Ford told me:

I can never be assured in advance what may "come through." Fletcher, my guide, a man I knew in earth life years ago, who monitors the spirit entities that are attracted to whoever is attending a séance, is limited by whatever persons show up. The sitting with Pike was arranged on the spur of the moment. We had met as personalities invited to appear on Spraggett's TV program, featuring a new book he had written on psychic phenomena. When Pike expressed a desire for a séance, an hour or more before we were due to make a live presentation, I said to him, "What's the matter with right now?" We went into the studio and made the tape that was later shown, in part, on the major United States and Canadian television networks.

While Pike had had reason to believe he had previously communicated with his son, James, Jr., by direct manifestations and through another medium, Mrs. Ena Twigg, an abundance of fresh material came through Fletcher, not only from Pike's son but also from other discarnates who had known the bishop.

Immediately after the Pike séance, telephone calls were made to persons as far apart as Los Angeles and London to check the discarnates' statements. All of them proved to be correct.

Naturally, the usual questions were asked—as to whether I might have picked up all this information by researching published materials or by reading the minds of living persons. Pike said he didn't think so, that some of the material was of such an intimately personal nature that it had to be erased from the film shown the public. It certainly could not have been published, and still is not published; yet it checked out, and the full significance was thoroughly understood by the bishop himself. He went on to state that some details that proved correct were definitely beyond anything that he could have known in his conscious mind—and, he suspected, in some cases, his unconscious.

Ford, in his book *Unknown but Known* (Harper, New York, 1968), tells of the initial evidences of James Pike, Jr.'s possible survival, in manifestations that took place in his father's apartment at Cambridge University in England, where the bishop was then studying.

Young Pike, twenty-two years of age, shot himself to death in a New York City hotel room in February, 1966. About two weeks later, physical phenomena began to occur. Most of these events were witnessed by, besides Pike himself, his secretary and a clergyman, the Rev. David Barr.

One morning, all the clocks stopped at exactly 8:19—the probable time, translated into Cambridge time, that the suicide took place. Then safety pins kept turning up throughout the apartment, bent open at the angle made by the hands of a clock at 8:19. Books having some connection with the dead son appeared in locations other than their accustomed places. Hymnals and prayerbooks were found open on verses having eternal life as their theme. Once, while Pike, Barr, and the secretary were working in the apartment, there was a commotion in a closet. Pike quickly opened the door; no one was there, but the closet was a shambles of scrambled clothing.

"If only," a visitor remarked on one occasion, "something of this sort would happen in the direct presence of witnesses." Immediately, in full view of the three witnesses present, the younger Pike's shaving mirror left the top of the bureau he had used while visiting his father, and floated gently to the floor.

On a recent visit I paid to Arthur Ford, with the actress Gloria Swanson, who is profoundly interested in this subject and has had extrasensory experiences of her own, we were given this amazing account. It is illustrative of the help that is occasionally received from the "other side" of life. Ford told us:

Last January, 1968, I was stricken with a heart attack, complicated by a severe case of the flu. I was in critical shape, and it was most uncertain as to whether I would pull through. I have had a serious heart condition for some years.

In New York City, Dr. Edwin Boyle, formerly associated with NASA, now research director for the Miami Heart Institute, Miami Beach, Florida, was at Grand Central Station, about to take a helicopter for the airport to fly back to Miami after having been away on an extended trip for some seven weeks.

As he was on the verge of taking the helicopter, a sudden compulsive urge hit him, and what amounted to an inner voice said to him, "Go to Arthur Ford—he needs you."

Dr. Boyle had read my book *Nothing So Strange* some years before. I had never seen him or even heard of him. Dr. Boyle did not know where I lived, but recalled that a colleague had once said I resided, he thought, in the east, possibly Philadelphia.

Dr. Boyle checked. My name and address were in the Philadelphia phone book. Acting under this compelling feeling and the repeated command, "Go to Arthur Ford —he needs you," Dr. Boyle canceled his plane reservation for Miami and took the train to Philadelphia.

When he arrived at my apartment, he found me in a

precarious condition. Himself a heart specialist, he took charge of my case at once and remained with me through Saturday, Sunday, and Monday, then flew me to Miami to his institute for treatment, and restored me to health. I have been under his care ever since.

I asked Arthur Ford how Dr. Boyle explained this most unusual psychic communication. He replied that Dr. Boyle had no explanation. He had never had an experience like this before or since, but the compulsion carried such conviction with it that he couldn't go against it. He *had* to act on it.

"Do you suppose that your guide, Fletcher, selected Dr. Boyle, possibly as the heart specialist you needed to save your life, and managed to reach his consciousness in this manner?" I asked.

Ford smiled. "I couldn't say. All I know is, some spirt friend made the contact for me, and I am very grateful."

This validated experience should demonstrate that those interested in your welfare, in the next dimension, can, on occasion, reach any mind anywhere, as needed, to bring aid of one kind or another. That it doesn't happen more often is undoubtedly largely our fault for lack of developed sensitivity and lack of faith.

The Psychic Experience
of a Philadelphia Lawyer

During our visit to Philadelphia to see Arthur Ford, Gloria Swanson introduced me to a brilliant attorney, a friend of hers named Joseph Sharfsin. He graciously took us to dinner and Gloria urged him to tell me of a psychic experience that changed him from an ESP agnostic to a believer in one night:

It was in the year 1941, after leaving political office. I received a special assignment from the federal government to commute to Chicago every ten days to supervise the expenditure of eighteen million dollars being used in the building of the first subway system.

I was having stomach trouble at the time and couldn't fly, so I made the trips by train. It was a boring job, going and coming, and I formed the habit of stopping at different hotels each time, to give me a little variety.

At one of these hotels I met the assistant manager, a woman, who invited me to have dinner. In the dining room she sat me down with young Marx, a grandson of the Marx with Hart, Schaffner & Marx, clothiers. In those days I performed mental memory feats, and I put on a little display of my prowess for Marx and his fiancée. They seemed amused.

Suddenly Marx grabbed me by the arm and said, "Come on. We're taking you to a woman who will make what you are doing look like kindergarten stuff."

I had nothing to do that night, so I said, "Why not?"

We took a cab, and in about fifteen to twenty minutes we arrived in an ordinary neighborhood of store fronts with apartments above them. In those days these living quarters would have brought about sixty dollars a month.

We went up the stairs, young Marx knocked on a door, and a black-haired lady of about forty-five answered the door. Marx and his fiancée had been there before. He purposely didn't introduce me by name, just told this woman, whom he called Sophia Williams, that I was a new friend of his.

We entered the apartment and I met Mrs. Williams' older sister. I didn't see any men around, and I learned that both of the sisters were working. We sat down and had pleasant chitchat for about an hour or so. I have been interested in music, and we got onto that subject, but no reference was made to anything psychic.

Finally Marx looked at Sophia Williams and said, "Have you been feeling anything about this friend of mine?"

She laughed, hesitated a moment, and then said, "Well, it's a strange thing—yes, I do feel—I see this man; it's so odd, I hate to mention it—but I see him surrounded by a great number of mechanical things: trolley cars, buses, trains, and electricity."

Well, Sherman, if I could have fallen through the floor, I'd have done it. Specifically, as I started to tell you, I had been hired by the head of the Federal Works Administration to dispense money as special counsel for the government, to pass on reorganization of the bankrupt system, and to watch how Mayor Kelly in Chicago spent that eighteen million dollars we were letting him have. It was the first federal subway-construction job . . . and of course we had to keep a close check on payments. How in hell Sophia Williams ever linked up those impressions of trolley cars, buses, trains, and electricity . . . the whole transportation picture, I haven't figured out to this day.

But this was nothing to the impressions Sophia Williams came up with next. She had me on the ropes right then—but she knocked me between the ropes, right out of the ring, on this next one.

"I have another feeling," she said. "It's entirely different —it seems that you are involved in a tragic situation. I feel the presence of a spirit here—she gives me the name 'Helen Fink'—it has something to do with legal matters concerning her—a will—some money—you are involved in her case—it's very complicated—it has some connection with Washington, D.C.—her mother—there appears to be some doubt as to who her mother was. . . ."

Sharfsin stopped in his narration. "Sherman," he said, "it gets too complicated from here on to give you a blow-by-blow account. I'll have to condense it, but this was just the start of a series of visits to this remarkable woman for sittings with her, during the course of which she told me substantially all I am about to relate, without any coaching from me whatsoever." Sharfsin continued:

In addition to this transit job, I had been hired by the city of Washington as special-causes counsel to fight a case in the Pennsylvania courts that involved the estate of one Helen Fink, who had served as secretary to Congressman Greist and to whom he had willed one hundred thousand dollars upon his death.

The case was unusual in that Miss Fink, who had later in a fit of despondency committed suicide onboard a ship bound for the Panama Canal, had left a will instructing the court to institute a search to determine the identity of her real mother, and, this failing, the money was to be given to the poor of the city of Washington. Naturally, Washington officials were interested in getting this financial plum, and I had been hired to contest those who might seek to obtain this amount.

The money had been left with the Gerard Trust of Philadelphia, and they were required by law to advertise for possible heirs as claimants to this money. The advertisements turned up three different sets of descendants, each claiming a relative who had been Helen Fink's mother.

The first claimants were descendants of a Baltimore prostitute; the second, descendants of a Buffalo woman who had died of a malignancy; the third, descendants of the Fink family with whom Helen had been reared.

The case dragged through many months and went up to the State Supreme Court, where I argued the appeals. There were thousands of pages of testimony, and Sophia Williams seemed conversant with the salient features of most of it. It was as though the spirit of Helen Fink were following this case from day to day and communicating it to this psychic medium.

I took the legal position that none of the three groups of defendants was predominant and that, therefore, none of them was entitled to the bequest.

When the case was decided, I wired Sophia Williams:

"The poor of the city of Washington have been given the money." She wired me back: "Helen will be satisfied."

Later, when I saw her again, I asked, "Between you and me—who was Helen's mother? Has she found out where she is? Do you know?"

I will never forget the expression on Sophia Williams' face. She sat quietly for a moment and then said softly, "Yes—the Baltimore prostitute."

Gloria Swanson and I exchanged glances and shook our heads. "Didn't I tell you that Mr. Sharfsin had a psychic experience worth relating?" she said.

"That's an understatement," I replied.

Sharfsin drew a deep breath. "Well, Sherman, I've never pooh-poohed psychic phenomena or ESP since. There were other things that happened. During many sittings in broad daylight I would hear voices around Sophia's head, and there were rappings on the table, beyond her reach. I would get down on my hands and knees under the table, and walk all around her while the voice was speaking—no tricks, I am positive. But how could this happen? Did you ever know—have you ever met—Sophia Williams?"

"Yes," I said, "I spent an evening with her in the home of Ivan Tors, the picture and television producer, in Hollywood a few years ago; she was just as baffling to us, and gave some messages to Ivan from a deceased uncle who had lived in Hungary."

"No kidding!" said Sharfsin. "I've lost track of her. Where is she now?"

"Still out west," I said. "She has not been well the past few years, I understand. You probably know that she was the medium who was made famous by her work with Hamlin Garland, author of *The Mystery of the Buried Crosses*. She located, through spirit communication, the places where many of the early priests had buried crosses and other artifacts—and they were dug up at the places specified." (Sophia Williams has since died.)

Despite such evidential psychic demonstrations as have just been reported, it is far more dependable and meaningful for you to rely on direct contact with people you loved, rather than seeking out mediums or fortunetellers who may or may not be genuine. You cannot force communication to take place. Instead, you must put aside your grief and sense of physical separation and accept on faith that people you loved are and can be near you at times. When a real purpose is to be served, or an urgent need arises, some sign or message may come through in a dream, vision, or actual physical manifestation of a deceased person.

There are simply too many thousands of case histories of a similar nature, covering a wide variety of psychic phenomena which point toward "survival," to write them off as hallucinations, flights of imagination, wishful thinking, or ordinary dreams. The fact that skeptical scientists cannot arrange to have these ESP experiences occur in a laboratory where they can be observed, placed under instrumentation, and controlled in no way discounts their significance or validity or reality.

The cases I have selected for presentation here indicate that people who have left this life are still concerned, at times, with living acts or intentions on earth, and try when possible to make this interest known. For example, consider this account:

Mrs. L. L. S. of Everett, Washington

Two months after my father's death in 1947, I was at a restaurant by the waters of Puget Sound, where my father had often fished. I was out to dinner with a boy of whom I was very enamored. I was engrossed in the boy's conversation when I suddenly had a very strong feeling that my father was seated beside me. The feeling was so intense that I was actually afraid to turn and look, and I debated strongly on whether or not I should tell my friend of my feeling. However, I finally decided to sit quietly and concentrate on looking straight across the table.

Still I felt my father close beside me, but he made no attempt to make me look in his direction or to talk with me. He simply sat there next to me for quite some time, and then his presence went. One minute he was there; in the next, I could sense that he was gone.

I later learned that he had spoken to my mother of his disapproval of the young man, but since he was the type of person who never forced others to share his opinions, he had never discussed it with me. The boy and I later split up with harsh feelings on both sides.

A few months later I actually "saw" my father walk into our kitchen, where Mother and I sat having an argument. Suddenly I saw my father walk into the room, dressed as usual. He stood looking at us both. Since my father had always disliked hearing us argue, I quickly told my mother what I was seeing. She said that she did not hear or see anything but asked how my father looked. I told her that he looked just as normal and that his expression was calm and not agitated, as it would have been when he was alive, had he heard us.

My mother fully shared my conviction that I had seen my father, as she herself had *felt* him. He had, in fact, made strong overtures to her to join him, and she had once even answered out loud, saying, "No, Sid, I can't come now. I still have things to do." She said that he never came again, nor did he visit me after that.

Her Grandparents
Appeared at Her Bedside

Apparitions of those who have gone on are common, and they are often associated with an attempt to convey messages, usually fragmentary due to the shock of the appearance on the person undergoing the experience, or his or her lack of receptivity at the moment. Mrs. E. S. of South Barre, Massachusetts, writes:

Strange things have happened to me all my life. The first one that I can remember took place before I had even heard of ESP, when I was fourteen years old. At that time my grandfather was just getting over an illness and was to return to work on Monday morning. On Saturday he had come up to visit us. I was his "pet."

That night I am sure that I awakened and saw my beloved grandfather standing at the side of my bed. His hand was on mine, and he said to me, "You are a good girl. You will always be a good girl. Don't be afraid." Then he was gone.

In the morning, as we were getting ready for church, the telephone rang, and as it did, "Grandpa's gone!" popped into my mind, and I began to cry. My dad came into the kitchen and told us that Grandpa had died in his sleep the night before.

When I told my father about what had happened, he said I was "just dreaming" and that Gramp always said this to me, and he had said it the day before. But he never said, "Don't be afraid" to me before. I felt then, and I do now, that I was not asleep and that I actually felt my grandfather's hand on mine, and that was what had awakened me.

Somewhat the same experience came to me again when my grandmother died, only this time it was in a dream. I was very close to my grandmother, too, and it seemed in this dream that I was at a funeral, standing beside a casket that had a glass top filled with flowers. I couldn't see who was in the coffin, but Gran walked into the room and touched my hand and said what my grandfather had said, "Don't be afraid. I have come to tell you something." I knew in my dream that my grandmother shouldn't be there, because she was already dead. But she said the same thing again: "Don't be afraid. I want to tell you something."

At this, she opened the casket, and I could see my grandfather sleeping in there, and he began to stretch and yawn. She then repeated once more: "Don't be afraid. I just came to tell you something."

I awakened after that, and it seemed like I'd really been somewhere, and perhaps what my grandmother was wanting to tell me was that she and my grandfather were not dead—they were both alive, and she didn't want me to have the picture in my mind that when a person's body was in a casket, that they, themselves, were dead. This left me with a feeling of peace that has stayed with me the rest of my life.

Her Dead Mother Was Actually There

There have been countless bedside visitations, undoubtedly because people are completely relaxed in the sleep state and the resistance of their conscious minds has been removed. They are thus far more receptive to spiritual influences. Here is a graphic instance reported by Mrs. N. P. of Bellevue, Washington:

Shortly after my mother died in 1965, she came to me and told me not to worry. She said everything was fine. I couldn't tell if I was dreaming or not, but I felt like I had awakened, and there she was, standing beside my bed.

I got up, physically, and put my arms around her and started to cry. I could feel her as if she was there, and my husband turned on the light and asked me, "What on earth are you doing, standing with your arms out like that, crying your head off?"

At the time I felt foolish, but the next morning I felt more peace of mind than I had had since my mother died. I am now sure she came back just to reassure me and the rest of the family.

It is characteristic, after experiences like this, that the person or persons involved, on this side of life, attest to a peace of mind, a knowing feeling that all is well. It is extremely doubtful that mere imagination or hallucination would leave such a deeply imbedded conviction.

Meaningful Reports

Mrs. H. S. of Canby, Oregon, has reported a series of remarkable visions wherein relatives have returned to show themselves to her psychic gaze and, once having caught her attention, to project a telepathic message. She told me that as a young girl she had married a much older man and had been unable to have a child by him. When he died, she became happily married to a man much nearer her age and was able to have four lovely children by him, which had been her heart's desire. Mrs. H. S. recounted:

Approximately sixteen years after my first marriage, I was out in my garden weeding, thinking of nothing in particular, my mind more or less a blank, when my eyes were suddenly drawn upward, as if by a magnet, to a spot of certain light above the ground. There was no vision, except inside me, as nearly as I can describe it—but there, surrounded by this light, was my former husband. He was attired in a loosely fitting white robe; his feet were bare, and so were his hands.

I wanted to reach up and clasp his hand, but since it was broad daylight, I was afraid if people saw me they would think me insane. I absolutely could not move. It was as if I were hypnotized. There were no visible facial features, not even in my mind's eye, but the rest was unmistakably clear. I knew it was my former husband's presence. I heard no voice, but his message seemed to flow from him into me, as if on an electric current.

He was telling me he was happy about my remarriage, and that I was happy and had the family I had always wanted so badly. Then, just as suddenly as the vision had come, it went, and I could go on about my work in the garden. I pondered on this many times but kept my secret to myself.

A few years later I was called back to Chicago for the funeral of my youngest brother, who had been very close to me. He had been in the service during World War II and was in Germany at the time of our father's death in December, 1942.

It was a military funeral, and my oldest son and I were the only members of his family present besides his wife. During the ceremony, at the folding of the flag for presentation, I felt this same electriclike impulse, and my eyes were drawn to a spot in midair, directly above his casket. There in an oval-shaped halo of light was my father's face.

He was smiling at me in a way I had always remembered my dad smiling when he was especially proud of us for some reason. Then I could feel what he was saying to me—how proud he was that I could come from Oregon for my brother's funeral.

Right after this, the vision faded as quietly and quickly as it had appeared. I told my husband about my experience and the one that had happened before. He was kind, but I could feel his skepticism. When a person has not had an experience of their own like this, I can understand their doubting it.

Three years ago my husband's mother, whom I dearly loved, passed away. I felt nothing at her passing but the usual sorrow for the loss of a loved one. I was more concerned with consoling my husband as best I could.

Six months went by, when the death of his stepfather occurred. His stepfather had simply gone to bed a week after Mom's death, and seemingly willed his own death, since the doctors could find no reason for his remaining bedridden other than his mental state of apparent grief over Mom's demise.

The next day my husband and I went to the mortuary where his body lay awaiting burial. The mortuary attendant was not there, so my husband phoned, and we were told to wait, that he would be right down.

While standing outside the mortuary, I felt this very same sensation of my eyes being drawn upward—always upward to a spot in midair.

There, in a halo of light, exactly as I had envisioned my dad, were my mother-in-law and father-in-law, smiling as happily as two children, in a field of wind-blown daisies. They were telling me, "We are together and we are happy. Everything is all right."

The vision was only of the busts of each, from the shoulders up, and I had the impression of their holding hands, as two happy children. Then, just as suddenly as it had happened, again the vision was gone.

After our visit to the mortuary, on the way home, I began to cry hysterically and told my husband what had taken place. "Am I losing my mind?" I asked him. "Why do these things keep on happening to me?"

Now, for the first time, my husband confessed to me that, six months before, while looking down on his mother's body in that same mortuary, he was torn with grief. While standing there, with the sensation of his terrible loss hitting him, he suddenly felt his mother's hand on his shoulder, exactly as she used to place it there in life.

And then he seemed to hear her saying to him, "Son, that is not me. That is only a piece of clay that was the body I occupied while I was on earth as your mother."

"At that moment," said my husband, "the greatest feeling of peace and tranquillity came over me. I can't explain it. I know my mother was a good woman, but she didn't take great stock in churches or religious training."

Mr. Sherman, these are true experiences, exactly as they happened to me and my husband. I hope you will believe them. I hope, too, they may offer some consolation and inspiration to others who have lost loved ones. As you can see, they are not far away, and they have not forgotten us.

Now a Story Can Be Told

At my time of life, it now seems safe for me to reveal this psychic experience of my own, of a somewhat similar nature. Because of the world prominence of the personality involved and the widespread public skepticism that existed in that earlier day, I have not thought it wise to report this earlier.

Leopold Godowsky, one of the great pianists and composers of his day, was introduced to us by our close friends Dorothy and Seymour Wanderman in New York City. We were living there at the time, and Godowsky was a patient of Dr. Wanderman's, who was and still is one of the outstanding physicians in the country. Both Dr. Wanderman and Godowsky were enormously interested in a study of psychic phenomena, and we attended many séances together, encountering the usual percentage of fraud as well as genuine phenomena.

When Godowsky died, his demise was headlined in newspapers throughout the world and brought out perhaps one of the largest throngs of celebrities and notables in every walk of life, especially the musical world, in the history of New York City. When I arrived at the Campbell Funeral Home, the auditorium where the funeral was to be held was already packed with mourners, and hundreds were milling around outside. Police tried to keep the lines moving so that all present could at least pass by the bier, even though all reservations were taken by those who were to attend the service themselves.

I managed, finally, to get in a few minutes before the service was to begin, and was soon halfway up the stairs overlooking the jammed lobby below, getting nowhere. As I looked around, it was not difficult to spot some of the giants in the musical world among the crowd, but I was not prepared for a glimpse of a most familiar figure on the floor below, moving toward the stairway, gazing interestedly about on all sides of him. I rubbed my eyes and looked again. It was Leopold Godowsky.

Such extrasensory ability as I possess does not ordinarily include psychic sight. I have seldom seen an apparition or the spirit form of a friend or someone I loved. But I testify that I unmistakably saw Leopold Godowsky in attendance at his own funeral.

I watched incredulously as Godowsky wove his way, apparently around and between many who had known him in life, who of course did not see him; he then began working his way up toward the turn in the stairway, where I was caught, unable to move in either direction. Fascinated, taking my eyes off him and then looking again to see if this were not some optical illusion, I watched until he suddenly reached a point directly in front of me. Godowsky was a vital little man with bushy hair and twinkling, alert eyes. He looked up at me, a light of recognition in his face, and somehow seemed to sense that I, of all the people present, actually saw him and knew of his presence.

Then his lips moved and he made, in a voice that I heard in my mind's ear, a comment that I will remember as long as I remain on this earth: "Hello, Harold—you might know there would be standing room only at my funeral."

With this, he vanished. He just was not there. The line on the stairway began to move. I passed the bier and looked at the still mask of the face that Godowsky's spirit had so short a time before shone through. It was not possible to remain for the funeral and to listen to all the deserved eulogies, although I am sure Godowsky was there, occupying perhaps a special box seat and enjoying every moment.

13

Communication with Cosmic Consciousness

PERHAPS THE MOST desirable and, at present, rarest of human experiences is the unpredictable ability of an individual soul to be instantly elevated to a position of sublime at-one-ness with cosmic consciousness. That this has happened throughout the centuries to a favored few, and is happening now, offers the most valid assurance that man has the potentiality within him to rise above his animal nature and eventually to evolve in the eternity ahead into a spiritual being.

Someday, in the far distant future, when man gains a deeper understanding of himself and leaves his limited material concepts behind, with all his hates and prejudices and fears and lusts for power, the human race will universally attain the cosmic-consciousness level. This level exists now, as a largely untapped area in most men's minds, ready to reveal itself to individual men, as they reach up to it through thinking and yearning.

In his remarkable book *Cosmic Consciousness* (University Books, New York, 1961) Richard Maurice Bucke, M.D., writes:

> The experience comes suddenly without warning, with a sensation of being immersed in a flame or rose-colored cloud, and is accompanied with a feeling of ecstasy, moral and intellectual illumination in which, like in a flash, a clear conception in outline is presented to the mind of the meaning and drift of the universe. The man who goes through the experience sees and knows that the cosmos is a living presence, that life is eternal, the soul of man immortal, that the foundation principle of the world is love and that the happiness of every individual in the long run

230

is absolutely certain. He loses all fear of death, all sense of sin, his personality gains added charm and he becomes transfigured. In a few moments of the experience he will learn more than in months or years of study, and will learn much that no study can teach. Walt Whitman speaks of cosmic consciousness as "ineffable light, light rare, untellable, lighting the very light beyond all signs, descriptions, languages."

The Experience of
a Remarkable Woman of Our Time

This highest form of spiritual illumination is by no means restricted to men, even though Dr. Bucke's book deals with fourteen selected cases that he feels are significantly demonstrative of this transcendental experience, taking place in the lives of Gautama, Jesus, Paul, Plotinus, Muhammad, Dante, Las Casas, John Ypes, Francis Bacon, Jacob Behmen, William Blake, Balzac, Walt Whitman, and Edward Carpenter. My files contain accounts from men and women who lay no claim to world recognition or even local prestige but who, through deep inner feeling and aspiration, have been momentarily united with the infinite, an experience so uplifting as to have changed the entire character and purpose of their lives. Rather than recite a number of these experiences, I feel it will be of more value to focus informatively on one of the most outstanding cases and permit the unusually gifted woman who underwent the great adventure of cosmic illumination to describe, as best she can, what happened—and also to indicate how you yourself may prepare, hopefully, for the attunement of your mind and soul with the presence of God within you. The woman is Gertrude Milton Walcher, of Colorado Springs, Colorado. Her cosmic-consciousness experience took place on March 29, 1947. As a result of it, her life interest in gemmology and crystallography was expanded into a comprehension of the structure of the universe as well as revelations of startling new theories now under study by leading scientists.

Mrs. Walcher gives the following account of her experience:

The house was quiet. No one but myself was up. It was a beautiful, sunny morning. I sat down at the dining-room table to study, but hardly got seated when the room seemed to be filled with the most magnificent yellow light.

Later I realized that my eyes were fluorescing. In all probability, my entire body was in a state of light. I was not aware of my body in any way. As I stood there, for I had risen to my feet in the wonder of it all, the whole plan of creation spread before me. The stupendous plan, the importance of crystallization in all its splendor and infinite forms in ineffable beauty, the gorgeous hues almost more than I could bear, and my heart was bursting with love and joy.

Standing there, I learned physics, chemistry, and a new mathematics, and from that moment on could converse intelligently with the most learned scientists, although what was revealed to me was far ahead of and very different from contemporary science. This knowledge was in the field of light and showed what the science of the future is to be.

I knew that this knowledge was given to me as a precious gift, and I received it with the utmost reverence, knowing that I would never do anything to degrade it or destroy it in any way.

While I remained in this highly attuned state, I learned about God, and this was the most wonderful and sublime experience that could come to anyone. The yellow light was as bright as the sun. I came to know that God is the nucleus of every atom, that He is the soul of every atom, every cell, every creature and organism. He is the universe. He is everything natural. I knew in that moment that we are God, that everything is God in one of His manifestations. The whole universe is God.

I saw how great is His love for everyone of His creation, and that man can climb to any spiritual heights he desires, provided his desire is great enough, and if he realizes that he is a part of God, and that God is right here within, and not in some far-off heaven, and above all, that God is love. I learned that God's love is beyond belief, because He is your soul.

The light began to fade out. I found myself in an unimaginable state of rapture and bliss, and cried for joy. Others could not understand, and I could not communicate. It is now twenty-one years since this tremendous experience gave me the greatest joy I have ever had.

It left me with the realization that the wealth of the whole world cannot compare in the slightest way with one short moment of cosmic consciousness. What would I say the necessary requisites are for experiencing cosmic consciousness? I would say, first, it is an overwhelming desire —desire to know the truth. The second is that one must adore the creator and nature and must have an inquiring mind. He must analyze and think for himself. When he does this, he can then begin to sense that he is reaching a state of inner excitement and higher consciousness, a prelude to the condition known as cosmic consciousness.

The experience of cosmic consciousness, once attained, is not the end, but the beginning of revelation. It is not extrasensory perception as we think of ESP, but something far more exalted and glorifying. One is uplifted to the highest pinnacle of reverence and love, and his ecstasy and rapture know no bounds. He is in seventh heaven, in a transcendental state, where his vibrations have been raised an octave, out of the material band of matter into the ultraviolet band of light. I believe that the vibrations are raised so high that the body assumes, for the time being, the properties of light, and it radiates and fluoresces with an intense illumination which glorifies and transforms the mundane being into a being of light who is in a condition of ecstatic holiness which cannot be even vaguely imagined by anyone who has not experienced it.

After having undergone the exquisite adventure of cosmic consciousness, one is aware that the vibrations of the everyday material world are very low. The green leaves of the plants, for example, seem very dull in comparison to the vibrant, vivid, and glorious hues that have been observed in the cosmic realm.

The Materialistic Trend Today

Today, as Mrs. Walcher has indicated, we are headed toward a computerized world wherein, scientists are predicting, everything will be done for us, including possibly the creation of human life outside the womb and incubator-raised offspring. Powerful drugs, so say some prophets, will make man gay or sad, suicidal or ecstatic. Man's thinking may be largely accomplished for him; his sex life may be controlled; everything may be taken into consideration but man's soul, which somehow will be lost in the dark, metallic, unfeeling void of complete mechanization. The world of the future, likely just around the new century corner, is not inspiring. It is frightening, even horrifying.

Perhaps nature itself will be revolted and shake man to his senses, destroying much of his vaunted wealth and power, bringing him back to a realization of simple, true, lasting values. This may cause man to create a new economic system that will permit him to escape from the soul-crushing congestion of the big cities—the noise and the smog, the polluted air and water, the poisoned foodstuffs permeated with insecticides, the radiation-infested atmosphere. Man may return to a common humanity, free of the hatred and strife now rampant, back to simple living, close to God and nature, where he can reclaim his soul and get back on the path of spiritual progress that has all but been obliterated in today's frantic, confused, war-mad world.

There are no shortcuts to heaven; no secret approaches to spiritual development; no exclusive and patented pipelines to God, despite the highly publicized promises of occult societies and so-called masters or adepts. The men and women who are truly developed spiritually are those who cannot and will not be commercialized; their gifts of the spirit cannot be bought. But they will freely share them with those who are willing to seek attunement with the presence of God within and to live in the world but be not of it, so far as hate, prejudice, greed, and lust for material power are concerned.

All great spiritual leaders, those who have attained to a consciousness of Christ on earth, have repeatedly stated that the path to progress of the soul is narrow but basically simple. It does not require rituals or ceremonies or mystic invocations sold in the marketplace, or any human intermediaries between the individual soul and cosmic consciousness. The door to higher spiritual realms is always open to the sincere seeker who puts aside external pitfalls and learns to depend on guidance and protection from within. This is the only basically true and unfailing source of supply and inspiration in the universe.

You can start from where you are and proceed day by day, through fine thinking and fine action, to where you want to be, in the care and protection and guidance of this higher power within, this portion of the cosmic consciousness of which you are an individualized, segmentized part. This power never fails to respond creatively to your need when called upon through proper visualization, faith, and a willingness to put forth your best effort, at all times, toward whatever goals you may have in life.

Disregard the commercial assurances of overnight riches, instant popularity, control over minds and hearts of others, miraculous healings, and so on. You unquestionably possess mysterious powers of ESP. These powers are inherent in you, and your wise development and exercise of them can bring you, within reason, all the good things of life you deserve and desire. The techniques have been outlined in other books of mine in different ways. They must remain fundamentally the same, because there is only one way that the mind basically functions.

The Keys

Here, then, once more, are the keys to your eventual mastery of your own mind. You will find that the faithful practice of these techniques will equip you, in time, to face and to solve all life's problems, as best they can be met. First, there is the technique for sending and receiving thoughts. Second, suggested meditative and visualizing techniques. And third, how to attune your soul to the consciousness of God.

A few minutes each day devoted to the study and utilization of these methods of thinking can bring about great and beneficial changes in your life. Avoid those who would tell you that you can learn to regress your mind in a few easy lessons and recall a host of your past lives; that you can, suggestively, progress from one plane to another in your consciousness, twelve planes in all, and arrive at the master soul that you really are, to discover your "Universal Name." These ways of so-called spiritual development are snares and delusions. They activate your imagination and often lead to mental and emotional upsets.

The Technique for Sending and Receiving Thoughts

Relax your body.

Make your conscious mind passive.

Turn the attention of your conscious mind inward.

Imagine a blank, white, motion-picture screen stretched across the dark room of your inner consciousness.

If you cannot easily visualize such a mental screen, let yourself imagine that it is there—as a focal point of attention.

When *receiving,* hold the screen blank, waiting with an inner feeling of faith and expectation that you will see and be able to recognize fleeting mental images from the mind of the individual on whom you are concentrating.

When *sending,* use your imagination to project mental pictures on the screen, or strong feelings of that which you wish to communicate.

Avoid all efforts to force, either in receiving or sending.

Usually, the first impression received is the right one. Record it at once, or speak it out—before your conscious mind has a chance to argue you out of it.

If you do not succeed in sending or receiving at first, clear your mind and try again. It takes practice to perform ESP, especially if it is an entirely new experience for you.

Remember that your subconscious mind, which contains your ESP faculties, is not limited by time or space. Distance is no barrier to thought.

In time, if you persist, your ESP powers, functioning through your intuition, can bring you hunches, premonitions, urges to do or not to do things, accurate visions or dreams that can guide and protect you in many ways.

Important: You must analyze each experience to make sure it is not made up of your fears, worries, wishful thoughts, or imagination before accepting impressions as genuine or acting on them.

Suggested Meditative and Visualizing Techniques

The way to live each day in the consciousness of God is to prepare for it in your meditation period the night before.

Give thanks for the protection and guidance you have received that day.

Picture what you wish to accomplish the following day.

Ask the help of the power of God within you to support your efforts to achieve goals and to solve problems.

Put aside all fears and worries.

Do not let them reside in your consciousness overnight, or they will separate you from contact with the presence of God.

Then give yourself over to the care and protection of this higher power while you sleep.

When you wake up in the morning, give thanks for your life, those you love, and the new opportunities waiting for you in this new day.

Resolve to do all you can for others as you move about your day's activities, realizing that, in serving them, you are serving this presence of God, which is serving you.

Look for good things to happen, and don't be disheartened by apparent setbacks.

Always remember that God's time is often not your time. He may say, "Wait," when you want to say, "Go."

But know that in God's good time, good things will come—if you hold to your faith and your willingness to help God help you.

How To Attune Your Soul To the Consciousness of God

The way to attune yourself to the consciousness of God is to make yourself quiet—without and within.

God does not speak with a loud voice or a compelling voice or a pleading voice. You often do not hear any voice at all.

But you'll feel a presence, if you remain still and receptive.

A sense of knowing.

A sense of direction.

A sense of rightness or wrongness.

And you, if you have put self out of the way, should act accordingly.

You'll reach a decision about a problem or a need, and when it is right, you'll feel a strength rise up inside you in support of your decision.

The fears and worries you may have had will begin to fade away.

They will be replaced by new courage and faith.

And you'll then get up from your meditation with resolution, ready to meet whatever is awaiting you in the world, in the consciousness that you are not alone, that a higher power is at your side, protecting and guiding you in all ways, in all things.

This is living in the presence of God.

This is knowing that one with God is always in a majority.

And that the presence of God is near you and ready to serve you at all times, dependent only on your willingness to enter the silence and just to listen.

As you practice these techniques, you will, if man does not destroy himself by erroneous thinking, probably see telepathy become a widely used means of communication between humans on earth, and perhaps between humans and higher intelligences on other planets. You will, I think, see a new understanding and harmony develop between all races as man recognizes his basic kinship and oneness with

life, not only with his fellow human creatures but with
other forms of animal and even plant life as well. You
should see mental illness reduced to a negligible degree
through man's developed ability to control his mind and
emotions.

You will also probably see a development of the healing
powers of man's mind that could substantially do away
with medicine as we know it. And a new knowledge of
foods and their effects on the physical body is likely to
bring about revolutionary changes in the health of the
world's populations; this refinement of the physical side of
man should lead to a more sensitized and effective approach to his spiritual side.

Communication between the earth and the next plane of
spiritual existence may be established to the point that fear
of death will be largely removed. Man might well come to
regard his life here as a means of preparation for a greater
life to come.

It will doubtless be a great day for you, should you arrive at the constant awareness, which is well within your
powers of attainment, that you are actually living and
moving and having your being in the consciousness of
God. When this day is at hand, your spirit will want to
sing praises to the great God of this vast and unlimited
universe, praises so well expressed in the old hymn:

> Oh, Lord, my God,
> When I, in awesome wonder,
> Consider all the worlds Thy Hands have made,
> I see the stars,
> I hear the rolling thunder,
> Thy power throughout the universe displayed.
>
> Then sings my soul, Jehovah, God to Thee,
> "How great Thou art,
> How great Thou art."
> Then sings my soul, Jehovah, God to Thee,
> "How great Thou art,
> How great Thou art."

Put this in your own words, if you will—but let your
soul sing when you get up each morning, with a fresh,
new opportunity to give a better account of yourself to
your fellow man and your maker. Remind yourself of how
very much you have for which to be grateful, that you, in
and of yourself, possess nothing of any lasting value but
your evolving soul, which is the real you—and which is to

accompany you in all the experiences awaiting you throughout eternity, in worlds or planes of being without number, yet to come.

A Code to Live By

In Old Saint Paul's Church, Baltimore, dated 1691, author unknown, is one of the most inspired codes of living that one could come across in any of the world's great literature. It says all I have tried to say here and more concerning self discovery. Let these kindly, loving admonitions become a guiding part of your consciousness from this moment on:

> Go placidly amid the noise & haste, & remember what peace there may be in silence. As far as possible without surrender, be on good terms with all persons. Speak your truth quietly & clearly; and listen to others, even the dull & ignorant; they too have their story.
>
> Avoid loud & aggressive persons, they are vexatious to the spirit. If you compare yourself with others, you may become vain & bitter; for always there will be greater & lesser persons than yourself. Enjoy your achievements as well as your plans.
>
> Keep interested in your own career, however humble; it is a real possession in the changing fortunes of time. Exercise caution in your business affairs; for the world is full of trickery. But let this not blind you to what virtue there is; many persons strive for high ideals; and everywhere life is full of heroism.
>
> Be yourself. Especially, do not feign affection. Neither be cynical about love; for in the face of all aridity & disenchantment it is perennial as the grass.
>
> Take kindly the counsel of the years, gracefully surrendering the things of youth. Nurture strength of spirit to shield you in sudden misfortune. But do not distress yourself with imaginings. Many fears are born of fatigue & loneliness. Beyond a wholesome discipline, be gentle with yourself.
>
> You are a child of the universe, no less than the trees & the stars; you have a right to be here. And whether or not it is clear to you, no doubt the universe is unfolding as it should.
>
> Therefore, be at peace with God, whatever you conceive Him to be, and whatever your labors & aspirations, in the noisy confusion of life, keep peace with your soul.
>
> With all its sham, drudgery & broken dreams, it is still a beautiful world. Be careful. Strive to be happy.

ESP RESEARCH ASSOCIATES FOUNDATION

For exploration of the origin and nature of man's sixth sense

1730 TOWER BUILDING
LITTLE ROCK, ARKANSAS

HAROLD SHERMAN
President

To Those Who Are Interested
in Further Exploration of
the Higher Powers of the Mind:

For years, it has been my conviction that many of the answers to the
mysteries of the mind can be found in and through the men and women
who have had and are having personal experiences with one or more phases
of extrasensory perception.

There are quite a number of individuals, of course, who are highly imaginative, hallucinatory, or self-deluded—often sincerely so—but I am
convinced that there are many more who truly have had extrasensory
perceptions.

I particularly invite the latter group of people to take a participating
interest in the program of ESP Research Associates Foundation as it unfolds.

You can now become an active member of the ESP Research Associates Foundation, an organization where you can receive guidance and instruction, take
part in ESP tests, form study groups, and be kept informed of
developments in the rapidly expanding field of mind-to-mind communication.

I also invite those with professional, medical, scientific, and religious
backgrounds, and those interested in the possible spiritual implications
and aspects of ESP—as well as those approaching the subject with an honest
skepticism—to join in exploring the mysteries of the mind that science
cannot adequately explain or classify yet.

If man is to achieve greater happiness and inner security and save himself
from self-destruction in today's world, then discovery and application of
the mental laws that govern the functioning of extrasensory perception
is of critical importance.

Please write me a detailed account of your own experiences in extrasensory
perception. State how you think you might be of service and what qualifi-
cations you feel you may have. In return, you will be sent a folder out-
lining the aims and purposes of the Foundation and describing the membership
services.

Sincerely,

Harold Sherman

HAROLD SHERMAN
Founder and President